"Squash has become increasi... ...*sions.
Raising Big Smiling Squash Kids is an excellent primer on how to get
children involved in squash, when to let the pros take over and, most
importantly, how to ensure that children are having fun."*
WILL CARLIN, Former US No.1

*"The book helps students improve all aspects of their game
tremendously and more importantly enjoy it!"*
MARK TALBOTT, Director of Squash, Stanford University

*"This comprehensive and unique guide contains a wealth of
information - perfect for every squash parent guiding the development
of a young squash player."*
ROBERT GRAHAM, Director of Squash, Santa Barbara Athletic
Club

*"We have been waiting for a book like this. Millman and Morque
cover every aspect of junior squash, from the first lesson to preparing
for college."*
JAMES ZUG, Author, *Squash: A History of the Game*

*"Richard Millman is a squash master. He and Georgetta Morque have
written a wonderful squash parenting book. Raising Big Smiling
Squash Kids is a jewel. I only wish that I could have read it 15 years
ago. I plan to keep my copy on the shelf next to Dr. Spock's Baby and
Childcare."*
SANFORD M. SCHWARTZ, Chariman, CitySquash – An Urban
Youth Enrichment Program

*"A wealth of information for young squash players, their parents and
coaches."*
PATRICIA FAST, Treasurer, CitySquash – An Urban Youth
Enrichment Program

*"We learn how to be involved, how to encourage the dream, and find a
balance with parental involvement."*
GINA RITTER, Westchester Parent Magazine

An Important Message to Our Readers

RAISING
Big Smiling Squash Kids

The Complete Roadmap For Junior Squash

Richard Millman & Georgetta Morque

Based Upon The Big Smiling Series Original
By Keith Kattan

Mansion Grove House

Richard Millman is the Head Pro at Westchester Squash Club and former Director of National Performance for the United States Squash Racquets Association. He coached the US national squash team and the university team at Cornell. As a player, Richard was the Norfolk Champion a record eight times, and a top 25 player on the ISPA world professional tour. Richard remains an active, enthusiastic player and has won the US National Men's 30s, 35s and 40s Championships.

Georgetta Morque is a prolific sportswriter, and a former squash league player. She is the daughter of the late Joe Lordi, a 1930s squash champion. Georgetta has fond childhood memories of squash, presenting trophies to the winners of the tournament named in her Dad's honor.

Raising Big Smiling Squash Kids

Published by Mansion Grove House. PO Box 201734, Austin, TX 78720
USA. Website: mansiongrovehouse.com
For information on bulk purchases, custom editions and serial rights:
E-mail sales@mansiongrovehouse.com or write us, Attention: Special Sales.
For permission license including reprints, excerpts and quotes: E-mail
permissions@mansiongrovehouse.com or write us, Attention: Permissions.

Printed in the United States of America
Library of Congress Cataloging-in-Publication Data
Millman, Richard
  Raising big smiling squash kids: the complete roadmap for junior
squash / Richard Millman & Georgetta Morque.number of
     p. cm.
  Includes bibliographical references and index.
  ISBN 1-932421-43-2 (978-1-932421-43-9 : alk. paper)
 1. Squash (Game) for children. 2. Squash (Game)--Tournaments--United
States. I. Morque, Georgetta II. Title.
 GV1004.3.C45.M55 2006
 796.343083--dc22

                    2005028181

Big Smiling Squash Team!
Copy Editor: **Pamela Garrett**
Cover Designer: **Bill Carson**
Cover Photos: **Stockton Photo, Inc** www.StocktonPhoto.com
Permissions & Book Design: **Maureen Malliaras**
Project Manager: **Uday Kumar**
Reviews: **Alex Linsker**

Credits: See Appendix "Credits"

Contents

Foreword

KEVIN D. KLIPSTEIN
Chief Executive Officer
US Squash Racquets Association

I am delighted to have the opportunity, in my capacity as the Chief Executive Officer of the United States Squash Racquets Association (USSRA), to write the foreward for Richard Millman and Georgetta Morque's exciting new book.

Squash in the United States is entering what is perhaps its golden era in the Junior game. We are seeing rapidly increasing numbers of both recreational and competitive players. New programs, clubs and courts are springing up everywhere across the country. The U.S. Junior Open attracts more players each year.

U.S. college squash, for so long a stable cornerstone of the game, is enjoying even greater growth now than in recent history. The addition of the Stanford women's varsity program in 2006 has made the American game of squash truly nationwide. And with so many leading colleges developing programs, the rest of the world is watching very closely as the opportunities for a first class education in the U.S. are enhanced for serious junior squash players.

Of course, with all of this new interest, there are many questions asked by new parents, teachers and students. Here, in Raising Big Smiling Squash Kids, Richard Millman and Georgetta Morque have come to the aid of squash associations, schools, colleges, clubs and programs around the world in offering answers to those questions in their comprehensive road map for young squash players.

We at the USSRA are pleased this book is now available as a valuable day to day tool in the development of our sport.

Kevin D. Klipstein
Chief Executive Officer
U.S. Squash Racquets Association

Introduction

*"Before I got married I had six theories about bringing up children;
now I have six children and no theories."*
JOHN WILMOT, Earl of Rochester.

S quash can offer your kid unparalleled benefits – opportunities to travel the world, a sport that can be enjoyed no matter what the weather, and a game where you don't always need a partner for practice. Plus: friendship, character building, and a lifetime of health and optimum fitness. Whether you know squash or not; whether your kid is 2 or 18 and just starting out, or has a few years of squash experience, this book offers a complete roadmap to all the game has to offer. You'll find practical advice ranging from the best age to get your kid started in squash, to pursuing a career in professional squash, to finding ways squash players can give back to their communities.

Picture a young boy of 12 on a competitive boarding school squash team in England. He's terrified of his coach, who is rumored to use the stump on slow learners. Four teammates just ahead of him won major tournaments and became the number one ranked player in England in his age group. That boy was, in fact, Richard Millman, co-author of this book, who won his first tournament at 18 and, unlike many of his former teammates, ended up dedicating his life to the sport. In spite of his rough start, Richard was persuaded to continue playing and eventually found that squash is more than just a sport, it's a vehicle that connects people from all walks of life and opens doors wherever you go.

My first experience with squash was not quite as dramatic but equally unusual. After my father's unexpected death when I was 6, the New York Athletic Club dedicated its squash courts to him and hosted an annual tournament in his memory. Those were the days when ladies needed to wear high heels to get into the place and were unwelcome as members. Each year, I would sit in the cold gallery and watch some of the country's best male players whip the hard squash ball around with wooden racquets. Afterwards, I presented trophies to the winners. Year after year, I began to wonder if squash was somehow related to my dad's incredible personality, drive, and success. In time, I began to understand that squash and important life skills did indeed work hand-in-hand

Squash is just as much a social skill as it is a sport. Squash can break down barriers and become almost ambassadorial in nature. Because it's a truly global sport, you can travel anywhere in the world and squash can be an entrée to an entire network of new friends and opportunities. You can be from Japan and go to a squash club in England, or vice versa, and say you play squash and immediately become connected with people, professionals and links to many new paths and discoveries. Whether you're a weekend warrior or world class pro, there is familiarity among players everywhere. And unlike some other sports, even the world champion is someone you can feel comfortable talking to.

Chances are, if you've picked up this book, you're beyond thinking that squash is a vegetable or a game played in a stuffy men's club. Perhaps you're a player who'd like to get your child started in this fun life sport. Or maybe you're a parent new to squash who has heard of its great benefits but don't have a clear picture of how to get started, or what it might be like.

Why this book? There have been numerous books written on squash drills and tactics, yet none have focused on junior squash or provided guidelines for parents. When you consider that kids invented squash back in the 1830s by hitting balls against walls in the schoolyard at the Harrow School in England, it seems appropriate that a book address the junior squash experience, especially since more kids are playing squash today than ever before.

But more importantly, Richard and I feel driven to help others help their kids enjoy the benefits of squash. Richard always feels great when players he has coached have gone on to coach others and is proud when players come up to him after many years and say, "the lessons you gave me were fantastic." Almost all the players he coached are still involved in the game. For me, I never had opportunities to play as a kid; I was always an observer. If I could go back in time, I would have made squash a big part of my childhood.

With the US converting from hardball to the international softball game over the past 10 years, squash has become easier for even the smallest kids to master. While the slower ball, bigger racquets and wider court have helped introduce squash to more players, longer rallies have brought a new set of challenges. The demands of fitness, skill and patience are much greater. Many kids are becoming proficient very quickly so reaching higher levels is keenly competitive.

Whether your child is heading for a competitive career, college squash or recreational fun, this book will guide you through everything from getting started to the mental strength needed for competition. You will be given simple steps to get through what could be a complicated maze. Squash parenting poses unique challenges and with our combined experiences—world-class coach and parent—we can help address these issues. Both of us have seen or been through the ups and downs of raising squash kids.

The overriding emphasis of the book is to offer a complete and practical guide for the squash parent and coach. "More info." This phrase, used throughout the book, will connect you to important Websites and references. Linking this way makes the book an easy read while allowing access to thousands of pages of up-to-date and in-depth information and contacts.

If your kids are not involved in squash, I hope this work inspires you to consider introducing them to the sport. This book will empower you to raise kids who swing the squash racquet with aplomb, their happy smiles a testament to the joy you helped them find in this great sport.

Richard and I believe every squash enthusiast is a kid at heart, and I hope you'll end up smiling, too, after reading this book. We wish your squash kid(s), and you, a joyous life. Your stories and experiences are of great interest to both of us; your comments are always welcome.

Richard Millman   Georgetta Lordi Morque
ricahardo@yahoo.com   glmorque@aol.com

Common Acronyms

AAASP: Association for the Advancement of Applied Sports Psychology
ABSP: American Board of Sports Psychology
AIS: Australian Institute of Sports National Athlete and Career Education Center
ANSI: American National Standards Institute
ASTM: American Society for Testing and Materials
AZSRA: Arizona Squash Racquets Association
BASES: British Association of Sports and Exercise Science
CASA: Caribbean Area Squash Association
CSA: College Squash Association
ESF: European Squash Federation
GAISF: General Association of International Sports Federation
IHRSA: International Health, Racquet & Sportsclub Association
ISDA: International Squash Doubles Association
MRT: Master Racquet Technician
NASM: National Academy of Sports Medicine
NCAA: National Collegiate Athletic Association
NESCAC: New England Small College Athletic Conference
NMSC: National Merit Scholarship Corporation
PASO: Pan American Sports Organization
PSA: Professional Squash Association
USSRA: United States Squash Racquets Association
WISPA: Women's International Squash Players Association
WISRF: Women's International Squash Racquet Federation
WSF: World Squash Federation

1

Getting Kids Interested

"You make 'em, I amuse 'em."
DR. SEUSS, on the subject of raising children

Johnny has a variety of sporting options next season – basketball, karate, soccer, squash and ice hockey. Mom encourages him to play two sports each season. Johnny tried basketball and soccer. He loved soccer and wants to sign up again. As his second sport, Mom wants to introduce him to a racquet sport and is considering squash. There are many good reasons why squash should be part of Johnny's repertoire.

Why Squash? The Right and Wrong Reasons

Pretend you're a squash novice. Ask any avid player why squash is his primary sport. Quite probably you just pushed his hot buttons. Brace yourself for an eloquent, emphatic and, of course, endless exposé on his complete addiction to hitting a small black ball against four walls.

His reasons will probably range from simple and sentimental to refreshingly innocent:

- *The simple:* Squash is fun and offers fitness for life. Easy, as it takes just two to play; social, as it takes at least two to have fun. Squash is truly a global sport and provides the opportunity to travel. It can also offer college team play and a future career. And squash can play a big role in developing character, self-confidence, decision-making and discipline.
- *The innocent:* Handle squash competition well and you can handle anything life throws at you. The sport can be played on the cheap, initially, and is relatively safe since it's not a contact sport. You can be tall or short - size doesn't matter. A player can pick and choose tournaments in which to participate, and even though squash is an individual sport, there are exciting team opportunities. And once you're on a squash team, no child sits on the bench at a match.

- *The sentimental:* Squash bridges the family generation gap, as old and young can play together. Squash brings together nice people from all walks of life, all over the world.

But don't get all teary-eyed just yet. There are also some negative reasons for introducing a child to squash, some very wrong reasons indeed. Prestige and rankings are valid motivators and their influence cannot be denied. Making an ivy-league squash team or attaining a world junior ranking is certainly impressive. However, playing solely for these external motivations takes the fun out of squash and is a perfect recipe for burnout.

It's important to have counter-balancing, less materialistic motivators, too – love of the challenge, a desire to do one's best and give maximum effort. Nor should a child play merely for parental approval. Enthusiasm for a sport cannot be sustained if every loss is equated with letting the family down. Fortunately, there are specific steps described in this book that parents and coaches can take to ensure that a child develops positive, intrinsic motivations.

As a parent or coach, choosing to introduce your junior to squash for all the right reasons, while excluding all the wrong ones, makes you part of a very special club – The Nice Squash People Club. Welcome. You may now burst into tears.

Home Away From Home

For kids with squash-playing parents, the squash club is sometimes a second home. Kids hang out, watch their parents play and get on the court and bat around the ball. Claire Rein-Weston, former US Women's Junior Team member and Seattle native, told *Squash* magazine that she grew up around the courts, always hanging around while her parents played. She developed her interest in squash naturally, starting around age 9 and then became more serious by the time she was 15. Top-ranked John White learned squash at a squash club owned by his parents in Queensland. White spent his childhood at the club and eventually turned pro at 18. As a child, Shabana Khan, a top woman player from the famous Khan family, could be found sipping lemonade at the squash club in Seattle where her father was pro. The happy atmosphere set the stage for her eventual love of the game, as well as her future success.

Once your child is old enough to hold a racquet, bring her along to the courts and let her try hitting the ball. Get her used to the place where you play. If you love squash, chances are she'll be interested in what you like too.

Learn to Love the Game

Enjoying squash yourself is a surefire way to jumpstart a child's interest. But even if you're new to squash and your idea of a racquet conjures up the Mafia, don't worry. You don't have to play to enjoy squash.

You can watch squash regularly on television in the UK and Canada. But in the US, unlike other professional sports such as football, tennis and basketball, squash is seldom televised. However in 2003, Americans began to have access to squash on television for the first time via The Tennis Channel. It is not nearly on the same scale as other professional sports, but it is an exciting beginning.

If you can't view squash on television in your area, there are many great squash videos and DVDs on the market. CitySquash, the successful urban youth program, gets kids interested in squash by playing a short video accompanied by music. In 2005, 112 sixth grade students tried out for the program's ten new available spots.

Squash British Columbia has a fun Website, Junior Jazz, (More info: SquashBC.com) just for juniors, with cool images and dynamite graphics. There is information on programs, tournaments, rankings and many photos of kids having fun. Since kids love the computer, you might want to let your child visit Squashtalk.com, where they can view video interviews with players and link to some of the players' Websites. On some sites, you can hear the ball pounding against the walls, see some amazing action shots and learn how these players got their start in squash. And soon enough, you'll be able to watch a squash match on your computer with on-line television. This is the future, according to those on the inside.

If you're new to the game, invite a squash-playing friend over to explain the rules, basic strokes, and strategies. Stump him with questions like, what is the difference between a let and a stroke? A couple of drinks and your friend should come up with a memorable answer. Two or three more educational sessions with your squash buddy and you may find yourself getting into the swing of things, so to speak. The point is, there is much in the game to love.

There may be initial stumbling blocks. Be persistent. Ask your friend if he has a copy of *Squash* magazine or *Squash Player* so you can read about the world of squash. *Squash, The History of the Game*, by James Zug is the first comprehensive book on the development of the sport in America and covers the key players throughout the past 100 years of the game. Another book worth reading is *Squash Racquets: The Khan Game* by Hashim Khan, where you'll gain insight into the ethics and values of this family of champions.

Before you know it, you'll be picking up on all the excitement squash has to offer. As you relax on the recliner, mesmerized by Peter Nicol's quickness, in walks 4-year-old Johnny, who asks, "Dad, can I watch with you?" Voila!

A postscript to this fairytale ending is in order. Don't be surprised if after a few minutes of watching squash your kid returns to his play dough. Remember, kids have short attention spans. However, when he does watch with you, patiently answer any questions he may have. Refrain from too much applause when your favorite player wins and from berating a player over a lost point.

Exposing Kids to Squash

As an infant, Amina Helal of England, sat in a basket in the corner of the court while her father, a pro, and her mother played squash. Amina ended up becoming No. 1 on the varsity squash team at Trinity College in Hartford, CT. Khawaja Maqbool of the United Arab Emirates was actually born *on* a squash court! His father was also a coach and his mother was nearby while pregnant. Maqbool, who is now a teenager, has won many events, including the US, Spanish, Nordic and Belgian Junior Opens. But you don't need to be born a player to become one. You can offer a positive introduction to the game to kids of all ages with enthusiasm, good coaching and the right squash environment.

Watch a Group Lesson

The best way to jumpstart a young child's interest in squash is by letting him watch a fun group lesson. Watching a tournament can also be fun, but a young child may not really understand what's going on and prematurely, and often subconsciously, begin to place undue emphasis on winning and losing.

Instead, choose a group-class where you know the kids are having fun. Take your child to watch five or six lessons. If an older sibling attends the class, this can be a convenient option. Plan to keep the young child engaged with off-court games, as her attention span is likely to be limited.

Learning by watching will give your child more confidence when she does get on the court. Observing a group lesson helps a young child realize the game is fun and that she too can learn to play. If all goes according to plan, your child will soon be asking to sign up.

Off-court Games

"It was a dark and stormy night. Two figures – one large and the other small, silhouetted by the light, were both at the end of a ping-pong table with one side folded up. The two were blowing a ping-pong ball against the vertical half of the table."

You probably guessed it by now. This is not a Stephen King excerpt; rather it's a description of a parent and child playing the game of Blow Out. Played indoors against a table with its half folded up vertically, Blow Out players aim to move a ping-pong ball along their sides of the table toward the vertical "wall."

Off-court games are a great way to introduce kids ages 4 and under to sports. There are plenty of fun games designed for young children that can help develop early skills suited for squash.

Stork

Balance is crucial for squash players. You can help develop your child's balance by playing this game. The player tries to balance standing on one leg with arms outstretched like a stork. Add a friendly challenge – see who can stork longer. The child is allowed to wobble if necessary, but the parent is not.

Medicine Ball

This game is designed to address the motor development patterns of children and develop a stronger foundation for squash skills. Use a two to four-pound medicine ball. A soccer ball or a large sized koosh ball works, too. Two kids, approximately the same height, throw the ball to each other using a movement similar to the overhead service motion.

As the kids develop this skill, have them use a forehand groundstroke motion. Then reverse the motion and throw backhands.

Jump Rope

Jumping rope can be fun and is good for timing and endurance. Look for adjustable ropes in durable plastic, with cushioned handles.

Balloon Ball

Even toddlers can bat a balloon around with squash racquets. You don't need a court to practice early pre-racquet skills. You'd be surprised how easy kids can learn to rally with each other.

Big Hand

Approved by the World Squash Federation as an official training aid, Big Hand (More info: bighandsports.com) is a pre-racquet training aid featuring a double-sided hand bat that fits over the hand like a mitt. It can be used with a spongy Big Hand ball. Big Hand is aimed at helping young children with hand-eye coordination and beginning racquet skills. Ken Watson, who designed Big Hand, explains that the device, by its design, encourages the development of correctstroking technique. Therefore, it can be helpful for young children to learn the basics before they start formal lessons.

Juggle

Teaching kids to juggle is fun. Start with two small beanbags and, after a few weeks of practice, progress to three bags. Juggling is a great way to develop soft focus.

Z-Ball

You'll have your kids giggling and chasing the Z-ball in no time at all. This rubber ball has knobs on it, creating unpredictable bounces. The Z-ball is great for developing hand-eye coordination.

Being the Court Crew

Retrieving balls that go out of the top of the squash court at a favorite player's match may be the most up-close-and-personal experience for a young member of a court crew. Sometimes, the player chooses to give the court crew a winning ball or a t-shirt; yeah, stars are humans too, you know. When that happens, be prepared for the inevitable barrage of bragging from the star-struck junior.

Court crews are not limited to professional tournaments. Say a younger sibling is watching her brother at match-play practice. The young girl can keep busy and feel like a significant part of the event. Most likely she'll go about the job with gusto.

Most tournament directors choose kids between the ages of 8 and 14 to work as the court crew. Usually, they are selected based on their behavior, both on and off the court. Prior to the tournament, kids get some guidelines from the tournament director. In addition to retrieving balls, the court crew is also responsible for wiping down a wet court in between games and matches and offering towels and water to the players.

Squash On Vacation

You can generally find squash courts wherever you travel. With more than 153 squash-playing nations, there aren't too many places where you won't find squash. Whether you're headed to Club Med, Bermuda, the Caribbean, the Maldives, Fiji, the Seychelles or even Iceland, squash courts await. What could be a better time to pique your child's interest in squash than during a fun vacation? Go on, experiment with squash on your travels. Your kid just might come home with the squash bug

The First Coach

Selecting a coach is a parent's single most important job. You can learn about teaching professionals from squash clubs and certifying organizations all across the world. In the United States – the United States Squash Racquets Association, USSRA (More info: us-squash.org); and in Canada, Squash Canada (More info: squash.ca); in England, England Squash (More info: EnglandSquash.com); in Australia, Squash Australia   (More info: squash.org.au); and in Asia, Asian Squash Federation (More info: asiansquash.com).

The United States Squash Racquets Association's coaching development program conforms to the World Squash Federation guideline, which establishes a standard across all nations. As a member of the WSF, the USSRA certifies squash coaches at four levels. Although certifications by themselves are not an absolute guarantee of coaching success, they are an important indicator that the coach has taken formal training and made a serious commitment to professional competence. Likewise, a coach from another WSF member nation, who possesses certification, has met the same standards and has the same competence as a USSRA certified coach.

On the other hand, some extremely competent coaches have no certification. They usually have extensive playing backgrounds and were coached as youngsters and competitive players. Experiences with these coaches are often very rewarding as they teach the lessons learned during their own development and playing careers. These coaches can be particularly effective when working with the intermediate and advanced player.

However, certification does guarantee a certain amount of consistency in coaching. Plus, certified coaches have gone through extensive ethical training, which is also very important. Make a point of knowing everything you need to about your coach and conduct background checks as necessary.

Over the years, some parents and children might find themselves choosing a coach at different phases of the junior's squash development: the beginner phase, the intermediate phase and the high performance phase. The first coach teaches the basics, the second oversees high school level competition, the third might be a coach skilled in working with a collegiate competitor and the fourth, a national team coach, who will be instrumental in international competition. Many players have such strong allegiances to their first coach that they never part with them and continue to look to them for advice and guidance. Others, once they've reached a certain level, feel the need to change to a different coach.

Obviously, choosing the right coach in the beginner phase is crucial because this phase determines whether the junior will even want to play squash. Besides, it's always easier to start with the right technique, rather than hustling through the early years and having to do a lot of fix-its later.

In a club situation, don't rely solely on the head pro's qualifications, although reputation is important. The character of the program is usually a reflection of the head pro's teaching philosophies, which are passed on to the staff. Keep that in mind, but make your decision based upon the coach that is actually going to teach *your* kid. There are specific qualities a parent can look for in order to find the right coach.

"Trust your child to a coach who is not only a leader, organizer and teacher but a good communicator capable of motivating and inspiring your child," says Bill McNally, men's and women's coach at Connecticut College. McNally, who has written coaching manuals and taught the USSRA Coaching Development Program, says it's not an accident that the most effective coaches seem to be the most articulate. In addition to being an expert on squash, the coach must be patient, enthusiastic, persistent, conscientious, sincere and humorous. Picking the right coach will instill a life-long love of squash with all its benefits, while a wrong coach may quickly extinguish any passion.

Certification

A good starting point is to find a coach who has earned credentials from a national squash federation, such as: the USSRA, Squash Canada, Asian Squash Federation, England Squash, Squash Australia or Squash South Africa. In the US, certification is available in three levels: Level 1 certification means the coach has studied and trained to teach beginning players. Level 2 certification means the coach is trained to take on intermediate players. Level 3 provides training for coaching advanced players. The Level 4 program, which is geared toward an elite or professional player, is in its formative stage. To reach one of the first three levels, the coach needs to attend an intensive weekend workshop with top squash professionals, complete a technical and practical course program, and pass a test covering what they've learned.

Squash Canada's coaching program has five levels of certification, ranging from the club coach or squash instructor to the high performance coach. England Squash offers four levels of coaching certification, from level 1, assistant coach up to level 4, elite coach. In addition, there are certification programs for mini squash, the fun introductory game for young children.

The World Squash Federation (WSF) sets the criteria for all certification programs, so that they meet the same standards. You can be sure that a coach with certification approved by the WSF has met all the necessary criteria for teaching squash. (More info: worldsquash.org).

Making It Fun

If you remember only one keyword for raising a successful squash kid, remember "fun." The ability to make a class fun is the most important qualification for a child's first coach. The coach should be able to communicate with kids lightheartedly, using analogies to explain shots and techniques. For example, a coach may use music so that every shot is a musical note and playing them together flows like a symphony.

Say you have to decide between a Level 3 coach who conducts his class with a serious poker face, and a new Level 1 coach who uses fun and games to engage the kids. Your choice is clear – pick the second coach. As long as a kid is having a good time, self-motivation and squash development will occur naturally.

A child is likely to have fun not only as a result of the way a coach teaches but also in response to his attitude. Look for enthusiasm – someone who believes in rewarding effort as much as outcome, creating an environment that encourages trying new skills, and who has the ability to focus on a particular child, even in a group situation.

The only way to make a good assessment is to watch the coach's group lessons. Short-list a few prospects and watch their classes. Ideally, pick a three to four week period and watch two or three lessons coached by each prospect. Include your child. This time invested up-front is more than worth every hour. After all, that first coach will determine whether your child gets in the game or not.

Making It Social

You'll have a lot easier time convincing Mary to join a squash clinic if her best friend Kate is signing up, too. Kids are more willing to try new activities as long as they can be with their friends.

If you get two or three kids together to take classes, it becomes an on-going activity that they can look forward to, especially if the program is fun. The squash facility offering weekly round robins and pizza will be more popular than the ones without any social activities. Once the club becomes known as a fun place, more kids will want to get involved.

Some kids are lucky enough to get invited to squash birthday parties. At the parties at Vassar College, for example, kids play all kinds of squash-related games, such as squash baseball and squash cricket, which are games that use some of the basic rules of other popular sports in a squash setting. When parents arrive after the cake is served, the kids have had so much fun they are totally excited and eager to start playing squash.

Mini Squash, popular in the UK, is another example of a fun introduction to the sport. Young children play with special racquets and balls on portable inflatable courts. There are several levels of play and opportunities for competition.

Parent as Coach

Parenting kids and coaching them are two of the most challenging roles any adult will ever face. Naturally, being a parent-coach is the toughest assignment of all.

It's understandable that a parent who is a professional coach or proficient player would want to teach his own child. After all, who better to assess the child's abilities and moods? There have been many successful parent-coaches in squash. Look at top player James Willstrop, former world junior champion, and his dad, Malcolm, or Canadian star Jonathon Power and his dad, John.

As a parent, you know your child and yourself. If you believe it can work, and no other coach is available, or you want to save money on lessons, the choice is yours. Some believe it's best to limit your coaching to the beginning phase. When it's time for lessons, go with the mindset of *playing* with your child rather than teaching him squash. Try to encourage and support the child, rather than give criticisms. Also, avoid initiating conversations with your child about his progress. Young children play sports for fun; learning is simply a by-product. Keep this simple truth in mind and you'll be your child's best coach ever.

Whether you choose to teach squash to your child or not, remain actively involved in the early years. Be a regular practice partner and do the drills the pro has taught. Let the pro do the teaching and never interfere during a lesson. But don't assume you can just turn your child over to a great pro and get him hooked. Children need to experience an emotional involvement if they are to choose squash as the sport of a lifetime. A good parent is clearly best qualified to offer the young child memorable squash experiences.

2

First Class

"As long as I can walk, I'll always be playing squash, and if I get to heaven and find out they don't play squash there, I'm coming back."
FRANK SATTERTHWAITE,
The Three-Wall Nick and Other Angles: A Squash Autobiography

Many a would-be James Willstrop, former world junior champion, and thousands of recreational prospects have been lost to the future of squash just because the sport was not accessible or their first class was not appropriately designed for kids just starting out.

Consider a 6-year old and a 10-year old who have never been exposed to squash. Both will be wielding the racquet for the first time, joining a so-called beginner group of 8-year olds who have been in the program for a while. Add to this mix a first lesson drilling forehands and backhands. Chances are, before long, either the 6-year old or the 10-year old, or worse both, will drop out, disappointed because they were unable to keep up.

The first few classes are critical in getting the child excited about squash and forming good habits on Day 1. Instead of jumping into a group lesson or clinic, allow your child to experience a potentially awkward first start with a few private sessions with a pro. This will enable him to get acquainted with the pro who will guide his development and give him the best chance to form good technical habits from the beginning. Additionally, the child will build some self-confidence before facing a group of new kids in a clinic.

The Right Age

Ask around for the ideal age to get your kid started in squash and you'll probably hear various responses. Some may say 3 years old, while others opine that ages 5 to 9 are perfect. Many will agree that a good time to start is when a child has developed some coordination

Sometimes, when a parent poses the "right-age" question, what he really means is, "What is the ideal age to get my kid started in squash *so he can get really good and make a top college squash team.*

And that, as they say, is the root of all trouble. Why? Because this places too much pressure on a child to reach a specific achievement. Kids should be encouraged to play squash because it's a fun, life-long sport that they will enjoy. College squash is incidental.

In reality, when should you start children playing? Here's the best answer: when they start bugging you to play.

Jumpstart Interest

Common sense dictates that a kid has to have basic comprehension and motor skills before considering any sport. That's about 3 years old. After that, you can use gentle and innocuous methods to jumpstart their interest in squash and begin to test the level of their enthusiasm.

There are simple ways to introduce kids to squash. Play a catch game with a foam ball, give your child a squash racquet and have him hit a balloon, or visit a squash club. Leilani Joyce, the squash star from New Zealand, got interested in squash at age 10 when her father showed her a video of top player and coach Susan Devoy. Watch players in action on a video or at a squash club. Try inviting a buddy to take a lesson with your child. Or, if it's possible at a local club, throw a squash party where everyone has fun. After a few of these jumpstart sessions, see if your child seems interested in the sport. If not, just take a break and try again another time.

Right Goal, Right Way

"My son is 18, is it too late to get started in squash?" It's never too late to start squash because it's never too late to have fun. And fun can progress into competitive enthusiasm. Look at the Vassar varsity squash teams. Some members never played squash before coming to college. They learned as freshmen and were able to make the team.

Some 50-year-olds have taken up the game and enjoyed it for the next two decades. Look at the late C. Howard Wilkins, Sr., who started to play squash in his 50s and entered his first tournament at 73. He was able to win more than a dozen USSRA championships in 70+ divisions. Start with fun and all kinds of things can happen.

When you look at some of the top players, their starting ages are all over the map. Natalie and Rachel Grinham, the highly ranked Australian sisters, used to chase a ball around an empty squash court when they were toddlers in the facility where their parents played. Top star Jonathon Power of Canada starting playing around age 7, and turned pro at 16. Kids participating in the urban youth squash programs in the US are introduced to the sport during middle school.

In no time, some are competing in national tournaments. At every level, a child has the opportunity to reach for the top. Once a kid achieves it, he can choose to challenge himself at the next level.

For every age there is also a right way to introduce squash. For a 3- to 5-year-old, simply playing with a balloon and a squash racquet is a great start. If you arrange a lesson for a young child, limit its length. Sometimes ten minutes is the maximum period of focus before a child loses interest. Always leave them wanting more.

Explore whether there is already an established system for introducing kids to the game in your area or country. The World Squash Federation (More info: worldsquash.org) can provide listings of national associations, which in turn will feature information on the hows and wheres of starting squash.

In England, for example, mini squash has proven to be an invaluable fun introduction to the game for kids ages 5 to 11. Playing on portable inflatable courts with three different types of balls and racquets, more than 10,000 young children in England have been able to participate at 100 approved mini-squash centers. The program is not only fun, but prepares kids who become hooked on the game to advance through the England Squash Player Pathway and progress to higher levels. Kids can even join a mini squash tour. Chris Simpson, a national champion at 17, started with mini squash when he was 8. The Mini squash program (More info: minisquash.com) features a progressive award system where players receive passports after each session to monitor their achievements and encourage progress.

In Australia, the Victorian Squash Federation introduces squash to children ages 5 through 7 with Totball, a fun program involving a wide range of games designed to develop racquet/ball skills. (More info: victoriansquash.com.au) In Canada, kids a little older, ages 7 to 14, have the opportunity to participate in a Skill Awards Program (More info: squash.ca), which lets them learn basic racquet skills at the club level and then progress through 12 award levels to eventually become high performance junior players.

The Right Class

The importance of a child's first squash lesson is key. Get it right the first time and the kid will come back for the next lesson, and the next. Before long, the child will take up squash as a lifetime sport. On the other hand, attempt to teach backhand, drop shot and boast in the first class and, chances are, the kid will turn to another sport.

First Classes

Forget about hand-eye coordination, footwork, and forehand technique. The first classes have one objective: get the kids to come back for the next ones. Tell jokes, play games, even those apparently unrelated to squash skills, and think up excuses to hand out candy.

Do whatever it takes to keep them giggling during the 30 minutes or so. Accomplishing this over the next few classes does more for the little one's squash development than any instruction.

Private Lessons

Private lessons can be an icebreaker and the way to go to first introduce a child to squash. One-on-one sessions with an experienced professional can cost as much as $50 to $100 an hour but may be worth it for kids to learn the basics first and receive individual attention. Semi-private lessons are beneficial when there are two or three friends starting out together. The best case is if the friends are all first-timers and roughly the same age. The downside of semi-private lessons occurs if the two players progress at different rates or need to focus on different areas.

Group Lessons

Once a child has a few private sessions, consider signing up for a group clinic, ideally run by the pro your child has gotten to know. Group classes should have up to six children of roughly equal ability who progress together, class by class. Kids love to learn in groups, especially when they are with their friends. However, in groups, some kids will progress more quickly than others. In that case, the coach needs to move the kids that are advancing to a higher-level group. Group classes work best when kids have already been exposed to squash or demonstrate roughly equal ability.

Class Format

Even in a small first-timers-only group, the emphasis should be on fun and group games. It's important to keep moving from one activity to the next to prevent boredom. Parents new to squash may find this strategy unconventional. An irate parent might demand money back, because no "squash" was taught in the class. To avoid this situation, coaches can incorporate a question-and-answer session, with parents as a part of the first class. A typical format might include a coach–parent conference to discuss the class objectives. This can be done in a social setting at an open house before the start of the class session. A typical class format might include:

- Stretches
- Coach–student conference: Q-and-A about court etiquette
- Games
- Cool downs
- Rewards to all kids. A favorite sports drink, a dollar bill they may have hit in target practice or watching their coach do push ups.

When kids leave with a smile, the first class is a success.

The Games Approach

In the games approach kids learn by playing squash games and discovering skills and strategies along the way. The approach itself is now old news, albeit a perfectly valid method of teaching.

The games approach works best for beginning and intermediate players. Let's face it, a young child attends a squash clinic not to *learn* squash but to *play* the game. Here are some examples of games for kids:

Game 1: Personal World Record

The coach counts the number of balls the players can hit back consecutively. On day one, it may be two balls. A few weeks later, it may be ten. The game can incorporate forehand drives or volleys, backhand drives or volleys, or boasts. The coach can add special rules as the players become more proficient. Initially, the ball needs only to land within a step or so of the coach Later on, the game can become more challenging.

Game 2: Beat the Coach

The coach has to hit the ball to the player while the player tries to keep the ball away from the coach. The coach gives forehand and backhand feeds directly to his student, but needs to run all over the court to return the ball back. Keeping the coach on his toes, the player learns about shot placement.

Game 3: Squicket

The coach feeds a ball to the first player, who hits it to the front wall. Other players in the group are fielders who must return the ball to the coach, who immediately gives another hand feed. The player who hit the ball must run and touch the back wall and then get ready for the next hand feed. The hitter scores a run every time he finishes the cycle of hitting, touching the wall and hitting the next feed. This game is part of Squash Canada's Skill Award program and is also popular in the UK.

Game 4: King of the Court

With 3 or 4 kids rotating, let them play out a point with the winner always staying in the game. The loser goes to the back of the court and waits his turn to challenge the king again. Many rounds can be played. This is a good exercise in developing shot selection, strategy and consistency.

Game 5: Target the Money

Place a five-dollar bill strategically on the court and have the kids aim for it. It can be very exciting for those who come anywhere close to hitting it. This is an exercise in early target practice.

Game 6: Heaven & Hell

This game is an expanded version of King of the Court with three courts – the heaven court, hell court and the purgatory court. There are six players on each court who play a game up to 9 or 15 points using three-fourths of the court. When the first kid gets 9 points, he shouts, "stop!" and the top two kids move up a court the bottom two kids move down a court, and play commences again. The angels won't necessarily go to heaven and the troublesome kids won't go to hell, but everyone has fun.

When kids understand what to do in a game, they want to develop the skills to play the game. The coach can then demonstrate those skills: practice using game-like drills and individually identifying player errors, thus helping to correct them.

The key to the games approach includes the questioning technique, games-guided discovery of rules and techniques, and problem solving. For example, a fun way to introduce kids to the court is during the warm-up. All kids stand in a line. When the coach calls out the names of the different sections of the court —tin, T, nick, short line, etc.—kids run to those areas. They get a warm-up and learn about the court, all with the emphasis on games and fun.

Once a Week

Usually children start out with a private lesson and then weekly classes. Even though a child has enjoyed his first class, he may require extra effort from a parent to get him to the next class. After a few successful classes, a child gets in the groove and, given a choice, may want to play more often. Some clubs have a ladder night or a round robin night, often with pizza. These evenings offer kids an additional playing opportunity combined with a social twist.

At first, sometimes less is more. Top-ranked junior Britt Hebden took it slow in the beginning, playing once a week to see if she really liked squash. Then, she stepped it up to twice a week after six months.

Finding a Court

Okay, so your 6-year old is all excited after his first squash class. Now it's the weekend and he can't wait to have some fun with you on the court. If you can't play where your child takes lessons—perhaps you haven't joined the club yet—check online to find courts through the Local Squash section on the USSRA Website (More info: us-squash.org), the Court Finder section on SquashTalk.com.), or through the World Squash Federation (More info: worldsquash.org and click on 'Squash Club Directories').

Also see if there are courts at high schools and colleges in your area. These courts are sometimes open to the public when students and staff are not using them, particularly in the summer and during school vacation periods. Private squash clubs, YMCA and YWCA are good places to find reserve-able courts. They also have great auxiliary features like pools and fitness rooms. When your kid begins to get serious about squash, membership in one of these clubs may be worth the cost.

Practicing with Peewees

When famous cellist Pablo Casals was asked why, at the age of 85, he continued to practice five hours a day, he replied, "I have the notion I am making progress." Practice is just as important as lessons. It can be a real source of enjoyment and an end in itself.

Schedule a practice session with your child and make it a regular activity, something you'll both look forward to. Use the same techniques and games introduced during the lessons. If you cannot be present during lessons, speak with the coach or have him provide a written lesson-plan so you know what he's worked on.

Practicing with peewees requires a lot of patience, but sessions should go a lot smoother when you use the games approach. If you have a question about or disagreement with something the coach has told your child, don't contradict him in front of your child. By doing so, you will diminish your child's respect for the coach. Speak with the instructor privately.

Try role-playing. Ask your child to pretend to be the coach and you his student. Both you and the child are guaranteed loads of fun. Always highlight accomplishments, not mistakes. And remember, let the squash coach teach squash skills. Your role is just to play and have fun. You are the teacher of things far more important – attitude, character, and life skills.

First Class

The wipers squeaked on the rain splashed screen
As our car pulled up some place I'd never been.
My mom said, 'Here we are honey! Won't this be fun!'
I felt kind of sick and my legs said 'Run!'
Then we got out and walked inside
With mom in front and me trying to hide.
The place was big and loud and white
With weird red lines and lots of light.
Just then this guy (who's kind of fit and tanned)
Walks right up and wants to shake my hand.
'Hi! I'm Jim and what's your name?'
'Katie.' I stammered and felt kind of lame.
'Great!' said Jim, 'and Katie how old are you?'
'Eight.' I whispered, though it wasn't true,
there were still at least four more days,
but Jim didn't care, because then he says:
Great Katie, well let's have some fun!
Let's get on the court and let's have a run!'
Next thing I know, I've got a racquet in hand,
A pair of glasses and my hair in a band,
And there we are walking right through the door
And I'm not on my own – there are several kids more.
I look round the court and would you believe
There's a girl from my school (she's called Genevieve).
She beckons me over and stands right by me
And whispers: ' Don't worry - It's brilliant! You'll see!'
And then - well, we started to learn
As Jim showed us positions and when not to turn.
I missed fairly often, but Jim said not to worry,
He said that was normal and that I wasn't to hurry,
That as long as I tried and just took my time,
I'd soon see improvement and I'd be just fine.
And after a while, well, wouldn't you know!
I hit two and then three and then five in a row!
In the end we did relays and a special 'cool down'
And next week, so Jim said, if I was around –
We'd all have a chance, if he liked how we played
To win us some candy or a red Gatorade!
So then it was over and Genevieve and me
Got to go for hot chocolate while our mommies had tea.
I can't wait for next time when I go to play
I think that my squash class might just make my day!

⚜

—*Richard Millman*

3

In the Groove

"I figure practice puts your brains in your muscles."
SAM SNEAD, professional golfer

A 10-year-old who receives motivation from a coach to learn, and support from a parent for practice, will grow into a 16-year-old who is more likely to be playing squash and enjoying it. Encouragement from and involvement by grown-ups helps kids get in the groove.

Getting Kids Hooked

Two words: parental involvement. There are tons of examples including many of the world's highly ranked players, such as David Palmer, Lee Beachill, Nick Matthews, James Willstrop and Nicol David. Without exception, these players can attest that, in their early years, their mom or dad was very involved in their squash. In some cases, they still are.

Some parents did all they could to support their kids' passion for squash. Indian junior champion Parth Doshi of Bombay became the shinning star of the varsity team at Williams College in Massachusetts. He credits his parents, who endured great sacrifices getting him up at 5 a.m. each day for fitness training and then taking him 90 minutes each way to practice and lessons.

Vicky Botwright, the top-ranked pro from England, remembers her dad arranging matches for her against players from neighboring clubs in Manchester. Top pro John White got his first taste of squash at his parent's squash club in Queensland. Some champions have squash bloodlines like the famous Khan dynasty, where squash has been passed down from generation to generation. Feeding balls to a child; playing games taught in a lesson; encouraging a child to practice solo; or watching an exciting tournament together can all be great motivators for a child.

When a Mom and Dad who have never played squash before take squash lessons, begin to play tournaments, and return from the club smiling and content, it sends a message to the kids that squash is fun to learn and to play. A parent can also get involved by volunteering at a community squash association. Anything a parent does to get connected to squash is sure to spark the child's interest.

The bottom line is, lessons alone will not get a kid hooked on squash. Practicing with a parent and developing a family connection to squash will. Whether or not the parent is a squash player is not important; what matters is involvement beyond paying for lessons and dropping kids off at the courts.

Learn to Handle Loss

At a parent-teacher conference for second-graders, the teacher was asked how parents could help their kids. The wise teacher replied, "Play a lot of games with your kids and play so they lose."

Why is it important to learn to handle loss? Face it, in a draw of 64, the odds are heavily stacked against a player. In singles elimination, 63 players are destined to lose. There's no guarantee that the player who wins will win again the next time. In an individual sport like squash, the player is solely responsible for the match result – fair and square. A loss not handled well can weigh heavily on a junior's self-esteem and enjoyment of the game.

Ong Beng Hee of Malaysia found the transition from junior play to the pro tour extremely challenging, yet his initial losses didn't get him down. "I get confidence from not only winning but playing well. Even if I lose, if I feel I played well and [gave] one hundred percent, that gives me confidence. If I lose to a player in three, then I work on it and next time I play him, I try to get a game off him and then take it from there." That strategy, as told to SquashTalk, proved successful as Beng Hee began to progress further and further in pro tournaments and in PSA rankings.

Britt Hebden, a top junior from Pennsylvania, had some unbelievable wins and some unbelievable losses. But Britt was able to regroup afterwards, says her mother, Jan. The Hebdens believe in looking at the bigger picture. "It is sports, not life," says Jan, who sees squash competition as a learning experience. "You learn to overcome obstacles. There will always be obstacles."

Fear of Losing

"My father," Chris Evert, the American tennis legend, has said, "taught me one important lesson: to not be afraid to lose." The best way to remove the fear of failure is to de-emphasize wins and losses, especially in the early years. That means don't over-celebrate a child's wins, and don't go ballistic after a loss. In either case, compliment the child's effort and ask, "What did you learn today?" Be genuine about it; a child can see through cover-ups faster than you can say let please.

The Four Step Solution

Any junior can follow this four-step process in order to handle a loss without feeling like a loser:

- *Handshake*: Shake hands with the opponent after every match, regardless of the result.
- *Cope with losing*: It's okay to be disappointed and a little hurt. After all, a lot of lessons, practice, and effort are invested and every child copes differently. Some sulk, others verbalize, still others take their minds off a loss by playing a video game or watching television. A parent should let the child work it out. It may be best to simply make a perfunctory remark or two and stay out of it.
- *Find redeemable qualities in a lost match*: Losing doesn't destroy self-esteem; the lack of ability to find redeemable qualities in a lost match does. Did you play your best? Did you stay relaxed? Were you focused on the point at hand? Did the match help improve your ranking points?
- *Put it in perspective*: What is winning anyway? What has your child gotten from the sport? If your child can look back in 10, 15 or 75 years and say, 'I won because I formed friendships,' then she is a winner.

None of these things come easily or naturally to an 8-year old who's just lost her first match. That's why it's important for parents and coaches to teach young players to handle losses, the earlier the better. Admittedly, there will be times when the child bursts into tears after losing an important match. Relax. Wait a day or two, and reinforce the four steps again.

Reward Effort

In many junior team sports, all players are awarded prizes for their participation and effort, regardless of a match's result. This is great practice for competition at the beginner level because young children are still learning to cope with losing.

When kids lose matches, help them learn to measure accomplishments in improvements and effort rather than simply in wins and losses. Plus, in a sanctioned tournament, players are motivated to win each round because they earn ranking points.

Parent-child Practice

Handling a loss can be practiced in an emotionally safe environment. A parent-child session is as safe as it gets. The objective is to handle the loss and find ways to improve.

Obviously, you *will not* say, "Johnny, let's go hit some balls and I'll teach you how to lose." You're going to be subtler than that, or perhaps you'll simply keep the game plan to yourself. Admit it – it's frightening to face your 10-year-old, knowing you're about to beat him. Gordon Anderson, President of Anderson Courts and Sports Surfaces and a former top touring professional, advises making the game close, so it's positive and fun. A handicap system is helpful, so you don't have to give the match away to make junior feel good. "You have to make it fun," says Dave Clarke, National Coach in New Zealand who once was Head Coach at Edgbaston Priory, a club in the UK. There, imaginative programs include crazy handicap events where one player wears flippers and the other plays with a frying pan!

You don't have to get out your snorkeling gear or kitchen utensils to make squash fun. Set up a point system to make it fair for your child. For instance, you could let your child start with a set number of points at the start of the game. Or, you could give yourself limits, such as scoring points only if you hit the ball before it touches the floor, or letting your serve land only between the service box and the half court.

Other common handicapping methods are allowing the junior to hit the ball wherever he wants while the parent just hits to the front wall. Or you could adjust the scoring so the parent can only score a point when he serves and the junior can score a point after every rally. Some families award a score of five to every point the junior earns, while the parent receives a score of one for each point he earns. Pick a formula that will allow the junior to compete hard. Reward effort. Soon enough, you'll be getting pointers from your child, which happens when top junior Lily Lorentzen plays with her dad.

Learning by Watching

Parents often complain that their children watch too many videos. One reason is that kids pick up a lot from watching and don't always learn the best things. So why not choose the videos that will teach them something worthwhile? Can a child learn squash watching a video?

While they certainly can't develop the game by watching alone, they can learn tips and strategies that can be applied on the court.

Training Videos

Squash involves many complex human motions. Training videos can be great teaching aids for juniors. Instructional DVDs, such as "Jonathon Power Exposed," the first instructional squash DVD, is a great example. Power shares his experiences in the game and demonstrates over 120 minutes of drills and training suggestions. Chris Walker's instructional DVD, "Raising Standards with Chris Walker," provides many tips, drills and tactical information with numerous demonstrations. You can also find other training videos, such as the three-set series with Mike Way, Canadian National Coach, who works with Power. Way describes the game as demonstrated by Power as he plays against Graham Ryding.

Fortunately, parents, junior coaches, and beginning junior players can find a choice of videos of key matches, such as the 2004 British Super Series finals and 2004 Tournament of Champion finals, produced by Canadian Jean De Lierre, one of the best squash producers in the world. You can also find historic videos of notable matches from the 1980s and 1990s featuring such stars as Hall of Fame legend Sharif Khan in the finals of the 1984 World Championships against Mark Talbott, who is considered the best American hardball player ever. These squash videos are narrated, which helps the viewer get a better understanding of some of the players' strategies and game plans. Videos can help even a non-playing parent appreciate what squash is all about.

Do keep in mind when watching videos that the techniques and practices of the pros are not necessarily right for every player. Advice from a coach who understands your child's game and his assets should always overrule what you may find on a video.

Tournaments

In the past, you were lucky if you could squeeze in a gallery at a club to watch a squash tournament. Now, with all-glass courts, which can be set up in arenas, theatres, and even train stations, there are opportunities for hundreds of people to watch the game. The Tournament of Champions in Grand Central Terminal captures the essence of New York City's energy and diversity as it offers squash competition among the world's best on an all-glass court, which can be viewed by millions of people.

When watching a match on a glass court, the best vantage point is slightly above the back wall, so you almost feel as if you are in the match itself. Try to avoid a corner seat so you don't view the match at an angle.

But squash aside, soaking up the hustle and bustle of a tournament can be a wonderful family experience. Sometimes there will be a Kids Day, such as at the Tournament of Champions in New York City, where kids take home a goody bag, poster, hat and other fun stuff. On a lucky day, Peter Nicol, the world's top-ranked player, just might walk up to your child and autograph the hat from the kid's outstretched arms.

Effective Practice

Grown ups practice to improve, kids practice to have fun. Understand this and there should be no problem getting your 10-year-old to practice.

Make a Plan and Stick to It

Practice with a purpose may be an overused phrase, but it is so true. Practicing without a plan encourages players to repeat only their best shots, overlooking all the weaknesses of their game. In the beginning, practice the drills and games taught in class. Once the junior has begun playing tournaments, have the coach suggest a plan to enhance strengths and improve weaknesses.

Shona Kerr, varsity coach at Wesleyan University in Connecticut, encourages her students to analyze their games technically and to create a chart as a practice guide.

Shot	Forehand	Backhand
Drive	5/10 hit a set target	6/10 hit a set target
Drop	5/10 hit a set target	4/10 hit a set target
Boast	5/10 hit a set target	4/10 hit a set target

Stick to your practice plan. Practicing a weak stroke for a few days does little to improve the stroke during a match. Repeat the new stroke technique until it is built into muscle memory. Then make it more challenging, says Kerr, who recommends working on technique at least four to six weeks before competition.

How Much, How Often?

Given a kid's limited attention span, it's best to limit practice sessions to 40 to 60 minutes with frequent breaks. In any case, stop while the kid is still interested.

No one can say how often to practice. The more hours of effective practice one puts into squash, the greater the benefit. Every player has to come up with his own practice schedule based on goals, commitment, and level of interest.

Many juniors want to compete in sanctioned events. The challenge for their coaches is making them willing to commit to the necessary hours of practice, according to former Squash British Columbia Provincial Junior Coach Phil Green, who is now a coach and club manager in Victoria. While some coaches would ideally like kids to spend four to six hours on the court each week, kids have so many competing activities, it is often difficult to find the time. Often, kids continue to play other sports and time management becomes an issue. Jan Hebden, mother of American junior Britt, found that squash helps kids learn organizational skills and manage their time wisely.

Kids and parents have to juggle a lot of schedules, from music lessons to sports to study time, and kids still need to be kids. Most teenagers want to have a social life, go to movies or just hang out with their friends.

"The amount of time for squash practice is also related to the opportunities available," says Green, who also coached the Squash Canada Junior Men's Team. Many clubs limit the times when juniors can play. Some facilities offer more clinics and match play than others. Sometimes, it is up to the child or parent to arrange his or her own practice matches.

Enthusiastic juniors should consider the following weekly schedule:

- Solo practice at least twice
- 1 private lesson
- 2 or more practice games, yet only 1 if a tournament is scheduled during the weekend

Some coaches say, "practice harder than you play matches and play matches harder than you practice." The point here is that practice and match play are equally important. Players should put the same amount of effort into their practice time as they do in their match play, but often they do not.

Practice Program

Parents often have to come up with creative ways to make a drill fun, while achieving a specific objective. Here are guidelines that will make practice effective and interesting:

- *Five factors*: Strokes are not the only techniques that must be learned. Practice movement, agility, mental toughness, and strategy.
- *Strong and weak points*: Practice the shots that are the most difficult.
- *100 percent effort*: Give it all during practice and eventually you're bound to do the same in a match. At some point, the shots will come naturally. Avoid injuries by limiting the length of practice sessions. A good practice session should have specific goals that a player can reasonably achieve.
- *Incorporate mental elements*: Simulate tough match situations and practice playing in a relaxed and focused state. The score is 9-all and your opponent is serving.
- *Spice it up*: Play games that make practice fun. Try conditioning games where one player has certain limitations, such as only hitting the corners. You can find great games and drills in Pippa Sales' book, *Improve Your Squash Game: 101 Drills, Coaching Tips and Resources* and *The Squash Workshop: A Complete Guide* by Ian McKenzie." There are also Websites that have drills and tips. (More info: khansquash.com and guide-to-squash.com).
- Develop specific goals that are performance-oriented rather than results-oriented. A qualified coach can assist players in developing specific, performance related goals. Phil Green says these goals should be short-, medium- and long-term. "A short-term goal might be achievable in one or two practices, while attaining a medium term goal might take a season. Success with short-term goals often lead students to take greater interest in medium- to long-term objectives. Success breeds success!"
- Think of goals in simple terms, like improving a volley, drop shot or return of serve. Don't predict your level for the entire year because you can get frustrated and end up struggling to reach a goal that may be unrealistic. Top American junior Chris Gordon, who is now playing professionally, always had goals along the way, but keeps them in perspective. "Don't let

it get you down if you don't achieve them as fast as you hoped. You have to use goals as motivational vehicles."

- Aim to see how well you played during your last match and try to play better the next time. Break down your performance in the match and try to develop better technical skills, strategies, physical movement and mental focus. Working on these areas will ultimately bring your game to a higher level.

Practice Partner

While kids are at the beginner stage, it's helpful for them to practice with a parent. Practicing with your child should be primarily fun and nothing more. Leave the coaching to the coach. When your child gets older, the same should hold true. Besides, teenagers don't often want to listen to parents' advice. Remember young Mark Twain's opinion of his father, "When I was a boy of fourteen, my father was so ignorant I could hardly stand to have the old man around. But when I got to be twenty-one, I was astonished at how much the old man had learned in seven years."

Finding a Partner

As children become more consistent, emphasize more one-on-one practice sessions. They can now begin to be partnered with players at various skill levels. And once they become physically mature, they will benefit from playing with adults. Against a more competent player, juniors will need to work harder and learn to play under pressure.

Practicing with a player at the same skill level will force both players to work hard and test their technical skills and strategies. Match-play practice with a player at a lower skill level will allow a child to be in control of the match, practice good technique and build self-confidence. Always reward the effort of both players.

One way to find partners of various skill levels is from the multi-level classes taught by pros. Consider kids in the class one level higher and one level lower, as well as kids at the same skill level. Another way to find partners is through any type of ladder play or round robin events that your facility might offer. Some facilities run leagues where juniors can play on a team, attend practices and compete against teams from other clubs. Teenage players will benefit from joining an adult league. When playing with adults, juniors will find longer rallies, which will force them to be more patient.

Solo Practice

In the book, *Squash Racquets: The Khan Game*, the famous Hashim Khan describes his youth in Peshawar where he played "Hashim against Hashim" at a squash club for hours everyday after school. Khan describes how he would often hit the same shot one hundred to two hundred times and then move to another spot to start again. "After a while, it is like court moves inside my head, I can close my eyes and see everything. Eyes shut, I stroke and the ball goes to that mark." (More info: Select References 2)

There isn't one top squash player who doesn't spend hours practicing alone. Squash coaches can't stress enough the importance of solo practice. Kids learn to play squash through several different avenues. They can learn a lot by listening to a coach and watching better players, but they also need to feel their strokes and grasp the sense of the ball as it hits against the walls. To accomplish these tactile sensations, players need to practice alone in the court, at least one to two hours per week.

There are many types of solo practice routines. Peter Nicol says he starts with easy volleys, hitting to the service box on each side to warm up. He then moves to the back corners to hit full-length drives on both the backhand and then the forehand side, using a medium pace to get a good rhythm. Afterwards, he practices low drives angled to bounce and come three quarters the way down the court. Next come volleys and drops and drop volleys, cuts and angles. He finishes up feeding himself short balls and coming in and playing aggressively.

Another type of solo practice, encouraged by Ashley Kayler, coach at the University of California Berkeley, is to play an entire match against yourself. Kayler says you can allow two bounces before the ball is down. He encourages players to play corner shots and if they play consecutive rails, he stresses the importance of getting to the T before hitting the next shot. Of course, you win every point, admits Kayler, who says the emphasis should be on making great gets while still being able to recover.

Solo practice also enables you to work on placement, while also serving as an important tool for developing variety, delay, and deception. Kids can arrange their own solo practice with the help of a coach. They should plan on allotting 45 minutes to one hour for each session and choose to concentrate on a specific shot or area of their game that needs work. Taping targets in key areas on the walls and floor of the court can also be helpful. Kids should keep a record in a notebook of their practice and go back to their notes for review at a later date.

In the Groove

Today I saw a player hit the sweetest shot I've seen,
And as I watched him strike the ball
I chanced upon this theme –
How many shots and how many hours
Combined to make this true?
And if it worked so well for him,
Then why not me and you?
A thousand balls on either side
Twice or more each week
And soon the shot that folks admire
Will be yours of which they speak.
And comments made so enviously
Will surely go to prove
That hours and hours of diligence
Have put you: 'In the groove'
⚜

—Richard Millman

Ball Machine

So your junior has gotten the hang of a drop shot. There are three ways to groove the stroke using a ball machine – practice, practice, and more practice. The Yale Varsity Team loves using the ball machine and the kids at SquashBusters (More info: squashbusters.org) are having fun with it, too.

It's helpful to have a coach or pro work with the player and the ball machine to make sure the player is practicing the right technique. Otherwise, the player will end up reinforcing a bad stroke. Pick a specific stroke for the practice session, say the backhand rail or forehand cross-court, and use it against a majority of the balls.

The ball machine can help the player practice any shot – rails, drops, lobs, boasts, return of serves and volleys, and feed a full range of shots from gentle tosses to hard drives. The machine can be maneuvered to place the ball to different specified locations on the court and can be set at speeds from 10 to 100 miles per hour, feeding balls as fast as every one and one-half seconds. It is therefore excellent for footwork and conditioning.

Easing into Competition

Fun is the name of the game for children under 10 years or so. After that children may begin to show interest in competing. A child will exhibit readiness for competition when they know the basics of the game and when they ask to participate in tournament play. Moreover, they are ready when they are able to deal with winning and losing. If the child gets upset when you as a parent win a game, then perhaps they are not yet psychologically ready for competition.

Learning about Competition

It does not matter whether a parent or coach had the opportunity to discuss the meaning and nature of competition with the child. Children learn about winning, losing, and competition from many others sources – television shows, for example. And remember the time when the squash class was challenged to a game of King or Queen of the Court? Even though the emphasis is on fun and games, children quickly begin to pick up on the competitive nature of sport. As long as there is less emphasis on winning and losing, children begin to thrive on competition.

The more time a grown-up spends with a child on the court playing games and match play, the easier it will be for the child to transition from drills and games to competing with peers. They should learn that it's okay to lose and okay to win. They can learn this by following some of the pro tournaments. Lee Beachill lost in the first round of the 2003 US Open, but came back the following year to reach the finals of the Men's World Championships and became the highest ranked player in the world.

First Competition

The best way to get started in competition is through internal club programs with kids of similar ages and levels. And if your facility offers it, try inter-club competition, where your child plays on a club team and competes against players of similar levels from another club. Once you've mastered these events, you can consider sanctioned tournaments.

In Canada, the Dunlop Power Tour Bronze events, out of Squash Ontario, are a great way to get children started in competition. Aimed a new and first year kids, ages 6 to 18, the program provides a fun introduction to competitive play with one-day events, complete with t-shirts and Big Mac coupons for all. Players are divided into categories based on levels. The format is flexible with matches of three or four out of five or by timed intervals, either with round robins or draws. (More info: squashontario.com).

In the US, Bronze Tournaments, formerly Future Stars tournaments, sanctioned by the USSRA, are open to all unranked players and those ranked 65 or below. Silver Tournaments, also designed for developing juniors, are open to players ranked 33 or below. The new bronze/silver categories, introduced in the 2005/6 season, were developed to promote play and offer a sense of accomplishment to players when they advance from one level to another. (More info: us-squash.org).

The England Squash Association has graded tournaments for both juniors and adults that emphasize fun and social play. Graded tournaments are part of an innovative pilot where players choose an initial grade that describes their level. They can then raise their grade by competing against players of a similar level in graded tournaments across the country. Players can follow their progress online. (More info: esgrading.com and englandsquash.com).

Players in Quebec will enjoy Junior Jesters Evenings, events that enable novice juniors to play with kids from neighboring clubs and schools. There are door prizes, refreshments and lots of fun. (More info: squash.qc.ca).

Keep on grooving!

4

Fun to Fiery

"Float like a butterfly, sting like a bee."
MUHAMMAD ALI, professional boxer

Winning is not everything, but winning is important. To keep this in perspective, remember that enjoyment of the game comes first, and then everything else, including winning. A class for young beginners is structured around fun and games. Sometimes, simply attending the class is fun. After a few years of squash lessons, a child gets in the groove and becomes more proficient. At this point the opportunity to participate and hang out with friends is a sufficient incentive. Approaching the adolescent years, kids develop additional motivators— competition and the desire to win.

The natural desire to compete and win ought to be accepted. A kid who experiences both wins and losses is likely to want to continue to play and improve his game. Acceptance of the natural desire to win, as opposed to emphasizing and pushing for a win, is in line with sports psychologists who advise parents to de-emphasize wins and losses.

Learning to Win

Top pro and coach Damian Walker says that players have to push, sometimes over their comfort level if they want to win. Winning not only requires giving your all during the match, more importantly, it means giving maximum effort preparing for the match. Encourage your child to become aware of his current strengths and weaknesses and shut out any unnecessary thoughts. Have him practice focusing on a few critical objectives, such as overcoming a weak stroke, improving a specific strategy, and achieving peak physical condition in time for the competition. "Even little tweaks can make a difference in your game in the long run," says Michelle Quibell, the top American junior from Georgia and now at Yale. "These little things also keep the player more interested during practice because they are working at improvement."

Raising the Bar

Michelle Quibell did what other juniors do when they dominate tournaments – she played up in an older age division. Since Quibell didn't have many juniors in her area to compete with, she practiced with adults. When she went on to play in sanctioned tournaments, there were few players in the US to challenge her. Quibell then took her talents to Europe and competed on the European Junior Circuit.

When the probability of winning is very high, a player's record may seem impressive but the accomplishment is clearly devalued. Squash development is sacrificed at the altar of easy wins. Often a kid loses motivation to improve and sometimes even to play.

When a kid is consistently winning the majority of his matches, it's time to raise the bar. Consider entering a few tournaments in a higher age group; practice and play with grown ups; or, try out for a team, either at a school, club or national squad, if you meet the criteria, Your kid may be overwhelmed by the level of play, but you'll get great competition along the way.

Becoming Assertive on Court

The Merriam-Webster dictionary defines assertion as "the act to state or declare positively and often forcefully." A player might be the nicest person in the world off-court and display excellent sportsmanship on court. To win matches, though, the player has to show assertiveness in his game. Being too careful or making tentative shots in a match may indicate the need for a talk with the coach about a more assertive game.

Mark Talbott, America's greatest hardball player and now coach at Stanford University, was known for his assertiveness in competition. He was calmly determined on the court and never let his emotions cloud the picture. Off the court, Talbott is the perfect gentleman. In fact, he is known in squash as a wonderful ambassador for the sport.

There are programs available at local community centers that offer assertiveness training for kids. Practicing martial arts is a great way to develop assertiveness.

Broadening the Definition of Winning

By definition, there is only one winner in a squash tournament – the winning finalist. If competition is to be beneficial to kids, they have to be taught to broaden their definition of winning and success.

A kid who has practiced his volley or drop shot and uses them effectively to win a third-round match is a success. Every junior who feels he played well on the court is a winner. Whether he wins a match or puts up a good fight, he's a winner. However, if the junior loses in the final round, after winning the first three rounds of a 16-player draw, he is a winner three times over and must be encouraged to believe that.

"Children should be encouraged to compete against their own potential," says Dr Alan Goldberg, a renowned sports psychologist. "Boys should focus on beating Mr. Peter Potential, competing against themselves, while the girls challenge Ms. Patty Potential."

Winners are also those who handle failure better. There is a widespread belief that great players were successful throughout their careers. Actually, champions probably just coped with their setbacks and losses better than their opponents did. England's Simon Parke had been one of the world's top players until he had ankle surgery. His ranking, which had always been in the top 10, dropped to 45 in 2001. The road back seemed long for Parke, who seriously wondered if he would ever play again. But his passion for the game outweighed his doubts and Parke steamrolled back to the top after physical therapy and fitness training. A few initial wins brought back his confidence and Park became a superstar once again. Parke never tried to predict where he was going. He just tried his hardest and played his very best in each match.

"A player learns more from her losses than from her wins," says Michelle Quibell. "It is also important to realize that every player has ups and downs, and in many cases she must take a step back in order to take two forward. This happens at almost every level."

Kids should look at competition as an exciting journey where you don't know the final destination. Be prepared and go as far as you can go. See how physically and mentally strong you are along the way. Find out which is your strongest stroke, the weakest, and learn how to improve them. Winning is a finite result and closed ended because after you win, what's next? Don't think of winning as the final stop. Keep discovering and see where that might take you.

I Don't Want To Win

Gordon Anderson, president of Anderson Courts and a former top touring professional, says his daughter would cry when she lost and cry when she won during her early days of competition.

We want to believe winning makes a squash kid happy and that losing makes her sad. Peel away the superficial emotions and you may be surprised to learn that your kid sometimes feels conflicted after a win – unhappy, anxious, and even guilty. Conversely, after a loss she may actually feel secretly happy and relieved.

Timothy Gallwey, author of best-selling book *The Inner Game of Tennis*, details possible reasons why a player could become conflicted about winning. Gallwey's advice applies to squash players as well. (More info: Select References 3). The challenge for parents and coaches is that these reactions to winning are natural for most kids:

- If I win and become the champion, I'll have to remain champion or disappoint myself and be criticized for not living up to expectations.
- If I beat my friend Harry, he'll be angry with me.
- If I win too much, I won't be able to keep my friendship with fellow players.
- I won't put in my maximum effort. That way I will have an excuse if I lose.

De-emphasizing wins and losses, especially during the early years, is a first step toward combating these attitudes. Encourage giving maximum effort and always celebrate the effort, whether the child wins or loses.

Find a quiet time away from the bustle of immediate competition and talk to your child about these pre- and post-match emotions. For example, while you chaperone the kid to and from lessons tell him what you know about fear of losing and fear of winning. Help the child understand that these are natural reactions.

Explain how he can overcome these negative attitudes by focusing on specific strategies and game plans rather than on the ultimate result of the match. Look at the performance in each rally rather than each point. Let the child know that giving maximum effort is your only expectation of him and that you will celebrate his effort regardless of the outcome.

Playing a Friend

In the relatively small world of junior squash, it's inevitable that players will have to face a friend on the court. Jenny Tranfield, a top WISPA player and sports psychologist, says it's difficult for the women competing on the pro circuit to be at each other like dogs on the court and then be friends later on.

Timothy Gallwey describes the nature of competition using a simple but enlightening example that even a 10-year old can understand and tuck away in his subconscious. Imagine the right and left hands to represent opposing players. Center the hands between your knees. Competing means the right hand aims to push the left hand past the left knee and vice versa. After pushing each other, say the right hand wins. Do you applaud the right hand and view it with respect and show disdain for the left hand? Of course not, you will simply accept the result. Also, say you do this five minutes each day, making sure each hand puts in maximum effort in the competition. Ultimately, both hands will become stronger, no matter how many wins and losses each hand has. (More info: Select References 3)

Help your child understand that giving maximum effort in a match is a way to better himself as well as the other player. He will be less anxious about competing against friends. After all, "compete" comes from the Latin word "competere," meaning "to seek together."

Courage of a Champion

Think of all the times
When someone said you wouldn't,
And add to those the other days
When you told yourself you couldn't,
Then gather up those occasions when
Some 'know-all' said you shouldn't.

Take all of this and pack it up
And put it in a box.
Then take the box and find a hole
As deep as it can be,
And over it lay a stone,
So that everyone can see,
And on that stone mark these words:

Today I start the journey of my life
And wherever I shall go,
I'll face the road determinedly,
For now I surely know
That should I meet adversity
I will never stall -
For I have the words of triumph with me:
I CAN! I WILL! I SHALL!

⚜

- Richard Millman

The Next Phase – Intermediate

A few years of fun and games have gone by and now your child is entering a new phase. In the beginner phase a coach's primary focus is to get the child interested in squash and teach the basics. While the game should never cease to be fun, the next stage requires new roles and offers fresh challenges for a coach.

The legendary Hashim Khan recalls how he coached players in his book, *Squash Racquets: The Khan Game*. Khan describes how he would play points with a player and try to make him think, giving him advice on better shot selection. "I put pressure on him to think more quick. My opinion, this is best thing coach can do for student." (More info: Select References 2)

Transitioning to Competition

During the kid's pre-adolescent years, a coach should be able to impart a higher level of skill and demand discipline. Working with kids through their teen years poses a unique set of challenges. Unless the coach has a successful track record teaching kids at both the beginner and intermediate levels, you may want to transition from your child's first coach to the next. However, in many cases, the first coach can take a child all the way through.

New considerations for the coach are as follows:

- *Commitment*: Coaching at this level demands greater commitment. Being available for a special pre-competition workout may be important. An adolescent may need emotional attention, outside of squash practice, to prepare him mentally for competition.
- *Emphasis on mastery*: The best coaches focus on fine tuning the strengths of a player and working on the weaknesses, rather than making the player better than a certain opponent. All-around development—psychological, physical, tactical, and technical—is more important than a good-looking record full of easy wins that will later crumble in the face of higher-level competition. The ability to guide kids toward performance goals is extremely valuable. For example, see if they can cut down their unforced errors to less than five per match.

High-Performance Phase

This phase represents national and international levels of junior competition. If a junior earns a spot in a team, either a national squad or a school team, he will inevitably spend more hours with his team coach in practice and tournament travel. However, the job of the team coach is dovetailed with the first coach, who still remains a mentor. There should be good communication between the first coach and the second.

Coaching kids, especially teenagers, is a challenge. Coaches can burnout, too. The coach needs to be able to take a personal interest in the player and provide a tailored, intensive program that will be motivating and exciting for both the junior and the coach.

From One Coach to the Next

Squash development aside, a parent may have to find a new coach because of relocation, scheduling issues and so on. Whatever the reason, try to make the switch from one coach to the next amicable and gradual. Ideally, let the kid continue attending classes with the first coach and start private lessons with the new coach.

Over the years, players may have several coaches. Top pro Jonathon Power started off with his dad as coach until he turned 15. He was then introduced to New Zealander Howard Braun. Later, he hooked up with Canadian National Coach Mike Way, with whom he still works today. Along the way, Power also worked with Rodney Martin in Australia.

Breaking the Mold

In the late 1960s, Dick Fosbury, a high schooler from Oregon and an avid high jumper, shattered the Olympic record, clearing 7 feet 4-1/2 inches. More significant than winning the Olympic gold medal was the way in which Fosbury won this event.

For decades, virtually all high jumpers were coached to use a method called the straddle. The jumper kicks one foot up and rolls with the next. The straddle method depended on leg strength. Dick Fosbury was taught to use the straddle method when he started high jumping. But his jumps were mediocre at best. He began experimenting with a scissors method, popularized by children leaping fences.

Eventually, he refined this technique and actually started to jump up and over backwards, knee, chest, and face to the sky. The technique needed less leg strength, produced higher jumps, and was so revolutionary it got its own name: the Fosbury Flop. The Flop earned Dick Fosbury Olympic gold.

Squash is no different. Some of the game's greatest improvements came about because a coach or player chose to break the mold and experiment with unorthodox techniques. Peter Marshall's two-handed backhand and forehand are still quite unheard of in squash. Yet, Marshall's power and consistency from using two hands put fear in the minds of even the top players. Although his strokes defied tradition and have been attributed to physical problems, he ended up as the world's No. 2 player.

Bedrock fundamentals won't change: good length, early racquet preparation, consistency, and so on. Still, there is tremendous room for innovation in technique and tactics. Go forth and experiment. Make sure your child has the opportunity for unstructured time on the court where he can be creative and take chances.

Legendary coach Jack Barnaby said, "No one can make a player. Teaching is only five percent of the process. It is the steering wheel, and it is therefore important, but the work, desire, determination, persistence, and character must come from the player." You can also add imagination to the list of player qualities espoused by Barnaby.

Measuring Progress

"You can't manage what you can't measure." The point of this famous quote by management guru, Peter Drucker, is that effective management requires feedback, knowing that you are progressing toward your objectives. Regular measurement is key to continuous improvement.

Drucker's theory is applicable to managing anything that has investments in time, money, and effort, including junior squash development. Win-loss records and junior rankings are some ways to measure a junior's progress. However, just as in the beginner phase, experts advise against over-emphasizing wins-losses and rankings once kids start competing.

When competition rankings and points are used as the sole measure of progress an unreasonable burden is placed on the coach and the junior. Easy wins will be emphasized over squash development. Junior competition is an essential part of squash development, but measure performance, rather than wins, and you will encourage the development of solid fundamentals and a love of the game.

Squash Canada Skills Awards

There are ways of measuring squash progress. Squash Canada, for example, employs a Skill Awards Program based on 12 levels. (More info: squash.ca). Adapted from the badge systems used in swimming and skiing, the program awards a badge to players after they reach

each level. The badges can be affixed to a squash bag, racquet cover or clothing. In assessing abilities and measuring progress, award programs provide junior players with goals while they recognize their achievements. The first few levels focus on basic hand-eye coordination, footwork and early racquet skills.

Table 4.1

Squash Canada Skills Awards		
Level	**Skill Assessment Test**	**Points**
1	**A. Hand Catch:** The player must throw up the ball approximately 3 feet with his hitting hand and catch it in the same hand. He then repeats the drill with the non-hitting hand. He must complete the task 10 times for each hand.	20
	B. Bounce & Catch: The player must bounce the ball on the floor from waist level with hi hitting hand and catch the ball with the same hand. This is repeated with the non-hitting hand. The task must be performed 10 times for each hand.	20
	C. Stone Throw: The player stands at the T and simulates the stone-skipping throw towards the front wall. The ball should hit between the cut line and the tin.	10
	D. Star Movement Drill: The player starts at the T without a racquet and is assigned six spots on the court he must move to, three on each side, front, middle and back, where most shots are made from. The player moves to one of the spots and back to the T as the coach points.	20
	E & F. Grips: Players must show the coach two ways of demonstrating the proper grip. **Racquet Roll**: The player holds his racquet flat and places a ball on the surface. He rolls the ball around the racquet clockwise 10 times and counter clockwise 10 times, while maintaining the correct grip.	10

2	**A. Racquet Bounce:** The player stands with his back against the wall and bounces the ball on the racquet, using his forehand and then his backhand 10 times.	10
	B. Two Wall Throw: Standing two racquet lengths away from the front wall, the player throws the ball to the front wall so it hits the front side-wall and then catches it after the first bounce. The player is given 10 tries.	1 per catch
	C. Frisbee Throw: Standing at the T, the player simulates a Frisbee throw towards the front wall. The ball should hit between the cut line and the tin. The movement is similar to the backhand stroke.	1 per throw
	D. Swing Motion: The player must take a full squash swing at an imaginary ball, using proper body position and racquet preparation. Points awarded at coach's discretion.	
	E. Bounce and Hit: The player bounces the ball on the floor and hits it to the wall. He then repeats this on the backhand side. Hitting does not need to be continuous. The player is given 10 tries on each side.	1 per hit
	F. Coach Hand Feed: With the player starting at the T, the coach hand feeds a ball in the service box. The player must hit the ball so it makes it to the front wall. The coach feeds the ball from 6 positions on the court, 5 per spot.	30
3	**A. Hand Feed – no movement**: The coach hand feeds the ball to the player from 6 positions around the court. The player gets 2 tries per position to return the ball.	1 per return
	B. Hand Feed – star movement: The coach hand feeds 5 shots from each of the 4 corners. The player must return to the T after each shot.	20
	C. Bounce and Serve: The player gets 10 tries per side to serve the ball. The ball can hit the floor before it is hit. The objective is for the player to throw the ball up high	20

	D. Single Racquet Feed: The coach gives 5 single racquet feeds to the player from each of the court's 4 corners. The player starts from the T to return the ball.	20
	E. Continuous Hitting: The player starts from any of the 6 court positions and tries to hit the ball continuously 3 times. He is allowed 2 tries from each position.	18

A passing mark is 75 points out of 100 possible points. As players progress through the 12 levels, the complexity of the skills increases. By the final level, players have achieved proficiency of high performance competitive play.

The Unsquashable Skills Awards in England and Scotland have also been helpful in junior player development. These awards, similar in scope of those of Squash Canada's, provide various levels of progression and include a question and answer segment to ensure young players understand rules and scoring.

You can also develop your own way of helping kids measure their progress. Squash pro Stephen Cox leaves it up to the kids to determine how well they're doing. "How many marks out of ten would you give yourself for that shot?" Cox asks his students when they hit the ball well. Sometimes the player will say 8 or 9. Cox believes this exercise helps kids start thinking about the game and begin critiquing themselves. This, he finds, helps accelerate learning and enthusiasm. At Westchester Squash, kids evaluate each other, giving style points as in gymnastics competitions. It becomes a game and something kids look forward to. When kids are finally able to make the shot they've been working on for weeks, give them a pat on the back. They'll be proud and so will you.

5

Competition

*"I've always had those little goals that I've worked toward—
they add up."*
STACY ALLISON, first American woman to climb Mt. Everest.
BeyondtheLimits.com

Why does my child hate sports? There may be many reasons, but competition is definitely not one of them. One of the big myths is that children hate sports because of competition. Just ask any child who is good in a particular sport if he would like to compete and the answer is invariably a resounding, "Yes!"

The reason competition gets a bad rap is because children are thrust into tournaments before they can become reasonably good at that level of play. A child will enjoy competing at every level—rookie to elite—provided he develops sufficient proficiency to sustain a good balance of wins and losses.

Is Junior Ready?

Most parents and coaches don't want to hurt or pressure their kids and risk burn out. However, in every sport there comes a time when the junior necessarily has to compete against an opponent, either a scoreboard, or a person, as in squash. It is the fundamental nature of sport that one must beat the opponent or lose.

Losing hurts, and though winning feels good, some children become anxious when they win in an early round because it means they have to face a tough opponent in the next round – fear of winning. The thinking process goes something like this: "If I win against this guy, I'll have to win against him every time or disappoint myself and be criticized for not living up to expectations." That's why players with better ability sometimes lose to less competent opponents. So the question is, when is a child mature enough to handle wins and losses without too much anxiety?

The other issue to think about is the child's level of competency in the sport. Consider a crossover scenario in which a 14-year-old soccer player switches to squash. She has been playing competitive soccer for several years and may be mentally mature enough to handle wins and losses.

Should the young soccer player take a few squash lessons and jump straight into competition? Most people would say probably not, because, although mentally prepared for competition, she is clearly not ready from the perspective of technical ability. Clearly, both technical competency and mental maturity must come into play when deciding if junior is ready for competition.

Technical Competency

As parents we are unabashedly biased when it comes to judging the technical ability of our kids. After all, Jill is the best squash player in her age group, right? Even though the world may think otherwise. Judging technical readiness for competition is best left to an experienced coach. Your child is ready technically if he's passed some of the skills tests, such as the Skill Award Program in Canada, where there are 12 levels, taking the child from the beginner stage up to the high performance phase.

Mental Maturity

America's Funniest Home Videos televised an episode in which a 3-year-old, frustrated with a computer challenge game, sobs and screams at the monitor, "I want to win! I want to win!" Psychologists say children 8 years old and under are not mentally mature enough to handle the rigors of competition. Between 8 and 10 years of age children can be eased into competition with club matches and inter-club competition. This is also the time when children need to be taught about handling wins and losses. Some kids develop the maturity necessary to want to enter and win competitions after age 10. More commonly, this happens at age 12 or 13.

Until then, they should be taking lessons and practicing match play. Having successfully completed the technical competency exercises, the young lady can't wait to enter the local tournament. It's time for her to enjoy the ride.

Having the mental maturity to face competition is less of an issue for older kids who crossover from other sports. Ellen Peterson of Denmark, who has hovered in the top 20 in the women's pro rankings, didn't pick up a squash racquet until she turned 16. Peterson had a childhood sports career as a soccer goalie and was a member of the Danish Junior Women's soccer team. When the family moved to Australia, where squash courts were more accessible than soccer fields, she took up the sport. Peterson's maturity and competitive background in soccer has helped her not only cope well with the rigors of squash competition but thrive on it, even though in squash winning and losing was her responsibility alone.

Draws

The Draw. Sounds like a Clint Eastwood classic, doesn't it? A junior squash draw can be just as exciting. The tournament draw determines who gets to play whom. The draw sheet published online and displayed at the tournament site may also indicate the place and time of matches. In a single-elimination draw, if a player loses, he is out; if he wins, he goes on to the next round.

So your junior has honed his technique, practiced match play, and is now entering his first tournament. You pay the registration fee, put life on hold for a day and drive 60 miles to the tournament site. In 30 minutes, junior has lost his first match. In a single elimination tournament, he's out of the competition and on his way home.

A first-round loss can be heartbreaking for a new junior player and frustrating for the parent. Fortunately, the double-elimination is the more common type of tournament draw in squash. With this format, if a player loses his first-round match, he is out of the main draw but can enter the consolation draw and play until he loses. The consolation format gives juniors a chance to play, even after losing, and therefore guarantees a player at least two matches. A Full Feed-In Consolation, which is most common within USSRA-sanctioned junior tournaments, places kids from the main draw into the consolations from the first round all the way through to the quarterfinals.

The best format to gain competition experience is the round robin, which is ideal for small draws of eight or so players. This format guarantees multiple matches for each player, as they play against all others in their flight. This format works well for clubs and beginner tournaments.

Junior Ranking

Put together a bunch of computers, a team of computer savvy folks, loads of experience and smarts from the USSRA and you've got the Junior Ranking system.

For parents who feel a computerized ranking system is sometimes unfair, consider the alternative: a mountain of avoidable paperwork for players, tournament directors, and the USSRA. Ranking and selection committees would inevitably be accused of playing politics and power mongering because the ranking computation depends on so many complex variables. And then there are the protest committees, who must give a hearing to players and parents who believe they got the short end of the stick.

The computerized ranking system is far from perfect but at least no one can accuse it of bias against a specific player.

Ranking Defined

A player's ranking is a number that reflects the quality of his match results compared to other competitors over a specified period of time. Tournaments that count toward the ranking are sanctioned by the USSRA on a national level. Likewise, Europe, Canada and other international governing bodies of squash have their own systems for ranking their junior players.

In addition to national rankings, some juniors can also receive rankings within their region. Each provincial association within Squash Canada has a ranking system for its players. In the US, some squash associations have their own program of ranking players, either regionally or by state. In Australia, juniors can receive state and national rankings. In England, players are also ranked by county.

Ranking is not intended to measure a player's skill level, nor is it a guaranteed indicator of future performance. If that were the case, a junior ranked No. 1 would become No. 1 in the professional rankings, which is not at all true. Consider ranking as simply an assessment of a player's past match record.

Ranking Systems

Depending upon how quality of a match is determined, there are two major systems of ranking players in squash – the Elo Algorithm system and the Points-per-round system. There have been rankings by committees in various squash nations; however, this type of ranking is becoming a thing of the past as newer and more objective systems come to the forefront.

- *Elo Algorithm System:* The USSRA uses this method based on the Elo algorithm system, which was initiated by Professor Arpad Elo, whose academic field was chemistry and computers. Mathematics is the backbone of the system, which has been applied to chess and a number of other sports and games, including bowling and golf. The USSRA (More info: us-squash.org) began using this system in the 1997-1998 season. It measures quality as results achieved playing against higher ranked opponents. The rounds reached in a tournament, or whether the player won the tournament, are all inconsequential for ranking.

- *Points-per-round Ranking System:* The number of rounds played and the strength of the tournament determine the quality of a player's record. The European Squash Federation uses this system to rank players who compete on the European Junior Circuit.

Elo Algorithm System – How it Works

The basic idea of this ranking method is to continuously change a player's rating based on whether she performs better or worse than expected in matches. The objective is to reward the winner (add points) and penalize the loser (subtract points).

Players come to a match with a rating based on their previous performances. If the player is new to squash, they are assigned a rating based on the results of their first tournament. The ranking systems simply sorts out the players by their ratings.

Whether the event is a closed championship or a bronze event, the type of tournament is not a factor. It also does not matter whether the player makes it to the second round or to the semi-finals. The ranking focuses on the matches between two players. The spread of ranking points between the two players determines how many points one gains or loses. If a player defeats an opponent who is well below him in the rankings, that player will gain very little. However, if a player beats an opponent who is much higher in the rankings, that player will make a big jump.

Just a couple of years ago, Squash Canada reevaluated its ranking system and adopted a Double Jump Ranking program, which is similar to the USSRA's system in that it allows players to move based on the level of player beaten and the time and ability level of previously recorded victories of the winner. (More info: squash.ca). The USSRA is continually evaluating and fine-tuning its system to ensure fairness and give equal opportunities to all players. (More info: us-squash.org).

Points Per Round – What it Means

Similar to the pro rankings, the European Squash Federation (ESF) organizes its junior rankings by how far a player advances in a tournament and the quality of the event. The number of points awarded per event depends upon the type of tournament, Junior Open, Circuit, Grand Prix, Super Series, or Gold, and the size of the draw. The farther one advances through the tournament, the higher the points.

Juniors, whatever their nationality, who have participated in just one tournament on the Circuit are given a ranking record in the age category played in. The ranking is based upon the player's four best results obtained in the preceding 12 months, divided by four. If a player has played less than four tournaments, the total is still divided by four to calculate the average.

At the end of the season, prizes are awarded to the top eight boys and top eight girls in the Under 19 division. (More info: europeansquash.com).

Earning a Ranking

Club play, long-term skill development, and mental maturity are important reasons why younger age groups are not encouraged to compete for rankings. Younger children can gain tournament experience by playing in tournaments that don't count toward rankings. Once a kid develops a level of competitive maturity, the rankings race can be an exciting experience for the junior.

To earn a ranking, players must accumulate a specified number of participation points by competing in sanctioned tournaments in their age category. In the US, once you're a member of the USSRA, it only takes one match to get your name on a ranking list. For a year-end or final national ranking, a junior needs to play in at least four tournaments in his age division.

In addition, before players can attain a final ranking, they must have a current USSRA membership and become certified as a club referee. To do so, they must study the rules and pass the USSRA's referee's test. At most junior tournaments, after juniors play their match, both the winner and the loser must also officiate a match. The USSRA believes it is important for juniors to become referees so they can gain an in-depth understanding of the nuances of the game and its rules. Juniors who have officiated matches usually have a different perspective about referees that is helpful during their own competitive play. There is also a social aspect to sitting with one's opponent and making decisions. This helps with social skills while it humanizes competition.

After playing in a sanctioned tournament and racking up the points, presto! Junior's name is up in rankings list. You can access the rankings list and your player record on the Web-based USSRA's Railstation (More info: us-squash.org.) It's important to verify player records and report any inaccuracies. Prior to Railstation, rankings were only published twice a year. Now they are available as often as twice each month. Under the previous system, only the ranking was published, not a detailed match history. Now, parents and players have the opportunity to review the entire playing record.

Playing lots of tournaments doesn't necessarily mean a higher ranking. Once kids compete in a tournament, the results go right into the data bank. A loss to a lower ranked player can impact standings significantly. Therefore, players need to be prepared for each tournament by staying healthy and fit to perform their best, even if it means missing a party or favorite TV show to get the rest they need. Welcome to the race! Keep it simple, don't over-manage rankings. Enjoy the learning experience. Have fun!

Perks

Obviously, there is no guarantee that a No. 1 ranked junior will win the next tournament he enters, but earning a high ranking sure has its perks:

- *Entries to tournaments*: If the number of entrants exceeds the draw limit, a Tournament Committee may bump out the lower ranked players. Many high-profile tournaments are restricted to a qualified number of ranked players

- *Better draw placements*: A highly ranked player may earn seeding in a tournament. This means he or she won't be confronting other highly ranked players in the early rounds. Like a self-fulfilling prophecy, this gives the player a better chance of winning the tournament, which in turn further improves his ranking.

- *Special opportunities*: Top players have the opportunity to attend training squads and become eligible for national selection tournaments that could lead to securing a spot on a national team.

- *Goal setting*: Rankings should show an improvement in performance and should not be a goal in and of themselves. The player who says I want to be ranked No. 5 is setting an outcome goal, rather than a process goal, which can actually limit him in reaching his full potential. See how the child can improve his performance no matter what number is attached. By consistently evaluating performance, the player will ultimately climb to a higher level.

Children are natural dreamers. A dream can be a great source of motivation to work hard. Encourage their dreams but help them understand the difference between a dream and a process goal. Children should be taught to chase process goals and enjoy each accomplishment. That is the practical way to make children feel successful, whether or not all dreams come true.

Of course being No. 1, even for a while, bestows never-ending campus bragging rights, too.

Finding a Tournament

It's great to be a squash kid – with hundreds of tournaments to choose from, and a good parent or coach driving to and from competition sites. And when the vehicle is equipped with a rear-seat DVD entertainment system, life can't get any better for a squash kid.

There are tournaments and leagues that cater to every skill level—beginner to advanced and all junior age groups under 11s-to-19s—with a variety of competition formats. The best place to start looking for tournaments is at your local squash club. Chances are, the club runs tournaments, leagues and links with a junior competitive structure. Many clubs have teams that travel together.

In the US, the best tournaments for new and developing junior players are Bronze and Sliver events, formerly Future Stars, which are sanctioned USSRA tournaments designed for mid- and low-ranked or unranked players. (More info: us-squash.org).

In Canada, juniors can start out with beginner level tournaments, such as the Dunlop Bronze events and progress to Silver and Gold tournaments for high performance players. Leagues are also great ways to get match play experience. Canada has active league programs in all of its Provinces, both local and regional. Canadian juniors have the added excitement of the Canada Winter Games, held every four years, which enable teams from all the Provinces and Territories to compete against each other. (More info: squash.ca).

The England Squash Association has graded tournaments for juniors up to and including age 15. Part of an innovative online pilot program, players choose an initial grade that describes their level. They can then raise their grade by competing against players of a similar level in graded tournaments across the country. Players can follow their progress online. After they turn 16, juniors can join adult tournaments. (More info: esgrading.com and englandsquash.com).

European Junior Squash Circuit

The ESF's Junior Circuit is often the next step in competition for many players who want to test the waters outside their homeland. Tournaments on the circuit take place in various countries, including Switzerland, Sweden, England, Belgium, Hungary, Ireland, Scotland, the Czech Republic, Slovakia, Denmark, Italy, France, Wales, Austria, Germany, the Netherlands and Spain. The British Junior Open is by far one of the most highly attended tournaments on the circuit and is sometimes referred to as "the unofficial world junior open".

The European Junior Circuit is open to boys and girls eligible to play in Under 13, Under 15, Under 17 or Under 19 age divisions. Players' entries must be endorsed by their national squash association. Juniors from all over the world have entered these competitions, earned rankings, and even reaped prize money. (More info: europeansquash.com).

Team Competition

Club versus club in league play, inter-state, or regional competition brings a lot of team spirit and camaraderie to an individual sport such as squash. Leagues offer great match play opportunities and a fun introduction to competitive play. Leagues are popular with players of all levels and ages.

Once juniors become the top in their age group, they can be eligible for a national team and compete against players from all over the world.

National Training Squads

For elite squash players, a real feather in their cap is to be invited to a juniors training squad. In the US, junior squads were established in 1996 and modeled after similar programs around the world. These squads prepare up-and-coming players for international competition.

In the US, the top six boys and girls from each of four age groups—Under 13, Under 15, Under 17 and Under 19—are invited, based on rankings. Once selected, squads train for two weekends each season at top-notch venues under the supervision of a first-rate coaching staff.

National Teams

One of the most sought after goals for a young player is to be selected to a national team to compete against teams from other countries. It is an honor and a privilege to play on a team representing your country. Playing on a national team also offers kids a chance to travel and meet new people. But more importantly, the opportunity enables kids to be on a team with those they have competed against all year long. Once adversaries on the court, they now come together as one. The friendships and life experiences gained are, in a sense, more significant than what transpires on the court.

In the US, to be considered for a team you must compete in three selection tournaments in each of the two age groups: Under 19 and Under 17. The tournaments have draws of 32 players only. One of the three selection tournaments is the National Closed Championships, which is limited to the top 18 ranked players in each division.

After the tournaments, a Junior National Committee will select four players in each age group for the team. In addition to reviewing the tournament results, players' rankings and coaches' recommendations, the committee also makes a decision based on other criteria, such as performance in national squads, particularly the player's ability to work with team coaches and fellow members. Another important factor is that the player has adhered to all world squash requirements and rules. Players must not have any on- or off-court violations of the Code of Conduct and must satisfy all membership requirements of their national squash association. In the US, players must pass the club referee course required for their ranking.

Should the committee be unable to make a clear decision, a special team trial can be arranged. In the future, there is hope that the USSRA will add more age groups, such as Under 15 and Under 13, to its national teams.

National squash organizations subsidize a portion of their team program, with additional funding through government sports commissions. In the US, some of the money comes from the US Olympic Committee and the USSRA's endowment fund. In many cases, additional fund raising is necessary. Team members get together to encourage their club or local sponsors to help out. Other teams participate in fundraisers, either by hosting a dinner or selling a product. The Victorian Squash Association in Australia has an active fundraising program to benefit its juniors. Team enthusiasts have sold travel mugs, led a Cadbury chocolate drive and hosted a Hall of Fame dinner, where proceeds went to the juniors. Juniors in Brisbane held an eight-hour Squash-A-Thon to raise money for team travel.

Here are some of the many competitive opportunities for top national junior team members:

- *World Junior Championships*: This biennial event is the icing on the cake in junior squash. The tournament has been around for 24 years and is always held in a different host country. The World Juniors includes both a team event and an individual tournament. One of the more recent world junior women's championships was held in Belgium and the men's in Pakistan, where armed guards manned the club. The unsettled political climate in this country deterred some American players from participating. From unusual court conditions to third-world environments, the location of the world juniors will bring a different experience for many young players. Some players have even met a Prime Minister!

- *Pan American Games*: These events bring together athletes from 42 nations from North, Central and South America and the Caribbean. The first Games date back to 1951. The motto of the Pan American Sports Organization, PASO, is America, Espirito, Sport, Fraternite, which in the four languages used in the Americas – Spanish, Portuguese, English and French – translates as "The American spirit of friendship through sports." The Games precede the Olympic Games by a year. In size and scope, the Pan American Games are second only to the Olympics.

- *Canadian American Junior Challenge*: Co-founded by the USSRA and Squash Canada in 2001, this event provides a competitive test match for the Under 19 and Under 17 national team candidates and one Under 15 developmental player each season. Players are selected for this competition based on rankings and the national team selection criteria. The idea behind the event is to give juniors from both countries better international match experience.

- *The Commonwealth Games*: The Commonwealth consists of nations from Africa to Asia, from the Pacific shores to the Caribbean. These are the only games where just one language is shared—English. The Commonwealth Games Federation, the governing body, has as its core values, Humanity, Equality and Destiny. These games were first held in Hamilton, Ontario, Canada in 1930 and the first Commonwealth Youth Games began in 2000. Nearly 600 athletes under 18, from 15 Commonwealth nations, participated in eight sports, including squash.

- *World Maccabiah Games*: Sometimes referred to as 'the Jewish Olympics," these games are held every four years in Israel, the year after the Olympics, bringing together the best Jewish athletes from over 50 countries. As many as 6,000 athletes participate in Open, Masters, Junior and Disabled divisions. Sanctioned by the International Olympic Committee and General Association of International Sports Federation, (GAISF), the Maccabiah Games rank among the five largest sports gatherings in the world.

- *World University Championships*: Held on even years, this multi-sports competition involves thousands of student athletes from all over the world. Hungary is the site of the 5th World University Squash Championships, featuring individual and team competition for both men and women.

Once juniors grow older, there are many opportunities for men and women's team competition. In addition to the Pan American Games, Commonwealth Games and World Championships, squash plays an important role in the Asian Games, the African Game and the World Games.

To get started playing tournaments, begin with your local squash club. The club can link you to your regional squash organization to find tournaments that match your child's level. If you don't find an appropriate level and format in your area, consider organizing a tournament or team competition. Gather up enough kids who want to compete and contact your local squash club. A little legwork, some financial savvy, and you can have a junior competition to call your own!

Tournament Travel

Kids, particularly teenagers, love competitive squash because it gives them a chance to travel, sometimes independently. At the higher echelons of junior competition—international team competition—a portion of the travel tab may even be picked up or one's national squash governing body.

Itinerary

There are tournaments just about every weekend in most squash playing nations, so it shouldn't be difficult to find nearby tournaments for a beginner or intermediate level junior player. As a junior advances in the rankings race, tournament travel is inevitable.

Crisscrossing the country, traveling overseas, meeting new people, and learning about other cultures is both fun and educational. It can also be a real eye opener. The World Junior Open has been held in places like Egypt and Pakistan, not countries many juniors would normally travel to on a regular basis. Kids learn about different ways of life, customs and food.

Since squash is so highly regarded in some countries, it is not unusual to have the Prime Minister and other important government officials as spectators. Different national squash organizations rotate in hosting international competition. Since there are 118 national associations of squash worldwide, there's no doubt you'll find an adventure at the next top international junior event.

Housing

When a parent accompanies the child, they might stay with friends or in a hotel. Even if the tournament is within a three to four hour drive from home, it may be advantageous to arrange an overnight stay so the player is better prepared for her match. Tournaments sometimes offer recommendations for hotels near the tournament site or provide an official hotel with a special rate for players.

Players sometimes stay at the homes of other players or with members of the host club. In this case, the host family assumes responsibility for providing meals, local transportation, and general supervision. A player who stays with a host family should be instructed to behave appropriately so the visit is a pleasant experience for both the host family and the player.

Advice for the Squash Traveler

- If your child is traveling internationally, it's a good idea to get medical coverage, as well as coverage for lost baggage.
- Keep all telephone numbers handy, including the hotel, tournament site, and any contacts you have in the area.
- If a junior is on her own, make sure she keeps in contact with people expecting her as to where she is in her travels and when she is expected to arrive.
- Find out if your child needs a visa. Some juniors have not been allowed on flights because they lacked the necessary documents.
- Americans should travel with a copy of the USSRA's Junior Guide to Squash (More info: us-squash.org).

Squash can literally take you and your child all over the world. Once she starts inching her way up the national rankings, it might be time to renew the passports and start packing. Bon Voyage!

6

Match Time

"To know how to do something well is to enjoy it."
PEARL BUCK, writer

Little things can add up when it comes to making those long hours of practice payoff on match day. For instance, knowing the tournament rules and code of conduct is a good idea. Checking equipment the previous evening and getting a good night's rest can make a difference on the big day. Arrive at the tournament site early and well fueled and always complete a proper warm-up routine.

Translating Practice to Match Play

When juniors start to play in sanctioned tournaments, they sometimes discover that even an early round match is played at a level several notches above anything they have ever faced. Start at the club level first and then progress to local events and, afterwards, larger sanctioned tournaments. As for a child's readiness, get the advice of your coach, but also put your child in the driver's seat. Is he asking to do this? If the answer is yes, your child is exhibiting critical thinking skills and will most likely put more into it, says top player and coach Damian Walker.

If a child is revved up and ready, it's a good idea to come up with a good practice plan to best prepare for competition. Practicing with different types of players and solo practicing are both important. Arrange practice with an adult or a partner who's at a higher level and encourage the junior to give it everything he's got. Practicing with weaker players allows your junior to hone his technique and build confidence. Shona Kerr, squash coach at Wesleyan University, suggests (Table 6.1) the benefits of practice matches with players of various abilities.

Practice Strategies

Teaching professionals urge their students to practice solo as often as they can. In doing so, a player gets the real feel for the game and can improve technique and consistency. Solo practice should be incorporated into a serious player's routine on a regular basis, with at

Table 6.1

Training Benefits	Competitor Ability		
	Weaker	**Same**	**Stronger**
Technical	Excellent: Allows time to focus on swing, movement adjustments	Good: Allows you to test how well and how long "good" technique will stand up to an equal player	Average: A stronger player will apply too much pressure for you to have time to consider technique
Tactical	Good: Allows you to practice being in control and to choose your shots	Excellent: It is here where you will see improvements in perception, anticipation and shot selection. Also test out and practice sticking to game plans	Good: Can be used for defensive game practice, working on patience in rallies
Physical	Average: Does not push you physically	Excellent: Pushes you physically hard and tests fitness	Good: More pressure equals more work
Psychological	Good: Builds confidence in being in control, shot selection and technique	Excellent: Good practice to remain focused in the moment and staying emotionally in control	Good: No pressure to win, good practice on hanging in a match and being patient

least two hour-long sessions per week. Get help from a boom-box blaring your favorite tunes or perhaps listen up on your sleek iPod. In no time at all kids will get in the groove, even while practicing solo.

In addition to playing matches, you should also encourage your child to incorporate drills into a practice session with a partner. Jonathon Power, like many top players, prepares for tournaments by playing conditioning games, where you practice certain game plans and playing styles. For instance, you can set limits for yourself and only hit the ball to the right front wall. Since your practice partner will always know where the ball is going, you will have some added pressure and have to put in a little extra effort. Or, you can arrange the game so that one player always hits to one of the four corners of the court and the other player can hit anywhere he wants. Set the conditions any way you like. You can find great practice drills in Pippa Sales' book, *Improve Your Squash Game: 101 Drills, Coaching Tips and Resources*.

Preparing for the Match

You won't find professional players that party all night long and head straight into a match early the next morning. If they do, it's guaranteed they won't be on the professional circuit for long. There are pre-match rituals most players follow so they can do their best.

At the same time, match preparation does not have to be a regimented boot camp. Rather, it is a set of simple, easy-to-follow routines, like getting a good night's sleep the night before match day. When parents encourage the child to follow a pre-match ritual it becomes a habit. Soon the child will start to prepare for the match without bring prodded. Help kids develop their own pre-match ritual to prepare mentally and physically for a match. What works for one may not work for someone else.

24 Hours Before Match Day

The USSRA's Railstation (More info: us-squash.org), for example, posts match times, as well as the tournament draw on the Internet. It's also a good idea to reconfirm the start time with the tournament desk a day before the match. The penalty for lateness varies among tournament directors. In some cases, if you're 10 minutes late, you might as well pack up your squash bag and head for home. Other tournaments may have different policies. Check with your tournament to confirm the match time. Is your kid on time? Better still, is he 15 minutes early? Then, there is a good chance he can perform to his potential.

Maintain a high-carb diet – whole-grain breads, cereals, and pasta, plus plenty of fruits and vegetables. Avoid fat and spicy foods. There have been several situations in top professional tournaments where a player had to withdraw due to stomach problems from eating the wrong food. Remember that kids react to foods differently. Certain foods may give them a boost, while others might slow them down. Top American junior Michelle Quibell must have protein the night before a match, while her mother, who was also a competitive player, found that bread made her lethargic before a match.

In the same way you encourage your kids to put homework and necessary supplies in their school backpack before going to bed, help them prepare their match bag with racquets, spare shirt, and so on the day before a match. And don't forget a book, magazine or game boy or whatever he likes to do in his spare time. You never know when the previous match might be delayed, bad weather has backed up all matches, or the tournament is running late for whatever reason. Be prepared to sit and wait it out.

Get as much sleep as possible the night before a match. Sometimes this is a challenge because of travel or the proverbial butterflies in the belly the night before an important match. Children need to know that it's okay to lose sleep once in a while. More important is that they not psyche themselves out before a match because of lost sleep.

Fueling for the Match

Go bananas, go nuts; salad with chicken, peanut butter crackers, non-sugar cereal, potatoes and pasta – all easy-to-prepare or out-of-the-box foods a busy parent can offer to ensure the kid is well fueled on match day. The high-carbohydrate plan helps store glycogen in the muscles and liver as fuel for activity. Once again, avoid high-fat and spicy foods.

Eat three to four hours before reporting time so food is completely absorbed from the stomach. Jonathon Power recommends pasta. He then enjoys a steak dinner afterwards for post-match protein. At the tournament site, a light snack of portable foods ought to keep junior happy. Healthy snack ideas include trail mix, rice cakes or mini-bagels.

Kids don't sweat as much as adults do and are less able to cool off. They also absorb heat more easily. These factors increase the risk of dehydration in kids. Give children a squeeze bottle of water or sports drink and remind them to take gulps before, during, and after the match. A sports drink is tasty, will supply energy, and turns on thirst; however, too much can be harmful. Encourage kids to alternate sports drinks with water.

Match Day

For afternoon matches, taking a catnap, playing board games with friends and family are all great ways to achieve some calm before the storm. If a child has an early morning match, parents ought to help him wake up at least a few hours before the competition. Don't allow your child to sleep within two hours of the match. You don't want a groggy player sleepwalking to the court.

If your child thinks a pre-match swim might perk him up, say no. Swimming can relax the muscles and cause the opposite effect. Save the swim for later.

Get to the tournament 30 to 40 minutes before reporting time and check in at the tournament desk. A new site and the hustle and bustle of parents and players can be intimidating for a young child. Fill up waiting time by getting to know other parents and players. Many lasting friendships have blossomed at tournament sites.

If the coach is available, an older kid may like to discuss the game plan, or if courts are available perhaps set up a short 15 minute hitting session to get grooved. KhanSquash.com provides a number of useful tips on technique, match preparation and conditioning. To get ready for a match, Khansquash.com recommends the following: Hit at a good pace until you break a sweat, but don't over do it. If a court is not available, find a quiet hallway to practice ghosting or try to imagine what it will be like on court. Visualization can be helpful. Have your child paint a mental picture of how he is going to hit the ball and how he sees himself playing. (More info: KhanSquash.com)

It's also helpful if you know a little about your competitor's playing style. Perhaps your child has watched the player previously and can get a grasp of his strengths and weaknesses. If not, the warm up and the first game will give your child a good idea of what he is up against.

Before the Match

Quiet time. Famous basketball coach Phil Jackson had his players take a ball into a locker room corner and visualize the game plan. Don't expect your bundle of energy to do that just yet, but make room in the schedule for some quiet time so you establish a good pre-match ritual for later years. A pre-match ritual of getting in the right frame of mind helps players feel that they are in the zone.

About 15 minutes before match time head to the tournament desk for the court assignment. Get to the court for warm-up. Find a routine of warm up and practice that works for you. A few minutes of dynamic stretching will loosen up the muscles and get the blood flowing before play. An example of dynamic stretching is holding on to the wall with your right hand and swinging your left leg up in front, then back behind you ten times. Then switch to the other leg. For the upper body, swing one arm up and back while holding the wall with the other hand, then switch.

Dynamic stretching uses controlled movements to increase the reach and range of motion while raising the heart rate and preparing the body for more intense activity. Static stretching, where you hold a position for a certain length of time, has the opposite effect. Static stretching releases endorphins that relax the muscles, encouraging them to shut down and preparing them for inactivity. The muscles therefore will not protect the joints, leaving them at risk for injury once they are stressed. Static stretching should be done after the match, not before.

After dynamic stretching, find a good pre-match warm up of on-court hitting. When world-ranked player Ivy Pochoda played her first junior tournament, her coach Geoff Mitchell recommended hitting each shot five times down each side of the court as a good pre-match warm-up routine.

As a junior develops, competition days will increase. There will be travel to tournament sites in different cities and countries. Travel is an exciting perk for a squash kid, but acclimating to a new city and culture takes some getting used to. Following a standard set of pre-match rituals will reassure the junior that every match is, in fact, like any other, allowing relaxed and focused play.

Etiquette

Good etiquette is not snobbish behavior. It's simply a way to allow everyone involved in a social gathering to have a good time. Translated to a squash tournament setting, good etiquette is required and means that players, spectators, parents, and coaches must accept certain behavioral norms so that everyone, including you, can derive maximum enjoyment from the match.

Racquet rage in professional tournaments and altercations among players and referees have been making the news in squash circles, so much so that the governing bodies of squash are condemning such behaviors and enforcing the rules of conduct more strictly. Bad behavior reflects negatively on the sport.

Pros Clive Leach and Blair Horler learned their lesson when they were not only suspended from a $30,000 doubles tournament, but also forced to pay a fine. Action was taken against the duo because of hot flaring tempers at a previous tournament where Leach disputed referee calls and returned his opponent's serve to the ceiling in a fit of rage that continued all the way to the locker-room. Subsequently, the pair calmed down. Everyone, both pros and amateurs, needs to be on the same page with regard to etiquette.

David Palmer, the popular Australian, was banned for an entire year from any World Squash Federation events, including the World Games, World Men's Team Championships and World Doubles Championships. This disciplinary action was a result of Palmer's inappropriate behavior at the World Doubles Championships in India. Palmer breached five codes of conduct and was penalized for verbal abuse of the referee and officials, foul language, abuse of equipment, not complying with the spirit of the sport and disrupting the game with poor conduct. Palmer had to forfeit his prize money of over $2,000.

The World Squash Federation has the most up-to-date rules, which include the acceptable behavior of both players and spectators. (More info: worldsquash.org) The USSRA has its Junior Code of Conduct in the Junior Guidebook (More info: us-squash.org).

Spectator Etiquette

What was once just a guideline has since become an official World Squash rule. If a spectator is unruly, a referee has the right to suspend play and remove the offending person from the court area. The World Squash Federation's Code of Conduct (More info: worldsquash.org) notes that the player can suffer if the entourage isn't following correct protocol. Keep that and the following ideas in mind at your next squash tournament:

- Don't yell or call the ball while the game is being played.
- Turn the mobile phone to silent mode. Step outside the spectator area if you must make a call and do it in between games.
- Go nuts when your favorite player wins, but only after you congratulate both players.

Parent Etiquette

Until a kid can pack her bags and fly to a tournament all by herself, the parent has to help junior prepare the match bag the previous night. On match day, get her to the tournament site in plenty of time so she doesn't feel rushed and is ready for her match.

- Resist the temptation to sit in the most visible seat, hemming, hawing, and tearing your hair at every point your kid loses.

Ready

One hour to go
'Til destiny and time to meet your fate.
Will you succeed or will you fail?
How stands your final state?
Now is the time
That all your work
Is finally brought to bear
Have you truly done enough?
Have really paid your fare?
If you have, then you will stand
And face the foe full strong
And if the other case is true
You'll feel everything is wrong.
For in competition you must know
That you must be prepared
Otherwise, despite your skill,
Your performance is impaired.
So as you stand in readiness
You must ask yourself this question:
Do you feel the battle's thrill?
Or nervous indigestion?
Whatever is the case this time
As today's heat turns to cold
Then organize your next year's plan
And make it plenty bold
And even think more than a year
Of two or three or four
So that one day, as you stand and wait
At the battle's brink once more,
You will say from within your heart:
I stand here feeling fine
For I have earned my passage here
And victory can be mine!

⚜

—*Richard Millman*

Officially called "one-of-those," parents who do this are an annoyance to other spectators and to players as well.

- If you don't agree with a referee's call, don't make an issue of it. The referee's job is hard enough. How would you like to be in that hot seat? Let the referees do their jobs to the best of their abilities.
- If you find the match disturbing in any way, including the opponent's behavior or anything else, don't speak directly to your child, the referee, or the other parent. Speak to the tournament director.
- Plan on devoting the entire weekend to the tournament. Don't try to squeeze in soccer or a birthday party. Once you commit to a tournament, honor that commitment. It's disappointing for the other competitor, who may have traveled a great distance if your child doesn't show up for a match.
- Try to clap for good points made by both players.
- Don't hesitate to have your child removed if she is misbehaving on the court. No match is more important than teaching a child life lessons.
- No matter the outcome, hug your child as she comes off the court. Congratulate his opponent for playing well.
- Should you bump into the parent of the other player, try to get to know them. If the two families live in different cities, the kids may choose to stay in each other's homes during tournaments, and it's always beneficial to develop an acquaintance. Squash is like that. You can have ferocious battles on the court with a player, but afterwards you can become best buddies. Pros Jonathon Power and Graham Ryding, both Canadians, have been referred to as best friends and arch rivals.

Coach Etiquette

Adhering to social graces guarantees an all-round enjoyable match, whether one is a certified coach or a parent who proxies for the coach. Squash is one of the few sports when coaching is allowed during the 90 second break between games, for both individual and team competition. If the coach takes more than the allotted time, the player could receive a penalty from the referee.

- Other than the break time, record observations unobtrusively, without distracting the players.
- Congratulate your junior after the match, regardless of the outcome.

- Put off speaking about the match until later. With very young kids, instead of talking to them about mistakes and improvements, simply make mental notes and incorporate appropriate changes into their lesson plans. Talking too much will be ineffective. For older kids, dissect what went wrong to see where the child got into trouble. Help the child see the choices he made in the match.

Player Etiquette

The World Squash Federation has a code of conduct that will not tolerate certain behaviors (More info: worldsquash.org). If Johnny feels like shouting the four-letter words he's picked up from the schoolyard, the squash court is not the place to try out his newly acquired language. He should make every attempt to hold his tongue. And if he gets mad enough to throw his racquet or worse yet, bop his opponent on the head, he's in for big trouble.

Taking too big a swing on the forehand or backhand that may get in the competitor's way or cause danger is violating squash rules. Because of the nature of the game, interference is a major issue. A player who feels his opponent is in his way can appeal to the referee by saying, "let please." The referee may allow a let or grant the player a stroke.

If a player is late getting back to the court in between games, or wastes any time, he could be penalized. If any activities like these occur, the referee can assign a penalty of his choice: a warning – conduct warning; a stroke awarded to the other player – conduct stroke, which means the competitor receives a point; game awarded to the other player – conduct game; or even the entire match awarded – conduct match.

Here's the rest of the story on player behavior:

- In the warm up, never hit the ball to yourself more than twice. When hitting to the other player, don't hit winners, hit a ball your opponent can return.
- Acknowledge your competitor's good shot by either a nod of the head or saying, "good shot."
- You can jump up and down crazily after a victory, but first remember to congratulate your opponent on a wonderful game and thank the officials.
- When you shake hands, shake firmly and look your opponent in the eye to show that you are sincere.

Let please, Ref!

I know you think I couldn't get
To where the ball was gone,
But where you thought I had to stop-
I could have carried on.
And if my dear antagonist
Had not unleashed his hairy fist-
My forthright try to persevere,
Had seen me through and in the clear!
What then is this ill-thought decision,
In light of which, like some incision,
You cut from me this vital score,
And leave me at this game's death's door?
By all that's just I must appeal
And ask you to restrain your zeal.
Allow us both to play again
And thus a true result attain.

—Richard Millman

During the Match

While a junior dukes it out on court, there is a lot a coach and parent can observe. A professional coach will go about his business, making notes on technical stuff like the margin of errors on the backhand, the follow through on the forehand and getting to the T.

Instead of getting all wound-up worrying about match results a parent can observe two factors on which he has the maximum impact—court behavior and mental toughness. Is junior displaying good player etiquette? Are there aspects of a junior's behavior that need to be discussed with her the next day?

When looking for mental toughness, observe whether junior is incorporating habits that sports psychologists recommend:

- *Focal Point*: Squash requires total concentration. Players need to focus solely on squash and avoid any kind of distractions. "Don't focus on the outcome," says top player Natalie Grainger. "Focus on hitting the ball."

- *Noise*: Learn to block out any distractions, even those squash related, such as worrying about the coach, parent or the way you look.
- *Concentration*: Focus on performance and conducting a game plan that will eventually lead to victory.
- *Pre Service ritual*: Develop a ritual before any point. Some players bounce the ball vigorously with their racquet before serving. Others take a deep breath and get their body in position before returning a serve. Each player needs to develop a ritual that works for him. Follow the ritual regardless of the match situation.
- *Loosen-up*: Enhance relaxation by holding the racquet in the non-dominant hand in between games.
- *Self-talk*: Avoid negative self-talk and berating after a mistake.
- *Attitude and Outlook*: Keep positive. Self-confidence is key.

There are a variety of established drills that work on mental toughness. Discuss observations with the coach and determine whether appropriate mental drills can be incorporated into lesson plans. If you suspect family or school issues may be affecting the ability to concentrate, try and get to the bottom of the problem as soon as possible.

After the Match

Following the match, junior should thank the other players and officials. If there is another match to be played, check the schedule from the tournament desk. After a tough match, it's a good idea to cool down by riding a stationary bike for up to 20 minutes. Some of the top players find that spending 10 minutes in an ice bath can help rejuvenate the body after intense playing. The bath can be half water and half ice. It's also important to refuel immediately. Research suggests that consuming carbohydrates within 30 minutes of exercising helps reload muscles within 12 to 16 hours.

Afterwards, assess what is, overall, the single most important factor: did your child have fun? Somebody is going to win and somebody is going to lose the match. Kids will be disappointed after a loss, and some will get very upset. Kevin Doucet, Vice President Technical Squash Canada, and a level 4 coach, says it's okay to be upset because it shows the child cares about the sport and his performance. But at the same time, kids need to keep it all in perspective, control their emotions and not think or speak negatively about themselves. Moreover, they need to learn that they can be winners in other ways. Maybe they hit some incredible nicks or returned some tricky serves. Make sure your child has a mentor who can help her believe in herself. With self-confidence, she will think, "If I don't win the match now, I've played well and perhaps I will win a match in the future." For a young child it's best to simply appreciate his effort and plan other post-match activities away from squash.

Allow an older child several hours—or better yet, overnight—before talking about the match. You will find a better listener when you do analyze the match. Avoid talking to your child about statistics that you or the coach might have recorded. Instead, look at the choices the child made and discuss what would have been better alternatives. Be honest with the child and don't let the fear of harming self esteem impact your ability to be candid.

And what about the winner of the match? The winner's behavior and attitude is also important. A handshake and acknowledging the opponent's performance are the marks of good sportsmanship. Bragging or negative remarks about the opponent are not.

An important element of match analysis is self-evaluation. Let your child look back and come up with his own opinions. Top American junior Chris Gordon, who is now playing professionally, likes to work things out on his own. Many players prefer not to over analyze a match or dwell on it, particularly if they weren't pleased with the outcome. Instead, they prefer to move on and focus on the next match. Sometimes this can have a positive effect. "That urge to not deal with a painful loss contributes to a stronger and more passionate desire to win," says Team Kneipp at SquashTalk.com.

Learning from a Match

Winning is important, but win or lose a player has to come away from a match with a "Eureka!" feeling of having learned something significant. Interesting gadgets and gizmos are available to assist players in learning more about their matches and how to improve for future competition.

Interactive software programs, such as Focus X2 lets the parent or coach videotape the match so the child can review it on the computer. Software programs, such as Peter Nicol's Interactive CD, allow players to compare themselves to the form of top pros, who offer technical analyses of shots and voiceovers.

Seeing yourself in action can be beneficial, particularly if a coach is able to watch with you and comment on the match. Viewing the tape within a few days of the tournament, when it is still fresh, can be helpful in building a program for improving in the future. Before videotaping a match, be sure to get permission from your competitor's family, as well as from the tournament director.

Think Outside the Box

In squash, each individual is allowed to bring his unique talents to the court. A player who is technically gifted, but not particularly fit, can compete against one who is more physically fit but lacking in technique. A good coach will build upon those talents and maximize the child's potential. Instead of putting players in a box, form a box around their talents.

Harry Cowles, the revered Harvard squash coach from the 1920s to 1930s, strongly believed in thinking outside of the box and tailored his approach to the individual needs of his players. Known as one of the greatest teachers in squash, Cowles took kids who were athletic but not squash players and taught them to play. They each had their own style and the team had tremendous depth. Under his reign, Harvard never lost a formal intercollegiate match in 14 years.

Learning About Life

A squash match can be a great learning tool for kids. It is there that, after hours of clinics and lessons, kids can put their practice to the test. Some will be immediate success stories, while others find they shine far better on the practice court than they do in competition, finding that it may take longer to get match savvy. Whether they win or lose, kids learn that those who work hard are rewarded, but rewards come in many forms, including the satisfaction of hitting great volleys, deceptive drop shots or perfectly executed boasts.

In match play, kids learn about getting along with others, making decisions, staying focused, building self-confidence, developing self-esteem and learning about sportsmanship. How's that for life-long learning skills? At this rate, we should be putting kids in squash matches instead of schools and we could be developing leaders of tomorrow in businesses and even nations!

All joking aside, kids will undoubtedly learn much about themselves from a squash match - the winning and the losing, and how to deal with both. It's how you manage the highs and lows that define character. The squash court can be a safe laboratory to develop the skills necessary to face the challenges life brings us all.

7

Camps and Resorts

"Just play. Have fun. Enjoy the game."
MICHAEL JORDAN, professional basketball player

K ids camps may bring back fond memories for grown-ups, but probe kids today and you'll be surprised. They either love 'em or hate 'em; there is no in between. If parent and child do their homework before selecting a camp, there's a much better chance the child will want to go back the next year.

Benefits of a Squash Camp

Squash-wise perhaps the most important benefit of a week of workouts for a young kid is the discovery of what it takes physically to play matches round after round, day after day. Kids also get plenty of practice against players with different styles and various strengths and weaknesses.

An advanced player can focus on stepping up to the next level through a more intense personalized program, perhaps concentrating on a particular strategy, improving a specific stroke, or correcting an error. Learning from a different coach, even for a week, may open up new perspectives on the game. Often, a kid accustomed to playing recreational squash returns from a week of fun with friends at camp eager to move on to competitive squash.

Some camps include talks by experts on topics like mental toughness, physical conditioning, nutrition, strategy, and tournament play. And don't forget the evening activities – movies, mini golf, and more.

Kids can progress to different camps as they grow older and become more experienced squash players. The typical progression is local day camp, sleep away camp and international camp. A local day camp is a good first step for a young player, who is likely to find familiar faces and can feel secure in returning home each day. After a couple of summers at local programs, you may feel the child is ready to get away. Once players have experienced a few sleep away camps and improved the level of their squash, the next opportunity awaiting is an international program that combines training and competition with sight seeing and travel.

Choosing a Camp

You can find squash camps in some very interesting places all over the world. In the US, where summer camp is an annual rite of passage for many kids, there are over 45 squash camps offering more than 200 weeklong sessions each year.

The Canadian provinces offer many junior summer squash camps. Add to this a gamut of camp choices in Europe, Australia and New Zealand. You can flip through *Squash Player*, the UK magazine, or *Squash* magazine to find camp advertisements. Or you can get a recommendation from a teaching professional at your facility.

Online directories are also good sources of information. (More info: squashtalk.com; us-squash.org and squashmagazine.com). These directories are usually up-to-date, easy to search, and include contact information. Many provide brochures and applications you can download. In addition to US listings, SquashTalk.com also provides links to camps in Ireland, the UK, Canada, Australia and the Universal Squash Camps in the Netherlands, Belgium, Italy and Spain. In the USSRA directory, you can find information on squash camps in Barbados, Bermuda, Canada and New Zealand. SquashTalk includes a preferred list of camps based on staff research and experience.

After reseaching your options, pare down your choices and make a short-list. Then determine whether the character and program emphasis are a good fit with your child's personality. The best way to decipher a camp's character is with an in-depth conversation with its director. Each camp has its own philosophy and mission. Some are more intense than others.

A reserved child might do better at a camp that is more relaxed or one that emphasizes instruction over competition. Kids seeking a fun vacation should look at the larger camps, which offer a variety of social activities. Those more serious about squash would be better off at a smaller camp that emphasizes squash over other activities and provides more individualized attention on the court. Some kids raise their ranking by 15 to 20 spots after training for several weeks at such intense squash camps.

Those ranked at the very top of their age group are more suited to Elite or Super Elite Weeks, high intensity training programs offered at select camps. For most of these camps, kids must qualify first.

If you're looking for something really different, try a squash and ranch camp in Montana. Squash coach Jack Halford built a squash court on a 15,000-acre ranch and offers a unique summer program for a small group of kids, or a family. Brand some cattle, hunt porcupines and lasso horses, while perfecting your squash game with private and semi-private coaching. Play tournaments while the steak sizzles on the barbeque and enjoy the wild-west experience of a lifetime all day long. (More info: Tibbetsranch.com)

Happy Campers

The number of returning campers is the best measure of camp quality. There is currently no way to determine return rate statistics for squash camps.   Don't be shy about asking the director of a camp you're interested in what the return rate is. Quality camps will proudly share these facts. Avoid camps that waffle over sharing this kind of information. You can also ask the director if anyone from your area has attended the camp. If so, these individuals can be a good source of additional information.

Instructors

Find out if the camp director will have a presence at the camp and try to determine who is actually going to instruct the kids. Are the instructors world-class players, certified professionals or college squash players? If they're college players, have they received training in the style and philosophy of the director and will they be closely monitored?

Fortunately for camps, the professional squash circuit slows down in the summer, so pros from various countries are more available to coach at camps. Some international players jump at the chance to come to the US for the summer. Camps with an international staff can offer your child more than squash.

Instructors who are college players from top teams can provide kids aspiring to play intercollegiate squash with valuable insight into varsity life.

It can be beneficial when the camp schedule includes a rotation of instructors for different drills. That way, campers can pick up a variety of tips. On the other hand, some camps provide daily private lessons with the same instructor, which can be invaluable in the progress kids can make. Working one-on-one with the same coach everyday gives players a personal prescription with a consistent message. There is no substitute for one-on-one training.

As in most squash clinics, the ideal student-to-instructor ratio is three to four students for each instructor. With any higher ratio, kids end up waiting around too much. Some camps offer an even better ratio: two campers to one instructor for a more personalized program.

Non-Squash Activities

Many kids will want to return to the camp the following season because of the evening activities and camaraderie. Campers enjoy first-run movies, bowling, mini-golf, swimming and more. A break from the squash court can often include hiking, kayaking, and visits to local museums. Or, in Bermuda, extra activities include snorkeling, jet skiing or relaxing on the beach.

If your child is shy, find out if the camp has specific getting-to-know-each-other activities or find a camp that assigns kids to the same instructor each day. A familiar face can break the ice.

Accommodations

Dorm is the norm as many camps are held on college campuses, particularly those with great squash teams, such as Princeton and Dartmouth. Here's a perfect opportunity for kids to get a feel for a school they might wish to apply to in the future. Plus, these schools usually have first class facilities with state-of-the-art gymnasiums, swimming pools and plenty of grounds for outdoor play. Camps in or near college towns can provide a lot of fun.

Some camps offer housing with families in the area, which can also be fun. At the end of the squash day, kids can enjoy going to movies or seeing the sights with their host family and may form lasting friendships.

International Camps

American juniors training for tournaments can benefit from camps in Europe and Australia. International programs, such as Bryan Patterson's Universal Camps, enable kids to practice with juniors from other countries while visiting historic sights and absorbing a new culture. Patterson, a pioneer in squash camps, runs his programs in conjunction with the various junior open tournaments in Holland, England, Spain and Germany, so kids can compete internationally and work towards a European Junior ranking. Also on the menu of choices are programs in France, Italy, Australia and Bermuda. Campers can participate in the South Australian Junior Open and the Bermuda Junior Open. There are various housing arrangements, including private homes and hotels. What an unforgettable learning experience for an American child to spend a week with a British family or to visit Amsterdam or Cologne.

There are other international squash tours to New Zealand, such as Mark Devoy's four-week camp for advanced players, usually those older than 12. Kids play in a tournament each weekend and stay in hotels or with host families. Players end up at the New Zealand Institute of Squash for the final week. Sightseeing in between tournaments is arranged. Due to the nature of the camp, it is limited to eight kids.

After New Zealand, Devoy teams up with Canadian coach Mike Way and the Bermuda Squash Association to lead a squash camp in Bermuda in August. This camp offers kids an opportunity to not only enjoy a beautiful environment and meet kids from other areas but to prepare for the coming fall squash season.

Pros are continually organizing programs for juniors in key squash areas worldwide. In 2004, Peter Marshall, former world No. 2, with the support of England Squash, started a National Squash Academy at Grantham College in the UK. Participants can study at the college while training. A division of the company iSquashMarketing, founded by Paul Walters, is iSquashAcademy, a series of weekly camps in England, in conjunction with Australia's five-time world champion Sarah Fitz-Gerald and two-time British champion Lee Beachill, who reached the No. 1 in the world ranking in 2004.

More Money

A one-week resident camp can run you from $600 to $1,500 plus. Day camp is more than half as much. The resident camp price includes lodging, meals, instruction, use of facilities, and evening activities. A bigger sticker usually means a smaller ratio of campers to instructors or a higher caliber of coaches. In most cases, coaching by world-class players and personalized instruction are the reason for a higher price tag. Yet, you can also spend more simply for better accommodations – private rooms and cutting edge facilities.

Despite all the detective work, you may discover the camp you chose isn't a good fit after all. A camp is more than the squash it offers. The social atmosphere is also important and that can be hard to figure out beforehand. It might take more than one try to find the best match for your child.

Brand Name Camps

You could shop for camps by looking at those led by famous players or coaches. Professional players and renowned coaches, such as Mark Talbott or Neil Harvey, all lend a sense of excitement to the program while they evoke their personal style in coaching the game. The Talbott Squash Academy in Newport, Rhode Island has the low-key, but effective style of Mark Talbott, the most famous American player

---

After Camp

Got home to day from being away
And Man! We had some fun!

Got home to day from being away
And Man! I'm glad I'm done!

It cost a lot, but for what you got,
It really was a deal.

The price of sense, Well! It's intense!
We got it at a steal.

What we did – it blew my lid!
I'll tell you later on.

But not to day, I've got to say
Right now my head is gone!

Thank you guys for being wise,
They sure knew how to teach.

But there's no way I'm going to play.
Until I've hit the beach.

But when I've done with soaking sun,
In a week or maybe two.

You wait and see how good I'll be!
You'll see what camp can do!

—Richard Millman

and coach of the Stanford team. The Princeton Squash Training Center, co-directed by Princeton's men's coach Bob Callahan and Princeton's women's coach Gail Ramsay, celebrates its 25th year in 2006, earning a reputation as one of the longest-running squash camps in the US. For its tournament training program, the camp brings in a special guest coach, the revered Neil Harvey. An individualized approach with small group coaching characterizes the Westchester Squash Personal Program with noted pro Kumail Mehmood of Pakistan. Mike Way, Canadian National Coach and coach of Jonathan Power, leads his program at various locations in the US and at the Canadian National Squash Training Center in Ontario

However, these aren't the only camps with top players and coaches. Most squash camps, on the whole, are associated with name coaches or players, some more prominent than others. Some camps offer special weeks with world class pros. Peter Nicol and Natalie Grainger are only two of the top pros on the roster at Squash and Beyond at Williams College. World champion Jonathon Power has been the head coach for three weeks at the Power Squash Academy at Dartmouth College in New Hampshire, which is run by his father. Check the schedule of camp sessions on their Websites and see where the pros are headed.

Expecting a celebrity coach to greet you at the camp entrance is about as likely as expecting Sam Walton to wave customers in at the nearby Wal-Mart. Yet, they are there, maybe not all the time, but they definitely have a presence, both on court and in running the program. You'll find Mark Talbott at his camp everyday.

Making Camp Count

Most squash camps accept children as young as age 8. You can gauge a kid's camp readiness by how well they handle sleepovers with friends.

Camp sessions can run four to five hours of on-court time. A kid practicing squash year-round may be physically conditioned for such an intensive schedule. Otherwise, players ought to get acclimated through a conditioning routine that begins two to three weeks prior to the start of camp. Evenkids who think they're in shape should do some extra conditioning prior to camp. That way your kid stays healthy and injury-free and won't be sore after the first day.

Some camps give kids a personal training program or report card to take home. At the Mark Talbott Squash Academy, kids go home with a pictorial CD of their week.

It's also a good idea to encourage kids to make notes about camp memories – their accomplishments, tips they learned, and contact info for all their new friends. Ideally, these notes can help them develop a program to practice what they learned.

Squash on Vacation

Most true squash lovers take their racquets wherever they go. And because squash is a global sport, played in more than 153 nations, you're sure to find courts in your travels.

If your family wants to play squash on your next vacation, check out the handy court finder on SquashTalk.com, which lists clubs and facilities geographically by the regions of the world. The listing also provides the number and type of courts, name and phone number of the pro and the facility's visiting policies.

You can find squash in some wonderful vacation destinations, such as St. Lucia, Jamaica and Barbados. Club Med offers squash in eight of its villages in Malaysia, Egypt, Brazil, Japan, Thailand, Indonesia and Brazil. Squash is enormously popular in many parts of Africa, Australia, New Zealand, the Middle East and Mexico. You can also flip through directories of the major hotel chains, such as Hilton or Marriott, and find that a number of hotels, particularly in European cities, have courts.

Professional and amateur tournaments also present opportunities for families to enjoy squash on vacation. Resorts sometimes host squash tournaments. Watching a professional event (More info: psa-squash.com and wispa.net), combined with daily clinics and social activities, is a great way to spend family time.

Bermuda, with its pink sands and turquoise waters has become a squash capital of the world. With its slogan, "Sun, Surf, Squash," Bermuda hosts the PSA Masters and World Open. Visitors watch the world's greatest players and can compete in the USSRA-sanctioned Bermuda Junior Open or the Bermuda Open Graded Championship, which caters to players of all levels. Surrounding these tournaments are special exhibitions, coaching clinics and many social events, creating a fun squash atmosphere for the whole family.

The Sharif Khan International Squash Festival in Barbados, now in its 4th year, provides squash players with a fun week of squash, entertainment, water-sports, golf and more. There is a tournament with divisions for all levels, plus practice clinics and a special 'Hits and Tips' with four PSA Pros, including 12-time North American champion, Sharif Khan. Kids who play squash will be able to play against other junior guests, as well as local junior players. The festival is held at the all-inclusive Almond Beach Village Resort, so you can take advantage of everything from banana boat rides to barbecues. A package plan includes special rates for children under 12.

Custom Squash Trips

If you can't organize a squash vacation yourself, leave it up to a squash pro turned entrepreneur to arrange one for your family. Gus Cook of Washington, D.C., who once lived in Provence and is a seasoned traveler and squash pro, puts together squash tours to France for small groups. Although these trips are geared primarily for adults, Cook can customize the program for families. Because of their extensive worldwide travels, squash pros have contacts in many destinations and those in the travel business can tailor a vacation to suit your needs and budgets.

The possibilities and opportunities are endless. Happy travels!

8

Gearing Up

"A racquet is like toothbrush, personal."
HASHIM KHAN, *Squash Racquets: The Khan Game*

Perhaps a minimalist can enjoy squash for a lifetime with just a racquet and a ball. But you won't find a kid who's a minimalist. Make stuff interesting, they'll enjoy playing a whole lot more. Racquets come in all sorts of appealing designs and colors. You can buy a racquet unstrung and have it strung with rainbow colored strings and paint it with a personalized logo.

Protective eyewear comes in many styles and colors. The clothing featuring wisecrack phrases always seems to bring a smile to onlookers. A bandana with a logo can be an inexpensive touch to make your squash junior look and feel special.

Virtues of Value

Your child has just got to have the latest tournament bag or the newest shirt. Well, if you can get hold of an affordable one, why not? After all, looking the part adds to the allure.

Racquets, however, are different. The racquet is the most important piece of equipment, so it pays to do your research wisely. Stay away from the highest priced racquets for a beginner player, but eliminate the cheap ones, too. A racquet with improper balance can lead to injury. Go for middle-of-the-road priced racquets.

The best source for finding a good racquet is your club or facility's squash professional. The pro can suggest different racquets for your child's size and game and will provide demos to try out on the court. Large retail outlets, which may have cheaper prices, may not have a knowledgeable sales staff when it comes to squash racquets. Internet stores have great deals and selections and are open 24 hours, but after sales service can be somewhat limited, depending on the store. If something is wrong with the racquet, you might be out of luck. A squash professional, on the other hand, will be able to provide a replacement. Besides, players should support their local pro.

Your child will undoubtedly want the really cool shoes and statement clothes. So why not establish a way for your junior to earn them? For starters, those tried and true chores like mowing the lawn or babysitting might do the trick. Squash outcome-related rewards for young kids are a definite no-no. "Johnny, you can have those cool shoes if you beat Brandon in the finals today." This is a sure recipe for disaster.

Instead, reward your 8-year-old for getting to practice on time. As your junior develops and becomes a competitive player, offer to buy those cool shoes when he takes the initiative to arrange practice games or completes several sessions of solo practice.

Racquets

Since the racquet is a junior's most important piece of gear, don't skimp on taking time to pick the right one. The Number One Tip for buying a racquet: have your kid try out a demo first for several games to really get a good feel for it.

Some pros recommend a junior racquet for kids starting at 3 and right up to 7 or 8. Junior racquets are very light, two to three inches shorter than adult versions, and have larger heads and smaller grips. They are usually made of graphite or aluminum and range in price from $25 to $150.

Other squash pros believe that kids should start right away with a lightweight adult racquet, if they can handle it, so they won't have to adjust later to the difference in length. There is a huge range in price for adult-sized racquets, with the high end models priced over $200. Yet you can find a high quality racquet for between $75 and $120. Check with your pro on what type of racquet to buy.

Balance and Weight

A racquet with the right weight and balance will help your child hit the ball most effectively and minimize the risk of injuries. A lighter racquet is easier for the beginning junior to swing and helps them acquire a better feel for the ball. A heavier racquet can be clumsy and more difficult to handle.

Balance is an important factor in your selection process, meaning is the racquet-head heavy or light? To check this, you can either test the racquet on a racquet balancing scale if your club or facility has one, or you can try balancing your racquet on your finger. If your hand needs to be close to the head, the head is too heavy. If your hand needs to be close to the grip, then the weight is in the butt of the racquet.

Grips

Unlike tennis racquets, which have many different grip sizes, squash racquets usually have a standard grip size of 3 and 5 /8 inches. But grips can be easily adjusted. If the grip is too large, you can remove it and put on a thinner replacement grip. If the grip is too small, which is more common, you can put an over-grip on top to build the grip up.

Adjusting the grip also affects the balance of the racquet. Adding more weight to the grip makes the head of the racquet feel lighter. Likewise, removing a grip brings the balance point more towards the head of the racquet.

Remember, kids will outgrow racquets fairly quickly if they play often, hit the walls a lot or have a big growth spurt. And as a junior moves to competitive play, you will need to buy more than one racquet at a time. It's not uncommon to break a racquet during play, or break strings during a match, particularly if your junior cuts the ball a lot. Two racquets are the absolute minimum for a competitive player and each racquet should be the same model and have the same balance. Even if the racquets look the same, they may not have the same balance. Test the balance to make sure both racquets are the same.

When your junior is starting to play more competitively, you should consider other factors when buying racquets, such as frame stiffness. A tête-à-tête with your junior's coach is invaluable because many of these factors depend upon the style of play. For example, a stiffer racquet can be good for those with a power game, as long as they have control. Players with very adaptable wrist skills will do well with a head heavy racquet. Players with who are not wristy will be better off with a lighter racquet for better touch and feel. It all comes down to personal preference, which will develop over time.

Racquet Care

When you learn of the existence of a select group of people called Master Racquet Technicians (MRTs) dedicated to the maintenance of racquets, you realize that caring for racquets is not for the faint of heart. For most junior tournament players, three racquets should last about one season, on average.

"Breaking racquets is part of the game," says Mike Hymer of Prince, noting that although today's racquets are durable, they still must withstand the impact from wall to ball. Hitting the walls while playing is one thing, but banging your racquet in frustration is something else. Prince technicians know immediately when a racquet has been abused and when it has simply reached its threshold of play. Tip: Juniors who keep their cool will find their racquets last longer.

Moisture and temperature also affect racquets. Keep damp clothes and wet towels away from racquets, especially those with natural strings. Likewise, keep racquets in covers or in squash bags for storage. Racquet strings are not meant to withstand extreme heat and cold temperatures, so it's not a good idea to leave your racquet in a car. According to experts at the United States Racquet Stringers Association, heat can cause the tension in the strings to decline and cold temperatures can make the racquet feel stiff and brittle. (USRSA. More info: racquettech.com). Keeping racquets at room temperature is advisable. You can also help keep the top rim of the racquet intact by putting light (not heavy) tape around the frame to protect the bumpers.

It's easy to understand why good strings are essential for peak performance. Jump on a concrete slab. Now jump on a trampoline. Which do you suppose will take you higher? The wear and tear of play causes strings to lose their elasticity and develop notches over time. When a junior begins to use a racquet over longer periods, have an experienced stringer restring it with a good replacement string. This returns power and control to one's game and extends racquet life. Replacement strings can range from $2 to $15, depending upon the type and brand. A string job, labor only, can be had for around $15. For labor and strings, expect to pay from $30 to $40.

The MRTs at the United States Racquet Stringers Association (USRSA. More info: racquettech.com) used to recommend that a tennis or squash player have his racquet restrung the same number of times per year as he plays per week. That means a player who plays three times a week should restring three times per year. However, the MTRs now suggest a newer and more accurate method of testing string tension. A stringmeter is a special device that measures the percentage of tension lost. A stringmeter can be purchased for about $30.00. (More info: stringmeter.com).

An easier way to test the condition of your strings is to tap your racquet head against the strings of another racquet. If you don't hear a clear ping sound, your string tension may have dropped and your racquet is due for restringing. As your child grows with the game, the type of strings and string tension will become more important.

Check the grip condition when restringing. If the grip is worn and slippery, you won't have the same feel or control. The more a junior plays, the more often the grip will need to be replaced. The pros often re-grip after each match. Replacement grips are inexpensive and can be ordered in packages of 24. Grips come with a variety of extras, such as more cushioning, anti-shock absorption, bumps for better airflow and grooves for improved traction.

Putting on a replacement grip can be do-it-yourself job, or if you're a novice, you might want to ask your squash pro for assistance. For right-handers, wrap the grip clockwise, for lefties, counter-clockwise. Start by wrapping the tapered end around the butt (bottom of handle), then work your way up the handle. As you wrap the grip around, turn the racquet in the opposite direction so the grip can stretch over the handle. Don't overlap or leave gaps as you go. If the grip is too long, you can cut it to the right size. Some replacements can just slip completely over your grip.

Protective Eyewear

"Playing squash without goggles is like riding a bike without a helmet – why take the chance?" says Phil Head, Asian Softball Doubles Grand Slam Champion and staff pro at SquashPlus.com, a comprehensive Website for purchasing squash equipment. (More info: SquashPlus.com) Besides, the USSRA now requires protective eyewear at their sanctioned tournaments, as do many other squash governing bodies.

Although eye injuries in racquet sports were listed as only 10 percent of all sports-related injuries in 1998 according to a study by Paul Vinger, M.D., the possibility of a severe injury if struck by a ball or racquet is high. When you consider that the average squash ball travels at 90 mph and a racquet can travel anywhere between 50 and 110 mph, it's no wonder that in a small squash court the risk of injury is great.

A ball went right into the eye of top US player Will Carlin in 1992 when he was not wearing protective eyewear. Carlin required two surgeries to repair his retina and missed two years of competitive play. He still has lingering problems. You can read gruesome stories about squash eye injuries, complete with graphic photos, on eyewear company Websites. Or spare yourself the details and purchase a high quality pair of protective eyewear for your child. Protective eyewear has become somewhat of a fashion statement, but should be viewed as an essential piece of squash equipment.

Be sure to buy eyewear that meets safety standards. In the US, there are two organizations that determine eyewear safety standards: the American Society for Testing and Materials (ASTM) and the American National Standards Institute (ANSI). Look for these stamps of approval when purchasing eyewear. International players should see that their eyewear meets their nation's manufacturers' standards as well. Also make sure the eyewear is designed specifically for racquet sports, not for skiing, cycling, or other sports.

Most eyewear is made with polycarbonate lenses, which can sustain the impact of a ball or racquet. Lenses must be permanently attached to the frame. Protective eyewear can also be made with prescription lenses. Many claim to be anti-fogging, but wearing a headband with the protective eyewear can sometimes further prevent fogging.

Other models, like I-Mask, can fit over the face like a shield, allowing for greater peripheral vision. They are lightweight and can fit over existing glasses. I-Mask is approved or endorsed by many of the squash governing bodies and top players.

Protective eyewear comes in adult and children's sizes. Prices range from the cheapest at $20 up to $150. Don't pinch pennies when buying eyewear. Avoid the cheap varieties but keep in mind that any pair over $120 is all about style and image.

Foot Care

An essential part of any good squash program is footwork. If you look at how the top players train, you'll see that speed work is one of the most important components. One player can dominate another simply because he gets to the ball quicker than anyone on the court. Footwork is so crucial in squash.

"Yet the stopping and starting combined with the length of the rally that keep the ball going are unique compared with other racquet sports and can contribute to additional stress on the foot," says Michael Schumacher, Chairman of the Medical Advisory Committee of the USSRA and podiatrist in New York City. In tennis, for example, the ball goes out of the court and the point can end sometimes rather quickly. But in squash, with the use of the walls, the point can last much longer, Schumacher explains.

Schumacher sees a number of foot injuries among squash players, but more in adults than juniors, who tend to recover more quickly unless they have a pathological condition. He finds it more common for juniors to suffer from fungal skin and nail infections, which happens when the foot sweats. Don't wear wet socks; change to a dry pair quickly. Powder is also helpful.

Shoes

Do we need fancy footwear? The start and stop motions, as well as the quick direction changes involved in squash require special features in footwear. A well-designed squash shoe is durable enough to protect against overuse injury and light enough that it doesn't interfere with agility and performance.

In all cases, avoid fashion sneakers or shoes designed for other sports. Running and cross-training shoes don't provide the lateral support so essential for squash. They put feet high off the ground, increasing the chance of ankle rollover. Brand name squash shoes are specifically designed for the quick movements on a squash court and have the necessary traction needed for the wood floor. A good pair of squash shoes can cost from $45 to $75.

Squash shoe manufacturers don't sell shoes in junior sizes in the US because they believe the market is too small and parents have many options for kids' ever growing feet. However, juniors can often fit into a small ladies squash shoe, where sizes run from 4 or 5 to 10. They are often identical to the men's models. Other options are indoor court shoes for tennis or racquetball, or volleyball shoes. Look for shoes with gum-rubber, non-marking soles for the best traction and leather uppers. Schumacher recommends tennis shoes if you can't find a squash shoe in the right size.

Since squash players need to be literally on their toes, a firmer toe area in the shoe is also important. Look for good support at the ankle and arch and adequate cushioning at the heel. Schumacher says active players should get new shoes about every four months. This is important, even though the shoes aren't worn outdoors and may not look dirty. Another alternative for keeping shoes fresh is to purchase two pairs at the same time and have your junior alternate them. This way, after one pair is sweaty, there is always a fresher pair the next time they play. This will double the life of the shoes.

Socks

There are more sweat glands on the feet than anywhere else on the body. A drenched sock can cause chafing and blistering, as well as skin infections. Athletic socks help wick away moisture to keep feet dry. Socks should also provide cushioning at the toe and heel for better shock absorption. Change them as often as you need to.

Insoles

Thierry Lincou of France, one of the world's top players, developed tendonitis in his left knee, among many other injuries, a few years ago. He was advised to try sport insoles, which provided quick relief. Sports insoles and inserts can cradle and support the foot, helping to stabilize the feet in the optimum position.   Schumacher doesn't recommend inserts for juniors unless their arch is very flat or extremely high.

Apparel

Squash apparel makes life easy: regular sportswear is absolutely fine for kids of all ages. Comfortable shorts and t-shirts work well and girls can opt for tennis dresses or skirts. Once your junior starts playing competitively, you'll probably need more clothing and you may find that some clubs require all white apparel.

There are several companies with specific squash clothing lines, but they do not offer children's sizes, mainly because parents don't need to buy squash apparel when regular sportswear will do and kids out grow clothes so quickly. Haseeb Anwar of Squash Design, an Italian based company with local distribution in the US, explained that by the time kids are playing squash seriously, around 11 or 12, they can fit into a small adult size.

The most important consideration in selecting clothing is comfort. Clothes should be loose fitting and made of fabrics that breathe. Very popular today are moisture-wicking fabrics. "These fabrics are engineered to transport sweat away from the body to the outer layers of the fabric, where the moisture evaporates away, leaving the sports garment dry, lightweight and comfortable to wear," explains Haseeb Anwar. "Proper active wear will keep your junior dry and comfortable – essential for any level of athletic training and competition."

Hair Care

Girls need to tie their hair back tightly so that it doesn't interfere with play. Boys with long hair need to do the same. If your child constantly needs to adjust his hair, it's a distraction. Don't let your child lose focus because of unruly hair. Try French braids, a tight bandana or clips.

Head to Toe: Accessories

Accessorizing is fun. Many accessories are useful and some are indispensable. A few, however, can cause problems. Remember, there is a rule in squash that no device can be attached to a squash racquet. Furthermore, should a junior drop an object of any kind, for example, keys or a cough drop, he will lose a point. So keep that in mind before a match.

Bands

Bandanas can make a fashion statement, and like headbands, they help keep sweat and wet hair out of players' eyes. Wristbands prevent sweat from running into the racquet handle and can be used to wipe a wet forehead. Look for bands made of a mixture of cotton and Lycra spandex.

Grip Enhancers

No one wants to lose points over a slippery grip. If your child complains about his grip, you can replace it with one designed for better absorption or use a grip enhancer, such as a resin-pad, a small pad filled with a mixture of high grade powdered resin. You can dab it on the grip as needed.

There are also liquid solutions in spray bottles that combat slippery grips. One application of a tacky solution is meant to keep a grip dry and firm for hours.

Racquet bags

Organize all that squash gear with a racquet bag. These bags are designed to hold two, three, and even six racquets. Besides making your junior look like a serious squash player, they're invaluable for protecting racquets. Manufacturers offer a variety of bells and whistles: zippered pockets to tuck away membership cards, toiletries, keys, overgrips, and other valuables, and ventilated compartments for wet shoes and clothes.

Some are weekender bags, large enough for overnight gear. Most have shoulder straps, but there are several models with adjustable straps that can be worn as a backpack. For serious tournament travel, you probably want to take two bags – the racquet bag with everything one needs for a match plus an overnight bag with items for the evening and next day.

Balls

Manufacturers use ball sales to gauge the growth of squash throughout the country and the world. Dunlop, the leader in squash ball sales, is the official ball of 95 percent of the squash regions of the world and is affiliated with the Professional Squash Association, Women's International Squash Players Association, World Squash Federation and College Squash Association.

The move from hardball squash to international softball in the US around the mid 1990s made the game easier for new players. The new soft ball proved to be much slower and extended the length of rallies, giving beginners an easier introduction to squash.

In the late 90s, Dunlop took this concept further by introducing a series of balls for different levels of play. As a result, Dunlop ball sales increased nearly 50 percent. Players today have a choice of balls to match their level of play and court conditions. (Table 8.1).

Table 8.1

Ball	Features	Player Level
Red Mini Foam	Light, Bouncy	Young Beginners
Blue Max	12 percent larger than standard, 40 percent longer hang time	Beginners
Max Progress	6 percent larger than standard, 20 percent more hang time	Recreational Players/Improvers
Single Yellow Dot	10 percent larger than standard	Club players
Double Yellow Dot	Standard	Tournament players
Green Dot	High Altitude	All players
White Double Yellow Dot	Glass Courts	Professionals/College Players

Squash pros have found several uses for the Blue Max and Max Progress balls. Although these balls may be geared for beginners, they can also be useful for other players, such as seniors or intermediate players trying to develop specific skills like getting the ball out of the back corner. Tournament players preparing for competition in warm climates will find playing with a slower ball helps simulate conditions expected in a hot court.

Check with your child's squash teacher on the best type of ball to buy. Sometimes kids rush right to the double yellow dot without taking advantage of the slower balls, which can lengthen the rally and make the game more fun. Stephen Hall, National Accounts Manager for Dunlop Sports, encourages players to make use of the range of balls and grow with them. "The single yellow dot ball is better for 65 percent of squash players."

Certainly not the big-ticket item on your squash list, a ball can be purchased for $3.50. Since squash balls are not pressurized, they don't need any special storage. On a warm court, the ball has more bounce. On a cold court, you can warm the ball up by rubbing it with your foot or by hitting it for a while. A squash ball has a fairly long life. If you play everyday, the ball can get slippery, so you might need a new one after a couple of weeks.

Training Aids

Can't find a practice partner? A ball machine that blasts balls every few seconds should do the trick.

Ball Machine

Ball machines are becoming a nice addition to squash programs and facilities. They can be helpful for pros in teaching children and coaching teams. They are also useful in solo practice.

Ball machines blast balls as fast as every 1.5 seconds for quick volleys and up to every 10 seconds for other strokes. With a capacity of up to 60 balls, the machine lets you adjust the speed to your liking and choose the shots you need to practice. A ball machine is great for footwork and timing and can be a big plus for pros, who don't have to feed balls from the backcourt, and can help adjust the strokes of their students. Ball machines can set you back about $2,000 but the investment may be worthwhile, especially for large group programs. Recently, some of the money raised for SquashBusters, the Boston-based urban youth squash program, went towards a ball machine.

Big Hand

Approved by the World Squash Federation as an official training aid, the Big Hand is a pre-racquet training aid featuring a double-sided hand bat that fits over the hand like a mitt. It can be used with a spongy Big Hand ball. Big Hand helps young children with hand-eye coordination and beginning racquet skills. According to Ken Watson, who introduced Big Hand, the device, by its design, encourages the development of correct stroking technique. (More info: bighandsports.com).

Interactive Software

Performance analysis software programs also help juniors learn the game. The Peter Nicol CD, for example, enables you to videotape your child's game and then compare the video with Nicol's game as you watch them both on your computer. You can also hear Nicol's commentary on his match and an analysis of his shot selection. (More info: Quintic.com). There are also helpful programs designed for use with a coach, such as Focus X2, which some of the top pros use to review their matches. Using today's advanced technology, these programs provide a variety of tools to view and assess a player's performance. This can be a fun way for juniors to see themselves in action and learn from their mistakes. (More info: elitesportsanalysis.com.)

Footworker

Footworker is an electronic device that helps squash players, both novice and advanced, improve their footwork and endurance on the court by making traditional ghosting easier. Placed in front of the court, the device has 10 lights that reflect typical positions from which a squash ball is hit. When a light is illuminated, the player moves to that position on the court and hits an imaginary ball. Footworker can be set automatically with random flashing lights designed to simulate a rally. It can be adjusted to four different skill levels. The cost is between $250 and $300.

Footworker is a new product invented by engineer Leonard Lye of Canada, father of a competitive squash player. Lye is receiving positive feedback from coaches and players on his product. (More info: www.footworker.ca) Using Footworker or ghosting on your own is most helpful if you focus on an imaginary ball. A practice session is effective only when you relate to the ball.

Targets

Setting targets is a tried and true practice method. Targets can be squares with red or blue tape on the walls of the court so kids can practice aiming their shots. Or you can purchase rubberized mats from physical trainers.

The Coach's Grab Bag

A coach will have plenty of tricks up his sleeve to get kids moving, encourage skills development and bring on the fun. In his grab bag you might find squash balls and racquets of different colors and sizes, cones, chalk, throw-down line markers, throw-down footprints, jumping ladders and more.

Match Play Bag

So your 11-year-old is raring to graduate from clinics and beat the stuffing out of his competitors on the junior tournament circuit. Before you let your little bull loose in the china shop, teach him how to prepare his bag for match play.

A carefully stocked bag will help your kid perform his best. Here are the top essentials:

1. Two racquets.
2. One or two balls.
3. Eyeguards: always.
4. Two pairs of shoes.
5. Water: Athletes can sweat half a gallon each hour. Don't just sip water, drink it.
6. Fuel: Energy bars, a bagel, and a banana can bring back the zip, especially when playing two matches.
7. Towel.
8. Bands, sweatband and headband.
9. First aid: Chemical ice for cramps and band-aids to deal with blisters.
10. A spare shirt: A shirt change can help a player look and feel comfortable again.
11. Extra socks.
12. Post-match change of clothes.
13. Money.
14. Mobile phone.
15. Paperwork: Membership card, tournament information, Rules of Squash
16. Leisure stuff: Walkman, Gameboy, or a novel for delays.

Fun Stuff

While kids love to hit balls, getting kids interested in physical conditioning is a challenge. Luckily, quite a few companies are introducing fun products with just this goal in mind.

Z-Ball

These rubber balls have knobs on them that create unpredictable bounces. They're great for building dexterity and hand-eye coordination.

Aeroprops

Get them by the dozen to increase tracking and catching skills and for just plain fun. Aeroprops are little plastic wings that soar as high as 50 feet and are easy and safe to use, even for the very young.

Finger Yo-Yos

Put on a Finger Yo-Yo the size of a squash ball. Bounce and retrieve to develop rhythm or practice serve tosses.

Jump Rope

This is one piece of equipment your kid is guaranteed to have fun with through adulthood. Look for adjustable ropes in durable plastic, with cushioned handles. Jumping rope improves agility, balance, and strength.

Frisbee

You can develop strength by running short sprints on the beach, or you can throw and chase a Frisbee.

Power Ladder

This is a 30-foot ladder you lay on the ground. Drills such as hopping in and out of each rung improve foot speed, quickness, balance, and coordination.

Obstacle Course

You can get hopping and jumping over cones and mini hurdles. Make it a fun game.

Tetherball

If you can find a tetherball in a park, on a beach or playground, take advantage of the game that pro Damian Walker enjoyed as a child. A ball similar to a volleyball is tied to a ten-foot vertical pole by a rope. Two players, each positioned in one half of the area around the pole, try to hit the ball with their hand repeatedly in one direction, trying to wrap the rope around the pole. It's challenging and requires strength and coordination

Best Buy

Imagine this. For a game that can be enjoyed with a racquet, a ball and a wall, squash stores are lined with literally hundreds of specialty items. Finding the best racquet or shoe for your kid may not be easy, especially for parents new to squash. Getting advice from a coach who works with kids can save you time and money.

Sporting goods chain stores rarely carry the range of items you need to explore. A high quality sports store or a local pro-shop may be your best bet, more so for first-time buyers. You can find pro shops in squash clubs, staffed by knowledgeable folks. Many also have stringing machines – nice to know when you need that racquet restrung.

Online stores can be great for research and repeat purchases such as replacement shoes, balls, and accessories. Many have been in business for decades and are run by dedicated squash enthusiasts. They supply all the usual squash stuff, as well as training aids.

Check with your racquet manufacturer about warranties. If your racquet breaks, some companies will provide a replacement during the warranty period. Racquet technicians examine returned racquets carefully to make sure the racquet was not abused and that the defects are the fault of the manufacturer and not simply the result of normal wear and tear.

Tips from the Pros

Juniors can learn from what the top pros wear and wield on court. Check out your favorite player's racquet and attire. Keep in mind, though, that what players use and wear are influenced by endorsement deals and there's no guarantee that junior versions of these brands will yield equivalent performance. And remember that the preferred racquet of a James Willstrop or a Nicol David may not be the best racquet for your child. Stick to your pro's advice. But it is certainly safe to assume that professional players would not risk playing with an inferior racquet simply because it meant a better endorsement deal. All the same, it's interesting to keep tabs on who is wearing and wielding what.

Future Gear

Racquets have come a long way from the wooden frames of yesteryear. Part of predicting the game's evolution is to look at where racquets might be, technologically, years from now.

While manufacturers attempt to enhance stroke power with racquet technology, the WSF and PSA, organizations responsible for equipment standards around the world, are determined to uphold the human element. In the future, racquets will continue to become even lighter and more durable because that's what players want, according to Mike Hymer of Prince. Hymer believes that companies will continue to reach the broad range of customers, offering a variety of styles and designs for all levels of play. "We've made the transition from wood to graphite and racquets have gotten better and better," said Hymer.

Shoe companies also strive for the lighter and increasingly more comfortable shoe. Who knows what the future holds? One thing is certain about the future of squash gear, though. A racquet will never hit the shot for you, not in squash.

9

Physical Conditioning

"You can never do too many sit-ups."
MATT RANKIN, swim coach

A study on Forbes.com rated squash as the number one sport for fitness. The online publication featured a special survey on the ten healthiest sports and squash placed at the top of the list. Ratings were based on consultations with fitness experts, including coaches, personal trainers, competitors and exercise physiologists. Criteria covered injury risks, energy expenditure and calorie burn rates. Experts gave squash the highest number of points. The remaining sports, in rating order, were as follows: rowing, rock climbing, swimming, cross-country skiing, basketball, cycling, running, modern pentathlon andboxing.

The study went on to report that 30 minutes of squash was a great cardio respiratory workout that also strengthened muscles in the lower body and increased flexibility in the lower back and abdomen. Squash proved to be an excellent calorie burner and had a relatively low risk for injury.

Playing squash regularly is great exercise and a way to keep fit for life. However, participating in other physical activities is also important. Pediatricians say that from middle childhood to early adolescence is the time to acquire and develop sport-specific skills.

Participation in a variety of sports and developing an exercise routine outside of squash will help strengthen different muscle groups. Risk of overuse injuries is reduced and, in many cases, all-around conditioning improves squash performance.

Scientific studies have validated, again and again, what the Greeks taught us about the mind-body connection. Physical fitness has a beneficial effect on academic performance.

Academic Achievement

Wanna become a better reader? Try doing some push-ups. A statewide study conducted by the California Department of Education (CDE) matched the reading and math scores with the physical fitness scores of nearly a million students in grades five, seven, and nine.

Announcing the results, the CDE's Delaine Eastin said, "This statewide study provides compelling evidence that the physical well-being of students has a direct impact on their ability to achieve academically." Students with high scores in fitness also scored high in reading and math. Furthermore, students who met minimum fitness levels in three or more of the six physical fitness areas showed the greatest gains in academic achievement at all three grade levels.

Reading and math levels were assessed using the Stanford Achievement Test (SAT-9), given as part of California's Standardized Testing and Reporting Program. The study used a physical fitness test known as Fitnessgram (More info: cooperinst.org) to assess health in six areas – cardiovascular endurance, percentage of body fat, abdominal strength and endurance, trunk strength and flexibility, upper body strength and endurance, and overall flexibility. A score of 6 indicates that a student is in the healthy fitness zone in all six performance-areas and meets standards to be considered physically fit.

Overheard In A Locker Room

Bill: Who do you think will win the district championships this year?

Bob: It depends if Johnson is training this year.

Bill: I hear he's been seen doing interval training on Hell's Hill.

Bob: Then he'll win. No one else can train like that. After a few weeks he starts to look invincible and everyone is scared of him. Even if you play great shots you know the ball is always coming back. Once he is in that state his confidence is so high he believes he can't lose.

Squash Performance

With the change from hardball to softball, squash has become more of a game of endurance. In the past, rallies were shorter and the court was smaller. Today, with a wide court, bouncier ball and bigger racquets, points last longer. Some professional matches have been known to last two-and-half hours or more. In the earlier days of squash, the longest match on record was Jahangir Khan versus Gamal Awad in England where the two battled it out for two hours and 46 minutes. More recently, some matches have lasted longer than three hours. A rally in a pro match can have as many as 100 shots.

Being in good physical condition not only helps a player last the match, but in many cases a fit player will be able to get to the ball quicker, hit with more power, and recover faster. American junior Lily Lorentzen, who took her talents to the pro tour before heading to college, started training with coach Rodney Martin of the Australian Sports Institute. She worked on strength training three times per week and speed work twice a week.

Lorentzen, who had never had a comprehensive fitness program under one umbrella, has seen tremendous results. She's able to hit the ball better and move faster. The results of her training have also paid off in competition. Lorentzen made it all the way to the quarterfinals of the British Junior Open, which attracts top juniors from all over the world. While the intensity of this training is more appropriate for a player who is committed to squash full-time, it does prove that conditioning can have an impact. Talk to your coach to determine a conditioning program that is best suited for your child.

Get fit to play squash; don't play squash to get fit," says Chris Walker, former top pro player, national coach and entrepreneur. Walker is a firm believer in training to play squash. But training doesn't mean lifting weights and running haphazardly. A plan, specifically designed to enhance one's performance on the court, as Lorentzen is doing so successfully, is important. According to well-known guru of sports specific training, Tudor Bompa, "when you fail to plan, you plan to fail."

When your coach feels your child is ready to work with a trainer, find one who understands squash and has worked with squash players. If you can't find such a trainer, find one who is willing to learn about the sport and develop a squash-specific training program. Make sure the trainer takes your child's entire profile into account, including other activities and their environment, in order to ensure a balanced program.

Good conditioning is key to on-court performance. Keeping fit also allows one to enjoy the game for a lifetime by reducing the risk of overuse injuries.

Participation in Other Sports

Perhaps the easiest way to ensure all-around conditioning is to encourage your child to play a variety of sports. This is especially true for the under 14s, who may more willingly commit to participation in other sports as opposed to working out at the gym.

Adding variety is a fun way to achieve total body conditioning and avoid burnout. "Squash players who also play golf, skate or do yoga are using different body movements that help overall strength and revitalize their physical needs," says Stephen Cox, NASM-certified (National Academy of Sports Medicine), and a teaching pro in California. With cross training, players work other muscles that can help improve squash performance. Swimming and cross-country skiing are perhaps the best sports to achieve total body conditioning.

Hockey, both ice and field forms, are great for coordination and provide vigorous workouts. "Name one Canadian squash player who hasn't played ice-hockey," says Cox.   Several top players, including Jonathon Power and John White, developed footwork speed playing soccer. American junior Lily Lorentzen continued with soccer, field hockey and lacrosse in various seasons of high school. These sports are similar to squash because they require quick changes of direction and have elements of deception. Chris Gordon, another American junior on the pro tour, played tennis before taking up squash. The advantage of playing tennis is learning to volley and take the ball early.

Dr. Ron Christie, a sports physician from Lewiston, Maine, believes that a period of rest, followed by an alternative activity and then a return to formal training, gives athletes an added edge. Each summer, Christie embarks on a vigorous canoe trip on Lake Temagami Ontario and invites the world's leading athletes, from all different sports, to join him. Nate Beck, a Princeton University varsity squash player, was one of them. The benefits were so pronounced that Beck has attended the camp twice and earned the most improved player award after each summer. Christie says canoeing is great for the upper body and core muscles and is also a fantastic cardio respiratory work out.

Think you should start Yoga only after hitting 40? Think again. Encourage your pre-teen to hit the mat and she'll continue to thank you well beyond her 40th birthday. Yoga reduces the risk of long-term injury by increasing flexibility and strength of the joints. It can also help sharpen focus during a match. And speaking of focus, how about Bruce Lee-style martial arts for concentration and a healthy dose of assertiveness training, so helpful in winning matches?

How about chess to improve on-court squash strategy? Like a chess game, a squash match requires complex moves, strategic planning and quick thinking. Golf also complements squash as the game relies on concentration and focus. Have you ever noticed how the golf swing is similar to the squash stroke?

There aren't many sports that don't complement squash, but bodybuilding will probably inhibit a player's ability to move at the quick pace that squash demands, and swimming, although great cardiovascular exercise, doesn't help one's on-court movement either.

By about age 14, a kid will usually narrow his focus and choose the sport he likes best. During these teen years, kids and parents find they can't do everything and it's time to choose one sport to pursue more seriously. You'll find that several of the top pros chose to focus solely on squash as they got older. John White gave up soccer and cricket at about 16 to concentrate on squash. Chris Gordon stopped playing hockey and soccer after age 12 and was able to transfer his passion for these sports to squash. Even if your child does choose to specialize in squash, see that he also takes breaks for some recreational soccer or Frisbee throwing, just for the fun of it

Making Exercise Fun

Kids get bored when they're told to exercise as a means to an end, in this case better squash performance. Instead, consider exercise an end in itself – make it a fun activity the child looks forward to for its own sake. Double the fun by joining in.

Shoot hoops on the driveway one day, play Frisbee after a day or so, and bike the next. Twirl around with a hula ring. Looking for a fun activity that will more directly impact conditioning for squash? Skip rope. Boxers have the fastest feet in the world and skipping is a major component of their training. It's also an unbelievable workout that demands control, endurance, speed, coordination, and strength.

Add variety by choosing a new activity for each season. Try sledding, skiing, or snowboarding in the winter, swimming or in-line skating during the summer, hiking and biking in the spring and fall.

Take a routine task and make it a fun activity for parent and child. Develop a routine of walking the dog together. It's simple, but it works.

Measuring Fitness

Squash performance demands various forms of fitness: strength, speed, local muscle endurance, agility and stamina. There are specific tests to determine one's fitness level in each of these areas. The results will help pinpoint weaknesses and target areas that need improvement.

The Beep Test is a fitness measurement routine that has been adapted to squash by a number of coaches. The test covers a variety of skills, such as broad jumps, sit-ups and sprints, set in timed intervals by audio tape. In the squash court, coaches place six cones in key areas and players run from cone to cone. The number of repetitions the players can accomplish within the time limit establishes the score.

Bryan Paterson, founder of Universal Squash Camps, and well-known coach Liz Irving use this assessment, sometimes manually.

Another test to determine fitness is the VO2 Max Test, which measures the amount of oxygen consumed during exercise. This test has been used on Olympic athletes and astronauts. Athletes wear a mask hooked up to a computer while they either run on a treadmill or cycle on a stationary bike with varying levels of intensity. High oxygen consumption means the athlete has greater endurance and can exercise at an intense level. Those who consume less oxygen may need to work on improving their level of fitness. The information gained from the test is then used to develop a personalized exercise program. After taking the VO2 Max test, squash pro Stephen Cox was able to design a new training program for himself so he could fully reach his fitness potential and achieve a better fitness level for squash.

Another more generalized fitness assessment protocol is called Fitnessgram, which has become the choice of thousands of schools for the annual physical performance testing of their pupils. Developed by the Cooper Institute (More info: cooperinst.org), the primary goal of the Fitnessgram test is to help students make physical activity a part of their daily lives.

Flexibility

Flexibility refers to the range of motion in a joint and its related muscle groups. Flexibility training increases the length and elasticity of muscles, reducing the risk of tearing a muscle when chasing down balls.

"Flexibility can improve squash performance," says David Behm, Ph.D, Professor and Chair of Graduate Studies at the School of Human Kinetics and Recreation at Memorial University of Newfoundland. Dr. Behm explains that you can stretch farther to reach balls when you are flexible. It also takes less energy to move a flexible limb than a stiff one, he adds.

Though most kids are naturally flexible, a regimen of both dynamic stretching for five or ten minutes before squash and static stretching afterwards goes a long way in helping performance and preventing injuries. Dynamic stretching helps prepare the body for activity, while static stretching helps the muscles relax. Forming a habit of stretching properly will pay dividends as kids grow older and their bodies become less flexible.

Depending upon your child's situation, it may be wise to enroll in a flexibility training class such as Yoga or Pilates. Flexibility aside, these programs improve agility and increase strength without bulking up, and work on the mind-body connection. There are lots of great videos and books on stretching, Yoga, and Pilates produced by specialists. Educate yourself and be sure to consult with your child's pediatrician before starting any physical training program.

Dynamic Stretching

Hold the wall with your left hand and swing your right leg up in front and then back behind ten times. Switch legs and do the same. For the upper body, swing one arm up and back ten times and then switch arms. Dynamic stretching uses controlled movements to increase the reach and range of motion while raising the heart rate and preparing the body for more intense activity. A proper warm up before squash should include dynamic stretching to help players loosen up, get their heart rates up and blood flowing.

It's not uncommon for eager kids to rush into squash drills as soon as they're dropped off for practice. If the coach is not including a warm-up routine at the start of every practice, it is the parent's responsibility to arrive five or ten minutes early and go through a warm-up routine with the child. A cool-down stretch after class is important, too.

Static Stretching

Static stretching involves holding a position for a certain length of time, such as the typical hamstring or calf stretch. In doing so, endorphins are released that relax the muscles, encouraging them to shut down and prepare for inactivity. Therefore, the muscles will not be able to protect the joints, leaving them at risk for injury once they are stressed by playing squash.

Static stretching should be done after playing not before. "Stretching statically keeps muscles and joints flexible, supple and healthy," says Karen Calara, Executive Director at BioSports Northwest, in *Squash* magazine.

Use "funny talk" to get kids motivated. For instance, stretching the quadricep muscles in the front of the thigh is a core component of a post-squash program. This involves raising one foot behind you and bringing your heel to your butt. Naming this routine "The Stork " is a fun way to help kids remember it.

Building Strength and Power

Young children don't have to take a class in strength training. Simply encourage them to play outdoors. Soon they'll be climbing trees or enjoying a swim in the backyard pool – activities that make the muscles work against resistance. They'll also be building muscle and increasing bone density.

Fitness experts recommend that older children begin to work on Core Strength Training (the obliques, abs and back muscles). These muscles help keep the body in alignment. Stephen Cox says most people are off balance, don't move correctly and are at risk for injury. Core Stabilization combined with exercises to raise the heart rate will help kids move more effectively, which is so important on the squash court. These are some of the principles outlined by the National Association of Sports Medicine. (More info: NASM.org).

Balance training using a balance ball is now being incorporated into more athletic training programs as fitness experts see the value of this method of building strength and maintaining equilibrium. David Behm has been studying the effects of balance training and has found the program beneficial not only for strength and balance, but also for improving running speed.

Body-weight Exercises

Bones continue to harden during the growing years. Up until adolescence, the area at the ends of long bones consists of soft cartilage known as growth plates. Near the end of the adolescent period the growth plate is replaced by bone.

Experts say strength training exercises that involve light weights can be introduced at adolescence. Body-weight exercises – squats, lunges, push-ups, pull-ups, crunches, resistance-band exercises, and rope climbing, with lots of repetitions, are safe.

Manual resistance exercises use a partner to develop strength. These exercises add variety to a workout and significantly increase the number of exercises available to the young athlete.

Interval Training

It may surprise you to know that a long-distance runner who can endure a marathon won't last through a vigorous squash match. Unlike slow distance workouts, squash requires repetitive bursts of intense energy alternated with longer durations of normal activity.

During short bursts of activity, the body uses energy stored in the muscles – glycogen and ATP. The by-product is lactic acid, which is responsible for the burning sensation we feel in our muscles during strenuous workouts. During periods of normal activity, the heart and lungs work together to break down any lactic acid build up. In this phase, oxygen is used to convert stored carbohydrates into energy.

Training for this form of repetitive activity, called interval training, leads to the adaptation response. Muscles develop a higher tolerance to the build-up of lactate. The body begins to build new capillaries and is better able to take in and deliver oxygen to the working muscles, thus strengthening the heart muscle. These changes result in improved performance.

Former pro and national coach Chris Walker recommends interval training as part of an overall squash fitness program. Walker likes to spend the first three weeks of a fitness program working on longer distance runs, and then afterwards switch to running shorter distances.

Plyometrics

"Plyometrics are exercises that enable a muscle to reach maximum strength within a short time," says Dr. Donald Chu, a leading authority on power training and author of more than half a dozen books on Plyometrics, including *Plyo Play for Kids*.

Plyometrics training enhances a kid's ability to increase speed of movement and improve power production. The exercises start with the rapid stretch of a muscle followed by a rapid shortening of the same muscle. There are many injury-proof Plyometrics drills using soft cones, medicine balls and other accessories designed for kids. Common games kids play such as skipping, hopscotch, and leapfrog; jumping jacks, bunny hops, and certain moves in aerobic dance are all forms of Plyometrics.

Plyometrics should not be the only type of fitness training for junior squash players, but should be part of a comprehensive program. Top-ranked pro John White found Plyometrics helpful for his endurance, as well as his reaction time. He was able to bring the explosive power gained from the exercises to his matches and stay on his toes more.

Light Weights

Building strength and endurance can greatly enhance one's ability to handle pace and hit more powerful shots. The goal is to increase muscular and bone strength while retaining flexibility and movement.

Use light medicine balls or dumbbells, resistance bands, and other free weights with lots of repetitions. In consultation with a fitness trainer or coach, design a variety of strength training routines including wrist curls and sawing. The general recommendation is to introduce weight training at adolescence or shortly after.

There has been a tendency for athletes to train the Prime Mover Muscles, those mainly responsible for joint movement, such as the deltoids (back muscles), quadriceps (thigh muscles) and hamstrings (back of the leg muscles). Yet it is also important to work the Stabilizer Muscles, those that protect and counter balance the stress of the bigger muscles. A training program needs to be balanced and ideally performed under the guidance of an expert.

Good Eats and Body Composition

You are not only what you eat, but also how much you eat. Most parents and coaches have become very aware of the importance of a well-balanced diet with healthful portions of proteins, fats, and carbohydrates.

Competition demands even more attention to good nutrition. Eating right the night before a match and three to four hours before reporting time will keep the player's energy high on the court. Energy foods rich in carbohydrates are solid fuels – lots of brown bread, potatoes and pasta, pancakes, bagels, raisins, and bananas.

Refuel with similar high-carb foods one to two hours after the match. In rating squash as the No. 1 sport for fitness, Forbes.com gave squash a score of 5, the highest on a scale of 1 to 5, in calorie burning. After 30 minutes of squash, you use a lot of energy, which needs to be replaced with nutritious foods.

Never forget the importance of regular hydration. Choose sports beverages, as well as plain old water.

Supplements

The scientific community has finally proved the efficacy of vitamin supplements. A multivitamin, antioxidant, and mineral complex are now an athlete's essentials.

Teenagers develop special nutrient needs as they experience tremendous growth spurts and hormonal changes. Individual likes and dislikes, as well as peer pressure can contribute to poor diets. Because of their eating habits and special nutrient needs certain food supplements may be useful.

Avoid supplements formulated to optimize hormone levels including testosterone and growth hormones because they may interfere with natural growth patterns. Meal replacement shakes and powders may sometimes be the only hope for a rushed teenager, but limit their use and seek medical advice before using these products.

Body Composition Tests

To be sure all that healthy eating is paying off, two simple tests are available to determine body composition – Skinfold and Body-Mass Index. A parent or fitness trainer can perform these tests. The results provide an estimate of a child's percentage of body fat when compared to body mass composed of muscles, bones, and organs.

- *Skinfold Test:* Using a basic device called a skinfold caliper, measure the thickness of the skinfold on the back of the upper arm. Use this measurement with the Skinfold chart to obtain body fat percentage (More info: cooperinst.org).
- *Body-Mass Index:* Based on height and weight measurements, a BMI table will provide an index number. The index will tell you if the child's weight can be considered healthy, overweight, or obese (More info: omronhealthcare.com and Tanita.com).

Speed, Agility, and Quickness

Speed is how fast a player covers ground; agility is the efficiency in changing direction; and quickness is the ability to get off the mark. The famous Hashim Khan was a master in action and these three qualities were his greatest assets. A player good in all three departments—speed, agility, and quickness— will be able to reach even the most well placed shots.

Simple ghosting, or running the court and simulating points is one way to work on footwork and is appropriate for young players, even if the movements are performed in two-minute intervals. Without the actual ball, players can run to the corners and to each back wall, swinging their racquets to stroke an imaginary ball. After each "shot," they always come back to the T.   When ghosting, players should always focus on the imaginary ball as though they are playing a real game.

Aerobic Capacity

Performing a physical activity for a long time without getting breathless requires good aerobic capacity. Keep in mind that the teen years are the most important time to develop aerobic capacity.

"Squash is a very demanding sport involving short bouts of intense activity (10-60 seconds) with very short rest periods (10 seconds) between rallies," says David Behm. A Player's heart rate increases to 80-85% of his maximum heart rate. Your 18-year-old would have a heart rate of approximately 172 beats per minute. In a tough, competitive match, his heart rate might stay around this level for more than 1 hour with only 90 seconds rest between each of the 3-5 games.

Short bursts of intense activity produce lactic acid that is associated with premature fatigue. During long and hard rallies lactate levels can double. In these situations, experts suggest, sufficient aerobic capacity is needed to remove the lactate build up, thereby increasing endurance. Behm says that the player who is less fatigued is able to put more pressure on his opponent, make better shot selections for a longer period of time and eventually win.

Cardiovascular training is important for squash. Swimming laps, doing step aerobics, and jogging are all activities that will improve aerobic capacity. Squash coach Tom Generous, in the Tar Heel Squash Web newsletter, says there's no substitute for running for optimum conditioning to help players get through the fifth game of a tough match. (More info: Select References 4). For even more squash-specific training, focus on interval training. Alternate between reaching maximum speed and returning to a normal pace.

Eye Injuries

Sports injuries are the number one cause of eye trauma in children under 15, says the *EyeCare Digest*. The report showed racquet sports, along with baseball and basketball, as one of the most injury-prone sports for eye injuries. Insist your child wear protective eyewear on the court. Protective eyewear comes in many colors and styles so your child may find one that makes a fashion statement while keeping him safe. In Australia, names of squash organizations have been emblazoned upon I-Masks, so the owners have a sense of prestige when wearing them. Other countries have followed suit to encourage more players to wear eye protection.

The average squash ball travels at 90 mph and a squash racquet, anywhere between 50 and 110 mph. And considering that two players are in a relatively small space whacking the same ball, it's no wonder that the risk of injury is great. Top-ranked pro Jonathon Power had two close calls last year with an eye injury. One time, a ball bounced off the wall and hit him in the eye. Another time, he was hit by his opponent's racquet. Will Carlin, a top American player, endured two surgeries and ended up missing two years of play due to a detached retina, an injury he sustained while competing in the 1990s.

Most squash governing organizations now require players to wear protective eyewear, especially for junior tournaments. It is important that the eyewear is designed specifically for squash and meets safety standards. You can learn more about eye injuries and how to prevent them in "The Practical Guide to Sports Eye Protection" by Dr. Paul F Vinger in the *Physicians and Sports Medicine Journal*. (More info: physsportsmed.com).

Good Pain, Bad Pain

No pain, no gain. A little discomfort is part of any sports and fitness routine. For a muscle to become stronger it must experience a higher than normal load. This slight overload is perceived as "the burn" and is the "good pain" necessary for improved performance. Onset of fatigue is another sign that activity is pushing the limits.

The discomfort associated with "good pain" is short-lived; it should not persist for hours or days. With rest, the slight fatigue should also go away.

Certain pain, though, lasts long after exercise. It affects sports performance, functions outside of sports like walking, sleeping, shaking hands or getting dressed, and does not go away after rest. These are examples of the "bad pain" one should always be concerned about. Discourage your child from playing through pain. Seek medical evaluation right away if pain persists.

Sometimes kids are less than honest about disclosing the real nature of their pain, either because they want to compete in an important tournament, attain a certain ranking, or make the team. The best antidote for this behavior is talking to the child about pain and injuries before they occur. Explain how to distinguish good pain from bad pain. Tell them why they need to be honest with you and with themselves about the bad pain.Make them understand how timely care of pain and injuries will enable them to enjoy the sport for a lifetime.

Common Pains

Pains associated with shoulders, elbows, and knees are common to squash. The parent, coach, and player should all keep an eye out for this kind of bad pain. At the first sign seek medical advice.

The most common injuries sustained in recreational squash, according to a survey by *Squash* magazine, in order of most to least common are:

1. Hip and groin injuries
2. Back and neck strains
3. Shoulder and elbow injuries
4. Foot and ankle injuries
5. Achilles and calf injuries

6.   Hamstring strain
7.   Knee injuries, such as cartilage tears

To help prevent these problems, it is important to strengthen the muscles around the joints with the guidance of a trainer or coach. Don't over train by doing heavy workouts on two consecutive days. Most importantly, warm up properly with dynamic stretching and cool down with static stretching.

Healthful Habits

The problem with most sports injuries is that you won't know you have them until joints become tender and you start to feel pain. Rehabilitation usually requires extensive treatment and rest. Once again, it is important to educate your child on good pain versus bad pain. Help him understand the importance of practicing good habits that will help prevent injuries that can appear, without notice, years later. Here are some healthful tips:

- Overall fitness is the best way to avoid injuries. Pay special attention to the demands of squash and those parts of the anatomy that are not worked as much by squash alone – Core Strengthening (the back, stomach, obliques and laterals).
- A cardio routine, followed by stretches before any workout and another few minutes of cool-down stretches afterward, is essential. Remember dynamic before static stretching.
- Always wear proper squash shoes. Cross-trainers and running shoes are big no-nos for squash.
- Wear protective eyewear specifically designed for squash with approved safety standards.
- Have racquet grip size and string tension checked by a racquet technician on a regular basis.
- Never play through pain. Seek medical attention right away and rest as many weeks or months as the doctor advises.
- Drink plenty of water during workouts.
- Have an extensive physical examination by a doctor every year or so. This is invaluable for competitive players.
- Play with proper technique – early preparation, racquet face open, shoulder rotation, and weight transfer through the ball and contacting in front.
- Rest. Take frequent time-outs from vigorous physical activity of any kind.

Summer Time Training

Because the squash tournament calendar is lighter in the summer and school is out, this is a good time for junior players to work on fitness. When former pro and national coach Chris Walker works on summer fitness, he spends the first few weeks on building stamina with running. From the fourth through sixth week, he adds interval training and for the final weeks, he concentrates on speed and power, working on court with practice drills and matches.

With any training program, it is important to balance hard training days with easy ones. The body needs to recuperate with 24-hour rest periods. Try a program of Monday, Wednesday and Friday with hard sessions and taking it easy on the days in between. On the easy days, don't play a hard match, concentrate on light hitting and stretching.

All bodies are not alike. Give kids the potential to build their strength, stamina and speed, but don't expect them to do the impossible.

Conditioning Roadmap

You can find loads of scientific research, books, videos, and television programs that discuss the nuts-and-bolts of physical conditioning. It's easy to get carried away. Educate yourself and keep current but remember to avoid too much structure at a young age. Keep conditioning simple and balanced. Above all, make physical conditioning enjoyable for its own sake. Jogging along a beautiful trail beats the treadmill hands down.

A balanced conditioning program will include training for flexibility, strength, power, speed, agility, quickness, and cardio. Incorporating all these elements in routines appropriate for your squash kid can be challenging. Table 9.1 provides a general roadmap that can help. Personalize the roadmap depending upon your child's physical growth and level of squash intensity.

Consult your child's doctor and a certified trainer before starting any physical training regimen. Complete physical examinations, by a doctor, once or twice a year are a must.

Most schools have physical education classes. In some areas of New York, students in grades 6 through 8 participate in more than three hours of physical exercise each week. Factor in such hours of exercise when designing a program for your child. You can find after-school sports and fitness classes at health clubs, YMCAs, junior camps, and community centers.

Happy moving!

Table 9.1

Age	Physical Conditioning Program
Under 13	Make a habit of doing warm-ups before squash. Start with dynamic stretching. After squash, perform a cool-down routine.
	Incorporate age-appropriate conditioning drills during squash lessons. Drills that focus on speed, agility, and quickness are best. Interval training.
	Participate in a variety of sports in addition to squash. Good choices are: soccer, lacrosse, field hockey, cross-country and swimming for all-around conditioning.
	Allow time for unstructured outdoor activities.
14-15	Add light structured training. Good choices are: Yoga, martial arts, and other flexibility and mind-body workouts. Body-weight exercises, Plyometrics, interval training, light weights, and resistance bands are good for strength and power.
16 plus	Hire a fitness expert and develop a squash-specific individualized training program.

10

Mind Games

"The game at the top is probably 80 percent mental"
Jenny Tranfield, sport psychologist and top WISPA player

Mental conditioning can be an emotional boot camp, but it doesn't have to be. When incorporated into routines like squash practice at an early age and fostered gently, mental conditioning can become a tool not only to develop a better squash player but also a better person.

Mental fitness includes three key components: mental attitude, emotional toughness, and mind-body coordination. Mental attitude can be nurtured on court by the coach and off court by the parent. Emotional toughness and mind-body coordination develop naturally with squash training, but if you want to up the ante, consider training in martial arts or Yoga.

Parent as Attitude Coach

A parent can make perhaps the most important contributions to a child's squash development in several ways—by acting as an attitude coach; by helping a child develop good sportsmanship; by encouraging off-court physical conditioning; and by playing regularly with the child.

Helping instill a positive attitude does not have to be complicated or time consuming. A simple insistence that the child smiles and shake hands after a squash match sends a number of positive attitudinal messages. This behavior helps the child learn relaxed play and to de-emphasize wins and losses, a critical component of the development phase.

The handshake also means the player is thanking the competitor for allowing him to give his best effort. The players should look each other in the eye to let one another know that they are sincere. The focus of competition is shifted away from beating the other player to challenging the child's own potential and reinforces the desire for continued improvement.

Choosing an appropriate time to speak to your child on the mental aspects of the game is important. You want to make sure he's an effective listener. If his mind is pre-occupied, you'll get an impatient nod or an "I know, I know." Talk to him during non-squash activities. A good time might be in the car, but not on the way back from a match or a lesson.

Here are a few questions to stimulate a lively discussion with your child. Just laying it out there will often work wonders with mental attitude and preparation:

- What is the true nature of competition? Is competition a threat or a challenge? Can competition help improve your game? How can competition help you become a better person? How is amateur competition different from professional competition?
- Johnny has won the championship two years in a row, why is he still afraid of competition? Could it be because expectations are too high? What should Johnny do to stay relaxed and enjoy the challenge?
- Jill is facing off against her best friend, Ashley, in the next match. Jill plays better than Ashley and wants to win. Yet she doesn't want to hurt her friend's feelings. Can Jill reconcile this dichotomy and approach the match prepared to win?
- The Jill and Ashley match result reads 11-9, 11-6, 11-8. The pair's previous match was 11-0, 11-3. 11-1. Can Ashley find redeemable qualities in her performance and truly feel she's a winner at different levels?
- At what stage of squash development are skill development and effort more important than the result of the match?
- Do you compete to please yourself, your parents and coach, or both? Why is playing for your own enjoyment important?

You will need to monitor the number of discussions you initiate about squash. Too much talk about squash can have a negative impact. Are you always giving advice? Do you have as many discussions about other aspects of your child's life? Tim Bacon, member of the Canadian Mental Training Registry and squash coach at Smith College, who has written extensively on mental conditioning, says more than once a week is too often. "Too much concern or feedback, even if it is positive, is likely to be interpreted by the child as I MUST do well."

Most squash coaches focus on attitude and sportsmanship during their lessons. If they don't, you can give a gentle reminder that this is an important aspect of learning the game.

There are websites and books that deal with cultivating good sportsmanship and positive attitudes in young athletes. Although not squash specific, The Center For Sports Parenting (More info: sportsparenting.org) provides helpful resources on some of these issues.

Mental Conditioning

Unlike golf, where there seems to be endless time in between play, squash is a fast-paced sport and players have to be willing to let go of negative emotions very quickly, observes Jonathan Katz, a sports psychologist and Director of Sports and Exercise Psychology at Altheus. Katz, who has worked with both amateur and professional squash players, says that players have to calm themselves in a very furious storm or they could let one bad shot in a match affect the next few points. "But at the same time, they can't get over-confident after a point well played either. They need to maintain an even keel throughout."

But some players can do this more easily than others. Katz takes a look at the entire profile of the child before recommending any techniques or exercises. "Two kids can come in with concentration problems, but the roots of those problems may be totally different," he explains. These roots, he says, also have to do with how kids approach other areas of their life. "Those who tend to be more critical about themselves might have more trouble letting go of negative emotions. Anger is often a mask for fear or sadness or some underlying problem. Those with a healthier sense of themselves can let go easier."

Different techniques can be used for different needs. For example, for players who are tense on the court, Katz recommends relaxation exercises, using the well known Jacobson Relaxation Technique, where the player tenses each group of muscles, one at a time from head to toe, and then relaxes them. But that may not be appropriate for all players. Those who are more laid back may need a vigorous pre-match work out to build up their intensity so they can become more aggressive on the court.

Appropriate goal setting is key to developing better focus. By de-emphasizing winning, Katz recommends players set more short term goals, such as changing a stroke to improve it, which will ultimately help kids plan and learn how to become better players. Most importantly, says Katz, is that parents often don't realize that while their child may be playing at an adult level, they are still a kid and will act like a kid. Parental expectation can be a big factor in a child's performance.

Noise

A thousand things may interfere
Unless you keep your focus clear,
When pressure mounts and things are rough
Considering your game's enough.
Don't think about your mother's sneeze
Or how you ought to win with ease.
Forget the scorer's lousy calls
On those clearly double-bouncing balls.
Don't worry that you're going to lose
Or how your coach will take the news.
No matter what the game and what the score-
Just work your game-plan – nothing more.
Be the ball and keep your poise
All the rest is simply noise!

—*Richard Millman*

On-Court Mental Conditioning

The Bounce Hit theory introduced by Timothy Gallwey in *The Inner Game of Tennis* can easily be applied to squash and has been helpful even for players who find hitting a squash ball extremely challenging. Bounce-Hit is a simple drill. Whenever the ball bounces, the player says, "bounce" aloud to himself. And whenever the player hits the ball, he says, "hit" aloud. This drill helps the player know when to hit the ball, thus his timing becomes more automatic and fluid. By concentrating on Bounce-Hit, the player is less likely to lose focus. Players who are nervous or too wrapped up in thinking about a match can try this exercise to calm down and get in a better rhythm. (More info: Select Reference 3)

Coming to the court in the right frame of mind makes a big difference. Take a look at top player Peter Nicol who often arrives at a tournament site tuned into his iPod, carrying his racquets on his back. At the Tournament of Champions in New York City, Nicol easily blended in with the crowd in Grand Central Terminal, indistinguishable from the other commuters. Yet Nicol was on his way to defend his title in one of the biggest events in the squash world. One would never have known it by his relaxed and easy-going manner.

The Other Parent

You can teach your kid all you want but you have to take into account the effect of his "other parent" – the television. Say you just talked to your kid about how effort is more important than winning during the development phase. He then watches a certain television show where little Tommy is the toast of the town because he won the little league championship for the home team. Maybe the show portrayed Tommy working hard, and that's good. But the fact that everyone on the show is completely focused on winning at all costs is not good. It may make for an exciting television episode, but it sends the wrong message, one opposite to what you want to teach.

Media so saturates our lives it isn't possible to protect kids from every message that runs counter to those of parents. Whether the television message is right or wrong, it undoubtedly plays a role in the development of your child's mental attitudes.

Setting good television habits can help. For instance, teach your young child to ask permission to watch television. Take advantage of the new gizmos that let you record the programs you're comfortable allowing your child to watch. Share television shows with positive messages with your child. Always be aware, for better or worse, your messages compete with little Tommy from the Tommy Show for your child's attention.

Drug Abuse

The three international governing bodies of squash—WISPA, PSA, and WSF—have come together to establish an Anti-Doping Policy that puts squash in a strong position against performance enhancing drugs.

In the past, the World Squash Federation has had professional squash players tested for banned substances at world events. The new policy extends the testing to PSA and WISPA events as well. An Anti-Doping program that covers the top events in junior competition is also in place.

A positive test results in a suspension. A second offense can lead to a lifetime ban. How's that for dissuading a player from ever considering drug abuse?

Avoiding Burnout

If there's one thing parents can do to avoid burnout in a young squash player it's to resist the temptation to coach too much. Lana Quibell, former national champion and mother of Michelle, two-time intercollegiate champion and former British Open Junior Champion, believes that too much coaching from a parent can be counterproductive. "Parents should be good and sympathetic listeners, models for conduct and sportsmanship and only give constructive and positive feedback. My best advice is to explain to your child that you will not give him advice or critique his play unless he asks for it. Follow this up by sticking to your word. If you do, they will ask and they then feel in control." Quibell is also a strong believer in teaching the importance of good sportsmanship. "Accept nothing less," she advises.

Another way to help keep burnout at bay is to manage the type and number of tournaments a child plays. During the early stages of competition, rewarding effort and de-emphasizing match results are certainly necessary. But nothing will help a player who is constantly losing in the first round. Before long she will burn out and quit the sport. Focus more on skill development and enter lower-level tournaments. Conversely, too much winning leads to boredom. A top-ranked teenager can become emotionally spent trying to stay on top, tournament after tournament.

Other Passions

Develop a passion for other activities—hobbies and sports. While the kid is into squash competitively, encourage her to participate in a different sport each season as recreation. Playing a variety of sports also exercises muscles differently and chronic injuries are less likely to occur.

"Children should not only play more than one sport, but also they should cultivate other interests such as computers, music or the arts so they don't always focus on that next tournament," says Michelle Klein, executive director of the National Youth Sports Safety Foundation in Boston.

Take a break from all organized sports for two or three weeks a year. Taking time out, going on vacation, or attending a family reunion will replenish the mind and body. Umm… at least *most* reunions are replenishing.

Have a Higher Goal

Religion, community service, and involvement in public causes can help keep squash in perspective. Setting priorities will ease needless pressure and may actually benefit your child's game by allowing her to stay relaxed. For example, explain that schoolwork comes first, and then sports.

Detecting Early Signs of Burnout

You have taken all steps necessary to avoid burnout—managed her tournament play, ensured her participation in other activities, and encouraged her to develop goals beyond squash. How do you know if these are working?

Burnout often kicks in when kids reach their teens. When they're young they generally go along with whatever their parents have planned for them. Meanwhile, years of junior competition and over-scheduling may have taken a secret toll—physically and emotionally. Around adolescence, kids begin to assert themselves more and express their true feelings. "Allow kids to participate in the decision making and let them own it as much as possible," says Lana Quibell. "This helps them to stay interested and not burn out."

Often, if parents are spending a significant amount of time and money on lessons, tournament travel and equipment, kids feel pressure to do well. You can relieve some of that pressure by putting squash in context, says Tim Bacon. Let your child know that you would gladly spend the same amount of time and money for art, music or other interests that the child might have.

Detect burnout early and make needed changes. According to experts, a child who asks to miss practice, or complains about her coach or the class, is really telling you there's a problem. Often a child suffering from burnout will show signs of sleep disturbance, headache, and muscular rigidity. She may also show signs of depression, such as sadness and lack of energy.

If you are reasonably sure that the problem is burnout, cut back on squash and extra-curricular activities. If the child has been exclusively focused on squash, encourage participation in another activity. Make that new activity, rather than squash, the focus of dinner conversation.

Redefine "Making It"

Okay, Mr. Jones, please lay down on the couch and let's talk.

In our hearts, we parents and coaches are conditioned to define "making it" in the world of squash as playing at an elite level, competing on an Ivy League college team or traveling on a national team. We visualize success in squash as a pyramid and subconsciously prod our kids and ourselves toward what we believe is the "pinnacle."

Instead of the pyramid, imagine the landscape as a beautiful valley of flowers. Surrounding the valley are gorgeous mountains. You and your kid are enjoying a beautiful hike up the side of one of these mountains. First you conquer one mountain, then another. Anytime you choose you can have a picnic on a rock or in the valley of flowers.

Each mountain presents different challenges. If one is the tallest, the other has the highest rock face; yet another tests navigational skills. In other words, there is no *one* Mt. Everest in this valley. You can enjoy an "ultimate" challenge by scaling each of them. Or you can choose to simply enjoy the beauty of the trek.

"Okay, okay, Dr. Filbur, I think I got the imagery – not a pyramid but a valley of flowers and mountains and all that. Now you expect me to read this passage to my 10-year-old? You must be kidding, right?"

Actually you don't have to say a word. Just believe in it and live it in your everyday words and actions. Trust me, the kid will soon learn to discover a Mt. Everest in every mountain he climbs. More importantly, whether you and your kid are climbing the mountains or relaxing in the valley of flowers, you will both learn to enjoy today's challenges and rewards.

You may get off the couch now. That will be $125, Mr. Jones. Thank you.

11

Pushing: How much is too much

"I believe you should push your child. Not only is it okay, it is your right, responsibility and your absolute moral imperative as a parent."
DR. JIM TAYLOR, Positive Pushing

Parents want the best for their children, and their goals usually center around helping the child to be confident, happy, and of good character. Why is it then that children, especially adolescents, resist our well-intentioned efforts to help? Why is it that loving parents sometimes feel the need to push—to direct the child to do something they don't want to do? These paradoxes are often most apparent in cases of sports parents.

Parental Goals

Sports psychologists trace many parent-child conflicts to parental goals that are outcome-based and confuse the child's goals with their own. Setting outcome-based goals is tempting and deceptively easy.

"I want to do everything I can to help my child become the next best thing the Harvard squash team has ever seen." Achieving this so-called "parental" goal is dependent on four actions:

1. The child has to take up squash, not as a sport but as a career.
2. The child has to put in the necessary practice hours.
3. The parent is able to provide the financial support necessary to reach the goal.
4. The parent is able to provide the time and emotional support necessary to reach the goal.

Clearly, 50 percent of the actions required to accomplish this goal successfully is dependent upon the child. If the child wholeheartedly embraces his end of the deal then everything should be fine. However, there will be trouble in paradise when an adolescent decides to change course to pursue other goals or to divvy up his limited time engaging in other activities. The outcome-based parental goal is suddenly no longer achievable, leaving the parent bewildered and frustrated.

Instead, revise the parental goal to something more specific and directly controllable. For instance, "I will provide the financial help to pursue serious squash development." Certainly setting such a goal does not preclude a parent from trying to pique the child's interest in squash or actively encouraging him to take up serious squash development. The process-based parental goal simply clarifies that the adolescent is the one in the driver's seat, while the parent plays a supportive role as far as squash development is concerned.

Process-based goals that a squash parent can set for himself include:

- Highlight the value of squash as a lifetime sport for fun, fitness, and skill development.
- Provide necessary time and financial and emotional support.
- Use squash as a vehicle to teach good attitude, sportsmanship, teamwork, discipline, and character.

Choose a parental goal that will offer you a sense of accomplishment, whether your child ultimately decides to take up squash, soccer, law, or medicine.

Why Parents get Pushy

After years of financially supporting a child's squash development and carting her to lessons and tournaments, even the most patient parent can be ready to explode. "Jill, win this match or else..." There is no excuse for actually saying such a thing, but it illustrates how parental pressure can fester. Parents feel that because they're contributing time and money, they're also justified in demanding a result: winning.

Measuring Results by Wins

Parents are perfectly justified in demanding results. At the very least, it helps them decide whether their time and money has been well spent. However, the trick is to measure results not by a young child's wins, but by the development of good attitudes and improvements in squash skill. Parents who measure results this way are less likely to push unjustifiably.

Winning is nice, but winning is only a desirable outcome. The purpose of sport for a child is to create an opportunity for fun and growth. The triumphs and heartaches inherent in sport can provide a child with the learning experiences and life lessons that help pave the road to adulthood.

Ask yourself – Is Jill regularly picking up on important life lessons on the court? Is the game emotionally healthy for her? Has it made her more mature and better prepared for life? And of course, is she having fun? If the answer to these questions is yes, your time and money have been well spent, regardless of the outcome of a match.

After a few years of squash, you can add a second component to monitoring progress – improvements in squash skills. Sports psychologists say that emphasis on sports mastery demonstrates a focus on performance, whereas emphasis on sports competence is used to describe focus on winning or losing.

An under-emphasis on mastery and an over-emphasis on winning account for many children appearing to fall short of parental expectations. When that happens, parents intuitively begin to push harder. Instead, measure the results as improvements in skill mastery – better strokes, strategy, physical ability, and mental toughness.

Life lessons and improvements in squash skills are the yardsticks parents should use to measure results. Chances are, you'll notice your kid has made great progress in vital areas, in spite of losing her match, making all your efforts worthwhile.

Early Parental Goal

Another reason parents are driven to push is that they decide very early on that they are going to raise the child to be a squash player, either at an elite, Ivy League or professional level. First, a parent is making a crucial life choice for the child that may not survive her adolescent years. Next, the pressure to constantly practice and perform takes the "sport" out of the game. Instead, it becomes "work" for the child. As a result, the parent has to push even harder to get the child to practice.   Michelle Quibell, the top American junior now at Yale, says it is imperative that the child plays the sport for himself, not for parents or coaches. "A child can be extremely talented, but if squash isn't something that he really wants to pursue, it isn't worth forcing."

Statiscally, 1 in 12 get accepted to Yale. A much smaller percentage become professional players. Notwithstanding the statistical long shot, there are parents who want their child to be an intercollegiate champion or the next James Willstrop, former World Junior Champion. Of course, parents would be ecstatic to see their kid reach the pinnacle of the game. By all means dream big for your child, but always remember that this is *your* dream, not your child's.

Undoubtedly, it takes tremendous effort to maintain a top ranking. But what differentiates the Top 10 from others is a burning desire and incredible ability, much more than simple effort. Fortunately, you can play a major role in nurturing your child's desire by providing positive squash experiences throughout her life. And emphasizing skill mastery rather than wins and losses during her developmental years can help develop the ability needed to compete at the higher rungs of squash.

For those who do desire a professional career, that decision should not be made on an emotional level. Periodically, as a child develops and is competing internationally, the parent, the coach, and an athletic trainer, along with the kid, ought to make an honest assessment about whether she has the true desire and ability, at all levels, to turn professional. Yet having said that, there are some instances where those who were perhaps less talented still made it due to tremendous passion for the sport and belief in themselves. As with anything else, there are exceptions to the rule.

Understand, the choice to become a professional should be made much later in a child's squash development and that it is a team decision based on performance at the time and, moreover, the kid's own desire. Doing so can help a parent be less pushy.

The trick is to keep the dream of becoming a professional player in perspective; look at it as just one of many equally challenging and ambitious aspirations you have for her. Perhaps, as a parent, you also have hopes that she will one day graduate from an Ivy League college, become a life-saving doctor, a public service lawyer, or head up a volunteer organization that gives back to the community.

And, it bears repeating, always remind yourself that these are *your* dreams and not your child's. Separate your dreams from your parental goals. And remember – you have little control over whether your adolescent child aligns her dreams and goals with yours. It's best to avoid verbalizing your dreams to the child or, as the British would say, "Keep mum." Instead, keep working toward your parental goals.

Gordon Anderson, president of Anderson Courts and a former top touring professional, said he had to take a big gulp when he realized his daughters would not follow in his squash footsteps. One daughter actually quit the game for four years. "They need athletic ability and desire," says Anderson, who saw that his children had a bit of both, but not enough to be the cream at the top. In the long run, although his daughters didn't turn pro, Anderson is happy that they both enjoyed playing on college squash teams and continue to play as adults.

That the journey is the reward might be a cliché; nevertheless, it is so true. The value in learning the game of squash and playing it has to be of the moment, in the present. "If today is the last day your child plays squash, it is still worth it." Repeat this to yourself and you'll find less reason to push.

Sacrifices – Too Many, Too Soon

"You have to understand that nobody in skating realizes, starting out, just how expensive it's going to get," advised World champion figure skater Kristi Yamaguchi's father, Jim, in the *San Jose Mercury News*. "It sort of creeps up on you, because as Kristi got better, she began to have more needs, so we got in deeper and deeper." Commitment to squash is no different, and an involved commitment has its costs. A squash career will require that the family make choices and compromises: missed social activities with family and friends; educational and career plans postponed; houses in different states or even countries—one for the working parent and the other where the care-taking parent lives with the child—a necessity for better coaching and competitive opportunities.

Reasonable compromises are okay, but only after a decision has been made to take up squash as a career. If not, the kid will think, "Jeez, my whole family is depending on me."

Sometimes parents make sacrifices very early on, when the child has just started playing squash simply as recreation and there is no evidence yet of desire, consistent performance or ability. And, most importantly, before the child has developed the maturity to weigh in on whether to take up squash as a career.

Hard sacrifices, including financial ones, made too early in a child's training add to the child's mental burden. And, at some level, squash development suffers. Once families invest so much of themselves in squash, it clouds decision-making. Children find it harder to quit if they want to.

We like to believe that anything is possible, but parents ought to look ahead to the financial demands of competitive sport. This doesn't mean you can't help your child succeed even if income is limited. A little planning goes a long way. Trade off a few private lessons for self-practice; travel to fewer competitions and, when you do go, stay with friends.

Britt Hebden, a top junior from Philadelphia, plays more than she takes lessons, and hasn't spent nearly the same amount of time or money as others have in training programs. She works a lot on her own and gets help when she needs it. Sometimes coaches put her up when she travels to tournaments. Hebden made the national junior team, earned sponsorship from a top racquet company, and is ranked both in the US and in Europe.

Playing Up

Opting to "play up"—the practice of competing in an older age division—can be quite an ego-trip for the parent. The decision to play-up a mature and competitive kid who is consistently trouncing his peers is cut and dried. To keep him challenged and interested, have him compete in an older age division tournament.

In the case of a younger child, the decision needs more careful consideration. A 9-year-old may be consistently outplaying his peers, but you have to consider that he's also having a lot of fun practicing with them. Maybe the kids have formed an adventure club and play together regularly after squash practice. Moving the kid to an older age group could be great for his squash, but may not appeal to him socially.

Another pitfall to watch out for is when a young child who is playing up begins to develop a convenient excuse for losing. Parents may also have a tendency to convince themselves the child is losing because his competitors are older. Such rationalizations can prevent kids from developing mental toughness.

Sometimes when kids compete in a higher age group, they end up losing tournaments they could be winning in their own age group. They might be missing out on some fun by moving up too soon. Michelle Quibell played up in practice and smaller tournaments to get better competition, but competed in her age group in the larger events to ensure a better ranking. She did this during the years when the older age group was a challenge for her.

Experts suggest that the best way to take advantage of the benefits of playing up, while avoiding the drawbacks, is to "mix it up." For younger children who are consistently outperforming their age group, start by phasing in practice sessions with the next older group. A kid practicing three times a week can be allowed to practice with the older group once a week, while continuing to practice with his peers.

In these instances, a wise coach will try to avoid creating the impression that one particular kid is being handpicked for promotion. In some cases, kids who are playing up may need to return to their own age group. They may not enjoy the new challenge or perhaps the coach will decide the kid is not quite ready. This can feel like a demotion to the child. Consider playing up as a part of the regular program and do it without a lot of hoopla.

When the kid develops consistency in the older age group and is able to win some practice games, he is ready to be phased in to a similar tournament schedule. Very rarely should kids be allowed to play up more than a single age group.

Kids develop faster when they play with adults or older children. Playing with adults is recommended when kids are physically older, at about 13. Playing with adults can help them develop a more mature game. Playing up is necessary to keep proficient kids engaged, but it is still best to mix in play in their age group so they continue to have fun and develop a social network at practice and at tournaments.

Played Out

Burnout is a reality in squash, as it is in other sports. Lily Lorentzen, the top American junior now at Harvard, says she's seen it happen, particularly when parents put on the pressure. Lorentzen, who is one of five children, said although her parents were supportive, they were never really that involved in her squash. "Sometimes I wish they understood more, but it's better this way."

"Parents putting pressure on kids is unhealthy," says Steve Hall of Dunlop, who used to play on the pro tour. "It doesn't create an environment for a kid to be independent or to have fun." Even early on, pushing kids into squash may cause more harm than good. Long time pro Tom Generous, now at Tar Heel Squash in North Carolina, says he put his 10-year-old in the mainstream too fast. Generous is now an advocate of making squash fun in the early years and showing kids basics rather than forcing competition to o early.

It's doubtful that most people can handle more than eight years of intense pressure. Nine years of intense pressure is about all anyone can take. If you start putting the pressure on kids at age 9, by the time they're 18, they've had enough. Christy Willstrop, older brother of top player James, started playing at 2 and was rumored to have had a game with squash legend Jonah Barrington, six-time world champion, as a present for his 4th birthday. Christy became the No. 1 player under 19 in England, but by his mid-20s, he was finished. Did he burnout? Many times, players you hear about constantly as juniors seem to disappear when they get older. Was it too much too soon?

Parents of some of the sport's top juniors know that you can't force the desire to play squash upon a child. "You have to separate yourself," said Jan Hebden, mother of Britt, a nationally ranked junior from Pennsylvania. The Hebdens like to put Britt's squash in perspective, acknowledging that it is a sport and not life itself. "We didn't do much, just supported her, got her in the right direction and saw that she was happy." Part of the reason Britt clicked with squash is because her personality matches the sport. "She's very self motivated," says her mom.

Squash can be an addicting game. In the book, *Squash Racquets: The Khan Game*, Hashim Kahn writes that he told his mother he could only think about the squash court when he was in school everyday. He was so absorbed in the game that he couldn't hear the teacher. Hashim Khan was a unique individual who developed a true passion for squash at a very young age. (More info: Select References 2)

While you don't want squash to take over your child's life, you want to encourage him to pursue what he enjoys and build on his talents.

Prevention

Kids who pursue a sport too intensely from a young age can get tired and want to stop altogether. Specific strategies can be employed by parents and coaches to help prevent the "I want to quit" syndrome before the fact.

- Avoid pushing young kids into a high degree of specialization in a single sport.
- Many parents believe coaching their child strains the parent-child relationship. Leave the coaching to a professional.
- Emphasize sports mastery over competence. Teach kids to enjoy the process of developing proficiency. Help them measure accomplishments by improvement in various skills rather than whom they beat or lost to. Today I hit great backhand volley returns or today I made less than five unforced errors in a match. These are better yardsticks for junior competitors than "Today, I beat Sally."
- Be prepared to lessen the degree of parental involvement in decision-making as the child grows older. Let the coach be the mentor.

Now What

A parent has done all the right things, yet sometimes the kid is ready to quit anyway. Sports psychologists say up until ages 10 to 12, a child will probably go along with what Dad and Mom suggest. Over the next couple of years, though, the child wants to begin making her own decisions, including those related to sports participation. By adolescence, the influence of peers is replacing that of parents.

Leaving squash behind might be the kid's way of asserting independence. "Mom and Dad want me to play, so I won't." Or maybe it's time to face the fact that they really don't like the game. Whatever the reason, parents ought to prepare for the day when their child announces, "I want to quit squash," whether that day actually arrives or not.

Remember, the choice to play should always be the child's. All you can do is gently nudge them in the direction that you believe is best for them. Let's say your young child has expressed some interest in squash. You think she might enjoy it and let her sign up for squash lessons. Three weeks into the lessons, she hates them. "All I do is hit walls," she complains.

At that point, the best choice is to make her stick with it. Often, after a few lessons, the child becomes more proficient and may want to continue. Younger children may be confused about the rules of the game. Explain the rules or practice with them so they feel more comfortable. In any case, she only has a few weeks to go and she'll probably learn a valuable lesson by following through on something she started but now doesn't enjoy. Be sympathetic, but firm. Don't force her to sign up for the next program, but make her finish this one.

Older children may have more complex reasons for wanting to quit. Help your child articulate those reasons. Talk to her coach. Study her performance at practice sessions and tournaments. Think about whether one or more of the following come into play.

1. *Squash isn't fun anymore:* Make sure the coach is compatible with your child. Tread carefully, but don't be afraid to try a new coach. Maybe your child has been played up too quickly and is unable to keep up, preventing her from having fun. Reduce competitions; instead, focus on casual practice with family and friends. Rekindle interest by taking her to watch a professional tournament. Sometimes simply taking a complete break from squash for two to three weeks can help the child return with enthusiasm.

2. *Too much pressure:* A kid can experience pressure from a parent or coach. Maybe it's time for the parent to get out of the advice business and leave the training to the coach. Praise effort, skills, and technique rather than focusing on bottom-line wins and losses. Find time to play squash with the family. Replace a weekly hour of squash with another hobby – music, photography, or anything else you know interests your child.

3. *Not enough time:* Experts recommend focusing on one extra-curricular activity at a time. Help your child prioritize. Instead of doing both soccer and squash each week, suggest she select one sport and put off learning the other until there's an opportunity to attend a related sports camp. Of course, as a loyal squash parent, you will instinctively guide her toward squash as a first choice,

won't you? Don't worry these things have a way of sorting themselves out.

4. *Mismatched skill level:* Again, this means the child has either been played up too quickly or placed in an inappropriate class where her skill level doesn't match that of others in her group. Perhaps not enough attention has been paid to learning the basics. Go back to the drawing board. A few months of private lessons and a different class level may be just what the doctor ordered.

Sometimes, though, even these methods don't work. It's not uncommon for children between the ages of 12 and 14 to lose interest in a sport. Rick Wolff, a well-known sports psychologist, says this is not always due to burnout. The child may simply have more of an affinity for another activity and wants to budget precious hours towards that activity. Squash is a complex sport that may not be suited to a child's personality. While it is okay to stop pursuing a sport, ensure that the child puts time and energy into another productive outlet.

If every squash lesson counts as a life lesson, then nothing has been lost. Remember that. Once you've exhausted all strategies and your child comes to you to announce, once and for all, that she's joining the band instead of her high school squash team, train yourself to respond: "Do your best kid, and have fun."

Key Parental Roles

Few players have reached their potential without support from their families. This support can be expressed in many ways—love, money, guidance, motivation, coaching, time, and travel assistance. There are other parental roles that may not be as obvious but, nonetheless, determine whether a child becomes not just a squash player, but a healthy young adult

Parental Involvement: Finding a balance

We hear a lot about Al and Kathy Gordon, parents of Chris Gordon, who have made great contributions to their child's development by staying involved. Generally, a parent's involvement ought to focus on financial and emotional support, character development, and education. In the early stages, parents can be helpful by playing with the child and reinforcing good sportsmanship and positive attitudes. Later on, parents are wise to loosen the reigns and let the coach take over. Having carefully chosen a coach, a parent should let the coach and junior player decide on lessons, practice, and competition structure. Periodic conferences with the coach and child will help communicate parental goals, assess progress, and synchronize tournament travel with family plans.

Sometimes parents get over-involved, scrutinizing every practice and agonizing over each loss. Called the "interference officers" by Mike Todd, owner of the Pontefract Squash Club in the UK, these types of parents can cause a lot of problems for coaches.

Physical Fitness

Physical conditioning is too often an after thought, even though any professional will tell you how central proper conditioning is to junior development. As the coach essentially works on the kid's squash and provides advice on conditioning, it's up to the parent to help carry out the coach's wishes.

Parental support can be a determining factor in whether a squash kid stays healthy, fit, and injury-free. Parents have to back up the coach's advice on proper warm-up and stretches, before and after practice. They may have to arrive a little early for a lesson so the kid can get in an effective warm up.

Encourage Your Child to Dream

Goal setting is about keeping feet planted firmly on the ground and choosing goals over which one has a reasonable degree of control. Children, however, are natural dreamers. The movie *October Sky* is the triumphant true story of Homer Hickam, Jr., a high school student in 50s rural West Virginia who refuses to give up his dream, regardless of how unrealistic it seems to the adults in his life.

Too small to earn a football scholarship, Homer is destined to follow in his father footsteps and become a coal miner. Until the Soviets challenge America with the successful launch of the Sputnik satellite, that is. With the help of his loyal band of friends, Homer embarks on a mission to build and launch his own homemade rocket.

Despite repeated setbacks and early failures that nearly get them shut down, the group of friends stick with it and do the impossible, successfully launching a functional rocket and winning prestigious college scholarships in the process. Their success inspires the whole town to believe miracles can happen, even in Coalwood, and that there's nothing wrong with shooting for the stars.

Children's dreams are the stuff of creativity; they are the fuel that motivates them to try the impossible. Dr. Alan Goldberg, a nationally known expert in sports psychology, advises parents to encourage children to dream. Inspire them. Tell them stories of all the "impossible" things that have been accomplished by people following their dreams.

Help the child understand the difference between goal setting and dreaming. For instance, developing a volley nick or an error free game are ambitious goals, but if one practices smart and hard, there is a good chance of accomplishing it. On the other hand, beating the No.1 ranked player in the world might be considered a dream because it presents too many variables outside one's control. For instance, one can't control how hard the No. 1 player practices. Encourage your child to keep a "shopping list" of all the things he'd like to do better. Keep the old "shopping list" and let the child review how much he achieved. Top player Michelle Quibell keeps a list that includes little things like improving rails or smoothing out movement.

By all means, encourage your child to dream big and chase his dreams, to set big goals and go after them. But also teach your child to measure success by goals accomplished rather than dreams realized. This is the practical way they learn to relish the process and lead successful lives, even though not all dreams come true.

Keep 'em Playing

Watching a group of squash kids play and grow together over the years is a fascinating study in physical and psychological development. One day you see them as 8-year-olds, playing and behaving similarly. Come back after the holiday season and at least one of the boys has probably shot up in height and has gotten stronger. His squash ability is now likely to be above everyone else in the class, too.

Give it a season or two; a couple of the girls will be starting to overtake him. Their squash ability may well follow. A child's squash development occurs in sporadic spurts, especially at and past the adolescent stage.

The key is to keep them interested in squash whether you think they have the ability needed for the sport at that time or not. More importantly, even if the child feels she lacks natural talent, encourage her to persist. When she catches the next growth spurt, she is bound to do better and her interest level will bounce back.

Basketball legend Michael Jordan did not make his high school team, even as a sophomore, because he just wasn't good enough at the time. A kid who is so-so at 10 years old may be a kid who is great at 16, and vice versa. It's a shame for a kid to drop out before he can find out how good he can be. Conversely, a kid used to dominating at an early age may drop out at 16 because he can no longer do so.

The best thing a parent and coach can do is to encourage squash mastery over winning or losing. Competing with one's own ability naturally discourages unnecessary comparison with other kids during the growth phase. Physical changes, especially in girls, can lead to uneven performance on some days. Gently nudge kids through the ups and downs of squash. Being positive and comforting is most important. Lana Quibell, Michelle Quibell's mother, always urged her daughter to challenge herself, but also tried to help her see everything in perspective. It wasn't the end of the world if she didn't play well in a match.

The Reserve Parachute

Life has a perverse way of throwing curve balls—injury, burnout, an unexpected move, financial fallout. Some parents feel they ought to help develop another talent, in case the child is unable to pursue his interest in squash, or at least pursue it as seriously as he wants to. Like a skydiver using dual parachutes, a child should be encouraged early on to pursue other interests, not as much for backup as for a more rounded childhood development.

All squash, all the time can become exhausting. A second passion offers an outlet to break away from the intensity of squash for a while and return rejuvenated. Pro, coach and squash entrepreneur Chris Walker took six months off to travel around the world. He came back refreshed and able to stage a dramatic comeback, making it to the finals of the British Open before eventually retiring from competitive play last year. "There is more to a person than squash, even if squash is life," says Walker.

Positive Pushing

The argument for pushing is really simple. Kids love any activity they're good at. Becoming good requires practice. As long as practice is fun, kids will do it. This is the "high" of the sport. Sometimes, though, they may need to practice skills that are a little hard to learn. Kids may need a gentle push to help them learn how to return tricky lob serves or hit off the back wall. It's during these times—the "lows" of squash—that a parent has to push.

The bottom-line is, for healthy development of a squash kid the highs have to outweigh the lows. When it becomes necessary to push a child through the lows, the parent or coach has to do so in a way that is deliberate and vigorous, but always with a positive message that reaffirms your unconditional love and helps to build self-esteem.

Dr. Jim Taylor is a psychologist who lived the life of a young achiever. A top-ranked skier, certified tennis coach, black belt in karate, marathon runner, and an Ironman triathlete, he has developed five tips for "positive pushing":

1. Set expectations that emphasize healthy values that will help your child become successful and happy. For example, focus on hard work, responsibility, cooperation, patience and persistence, rather than expectations that stress grades, results and other outcomes.
2. Allow your child to experience all emotions, don't assuage, placate or distract them from their feelings. Help them to identify, understand and express their emotions in a healthy way.
3. Actively manage the child's environment and activities—peer interactions, achievement activities, cultural experiences, leisure pursuits—in ways that reflect the values, attitudes and behaviors you want the child to adopt.
4. Create options from which a child can choose a direction. Stress that doing nothing is not an option.
5. Help your child find something they love and are passionate about in their efforts. They will be successful and happy.

Achieving success in almost anything requires a sustained effort that will always have its highs – the fun parts, and lows – the parts one doesn't like to do. The trick is to maximize the highs and ride out the lows through positive pushing.

The Squash Parent's Prayer

Dear Lord,
give me the strength to watch without twitching,
to encourage without shouting,
to congratulate without embarrassing,
to enquire without putting my foot in my mouth,
to drive without losing the way,
to pay the fees,
find the hotels,
clubs and best restaurants in cities both old and new,
socialize with the opposition's family,
forgive junior referees for what seem like **outrageous** decisions,
never make
any comment that could conceivably be construed as derogatory
(especially to my own child)
and above all believe that the algorithm of the ranking system will
finally come good by the end of the ranking year!
Grant also O Lord that the boy from our club that he plays twice a
week and has a mental block against,
doesn't enter **every single tournament** that we enter again this
year.
Thank you Lord,
Amen

—*Richard Millman*

12

Money Wise

"Don't worry about money. If we do the right things,
there will always be plenty of money."
ROBERT KIYOSAKI, Rich Dad's Guide To Investing

W hat's nice about squash is that the cost of getting started is relatively manageable. Once you own the initial equipment—a racquet, ball, shoes and protective eyewear, which are, for the most part, fairly affordable—you need a place to play, either a private club or a public facility. Where you live makes a difference. In parts of Europe and Asia, where courts are so plentiful, the cost for using them is very small.

In the US, clubs tend to be in high-income areas and can be costly. Once you've found a facility, it doesn't take a whole lot of time and money to play the game. Aside from a few initial private lessons, which experts recommend for beginners, an eight-week program of weekly group classes is all a kid needs to pick up the basic strokes. And for those who can't afford to play, there are more and more urban youth squash programs developing in the US, enabling youngsters in inner cities to learn the game.

The Cost of Raising a Squash Kid

As a kid begins to show serious interest in developing his game, a little initial budgeting goes a long way. However, plunging into competition at the national and international level can take serious bucks. Parents report an annual outlay for the serious junior player ranging from $5,000 to $20,000, depending upon how far away the major tournaments are held and the intensity of coaching. At the higher echelons of junior competition the real kicker is the tournament expense. That includes travel for the player and his entourage—a parent or coach—and accommodations. Private lessons, group clinics, and camps are a close second, expense wise.

The Good News

If your jaw is beginning to drop, lock it back into place – there's some good news. Many countries are helping to support their junior players through government sport commissions or Olympic committees.

The British Government set up a lottery fund for Sport England to distribute to priority sports, including squash. In England, and other European countries, national lottery money provides grants for local communities through to national level projects and programs.

In Canada, Squash British Columbia, like many of the provincial squash associations, has a junior development program that helps smaller clubs and communities get programs off the ground by supplying equipment, instructors and even busing kids back and forth for club matches.   In the US, the US Olympic Committee works closely with the USSRA and helps fund programs to support elite players and national teams.   The USSRA is also exploring ways to support an environment that fosters the development of more urban youth programs.

Individuals also play a big part in developing players, particularly coaches who are flexible with fees. Neil Harvey, the renowned coach of the world's top players, sets his fees according to what players can afford. He charges more money to those who can afford his prices so he can help players who don't have the funds. If those with money are really serious and want to continue with him, he'll lower the price. (Select Reference 5)

It is not only the famous coaches who help out financially. In the US, squash clubs and coaches often provide scholarships for kids in urban youth squash programs and subsidize tournament entry fees. Teaching pro Tom Generous, now a retiree, moved to North Carolina, where he runs an active junior program at Tar Heel Squash, a community squash program at the University of North Carolina.

In addition to coaches, there are players from affluent areas and backgrounds who are happy to help an up-and-coming young player in need of financial support.

In certain areas, scholarships for training at academies are available. The Australian Institute of Sport offers   scholarships to elite squash players who have demonstrated their talents at a national and international level.

The very top ranked juniors can expect free racquets and clothing from squash equipment manufacturers like Dunlop, Prince and Feather. Others on their way up the ranks might qualify for special prices on products.

In the early years of squash development, the costs are more or less the same as they are in other sports. However, as the player progresses to competition at the national and international levels, the bucks can add up fast. With some smart planning and savvy saving tips, parents should be able to see their squash kid through.

On the Cheap

Manufacturers' shipments of sporting goods in the US rose 4% in 2004 to $52.1 billion according to Sporting Goods Manufacturers International. That includes sports and fitness equipment, athletic footwear, and sports apparel. It's not hard to find the reason for the astonishing sales. Just check out the price tags of the equipment and clothing of today's top players.

If you don't have money to burn on the extras: designer attire, expensive equipment, brand name lessons, and costly accommodations – take heart. With a little creativity you can limit the costs and stay within your means. Being money wise can also teach your child an important life lesson.

Racquets

Whatever else you skimp on, experts will tell you not to skimp on racquets. An ill-suited racquet can cause long-term injuries, but you don't have to splurge on high-ticket racquets either.

Quality models are available in the mid-price range, around $75 to $120. They don't break the bank and are perfect for a child's growing years when children go through one or two racquets each year. You can often find great buys at Internet stores plus package plans that will throw in a shirt or a ball with a racquet purchase. There are plenty of racquets that will be fine for kids who are just getting started in squash. Since racquets can break, plan on getting two of the same model, particularly for tournament players.

Both online squash stores and local pro shops sell closeout models and slightly used demo racquets at bargain prices. They're worth checking out, but get good advice from a pro in making your selection.

Another smart way to save is to turn necessities into presents. Buy your aspiring Sarah Fitz-Gerald a new squash racquet for her birthday or give her a gift certificate to her favorite pro shop.

Court Time

Saving on court time comes down to whether you play at a private club or a public facility. Private clubs can be costly with annual dues, court fees and minimums. Yet in some areas, this may be your only option. Public facilities are less expensive and sometimes you can save yourself a bundle by paying the annual dues in one lump sum. Be sure to check out the schools in your area to see if they open their courts to the community, which can be the least costly alternative.

Lessons

Private lessons are important and can range from $35 to $70 per hour with a staff teaching pro to $100 with the head pro. You can cut lesson costs by alternating private lessons with semi-private lessons, on a weekly basis. By pairing with another student in a semi-private setting, you not only save money, the child is likely to have more fun when he has another kid his age to learn and practice with. Playing with a stronger practice partner can be a lesson in itself. Try to find partners so your child can practice what he's learned. Stick with the staff pro until your junior becomes more advanced and needs specialized attention.

Tournaments and Travel

To play in national-sanctioned tournaments, your child usually needs to join his national association for a nominal fee and pay an entry fee for each event. In the US, you must be a member of the USSRA to enter national-sanctioned tournaments. However, for events other than nationals, membership is not required, but non-members pay an addition $15 on top of the entry fee. There is a wide range of entry fees, depending upon the event. The entry fee for a national junior tournament can reach $95.

When your child moves from local tournaments to ones further away, take advantage of the hotel discount deals some tournaments offer. Tournaments may also offer private housing. Staying with a local family is a big cost-cutter in tournament travel. If you're looking for a host family, ask your coach for some suggestions.

Parents often develop friendships with parents of squash children from other cities and host each other's kids. Join the frequent flier and frequent-traveler programs offered by airlines and hotels. Tournament travel is an easy way to rack up additional points. Cash in the earned points for free hotel stays, air travel, and upgrades.

Savings on Stuff

Some companies are committed to providing special discounts to players associated with a scholastic organization. Prince provides equipment to the College Squash Association and Dunlop provides the squash balls. Some apparel companies, such as Squash Design, have sponsorship programs for junior and scholastic squash players. Squash Design has several promotional programs, including volume discounts, referral credit programs, and buyer group discounts. (More info: squashdesignusa.com)

The Lemonade Stand

Sidewalk lemonade stands are a cherished memory of childhood. This American rite of passage embodies hard work, dedication, and reward. Once upon a time, the only regulation for lemonade stands was that you had to be home for dinner by six.

Today, Baby Boomers may lament the fact that this simple childhood enterprise now seems to require licenses, liability insurance, and permission from three different government agencies. But when you see that some youngsters are finding ways to negotiate court time, you realize that the lemonade stand lives on.

An enterprising junior can find many opportunities to save on squash training and earn pocket change at the same time. A 14- to 18-year-old advanced junior can assist with younger kids, sell drinks at a local adult tournament, and mop up a court after play. She can work at the reception area at a local squash club in return for court-time, or discounted lessons.

Grants and Scholarships

Some junior players are lucky enough to live in areas were there are grants for player development. In England, through Sport England, there is a Lottery–funded World Class Performance Program designed to provide athletes with funding for a wide range of services, from coaching to sports medicine. In Canada, through Sport Canada, there is an Athlete Assistance Program that helps fund the training needs of international-caliber athletes. Since squash is considered a priority in these countries, players are able to receive the support they need to pursue a squash career. In Malaysia, 9 out of the 18 development grants from SportExcel went to junior squash players. In the US, where squash is not a high profile sport, there is limited funding, yet the USSRA continues to support its elite junior players through national junior squad development and national junior teams.

Private Scholarships

Thanks to creative and concerned squash players, there are programs that reach out to the underprivileged. Because urban youth squash programs have been so successful in Boston, New York and Philadelphia, more are cropping up in other US cities.

Corporate Sponsorships

With smaller promotional budgets than other sporting goods manufacturers, squash companies keep a keen eye on what they give to players and why. You won't get money from equipment companies, but you can get on a free list if your child makes the top of his age group in national rankings.

Some companies like Prince will provide just the top one or two juniors in the nation with a full package of products, from racquets and bags to shoes, clothing and accessories. There is also a Preferred Player Program, where you can purchase products through the manufacturer at wholesale price or below. For this to happen your junior needs to be recommended by her coach, who in turn has to have relationships with equipment representatives.

If your child is Miss Popularity and you see her as a model player among her squash peers, talk to your coach or pro shop manager to see if she might be eligible for free or reduced priced equipment. Company spokespersons advise parents to work through their child's pro rather than calling up and asking to be on the free list.

Companies rely heavily on suggestions from coaches on potential recipients of free or reduced priced products. Greg Reiss, an independent representative of various squash products, says companies not only look at rankings but also at players who can help sell products. "If they have a temper, or they are too quiet, they won't be good salespeople. What is the individual like both on and off the court?"

Private Sponsorships

Support from a grandparent, other extended family member, or a community group is a quick way to cover a large, one-time expense such as travel to an important international tournament. If the financial support comes from family members, it's probably best to keep the amounts reasonable so you and your child don't end up feeling uncomfortable about accepting help.

Some companies have a special fund for community outreach programs and may be willing to use some of that to help out employees and their children. There's no guarantee that a company will contribute, but a parent shouldn't automatically assume it won't either. It never hurts to ask.

Publicity for Your Junior

Who wouldn't enjoy reading glowing newspaper articles about themselves? Media coverage that highlights a young player's efforts and accomplishments can be exciting. As long as the coverage doesn't turn the kid into a prima donna, publicity can provide healthy motivation, attract potential sponsors and college coaches and inspire other kids.

Make it Unique

Media experts advise potential publicity seekers to look for something unique in their story. There are probably lots of young, aspiring players in many different sports in your area. What's special about your youngster's story? Squash is not always in the headlines in most newspapers, particularly in the US. Local papers and school newsletters are always looking for something different. What's more, these publications like to report about successful youths. Chances are, the editors are unaware that a squash tournament is happening close by and that juniors from the community are involved. Be your own public relations rep and let them know about it.

Tools of the Trade

Establish direct contact with journalists, but before you do, assemble the communication tools you will need:

- *Targeted media list*: Names, e-mail addresses, phone and fax numbers of reporters who cover sports and youth-related stories. Newspapers, magazines, television and radio stations, and Websites are the media outlets you should consider contacting.
- *Prepare a media kit*: Include information about the player's record and planned activities, points you would like highlighted, photographs, and third-party quotes.
- *Identify a spokesperson*: Designate a parent, coach, or relative as the exclusive contact for the media.

Create your own buzz. Develop interesting story angles and pitch them to the media on an ongoing basis.

Crossroad: College Squash Vs Pro Tour

For most American junior players, attending school and getting good grades is extremely important, and academic achievement combined with squash can be the ticket to a top college. While college squash is a laudable goal, it won't necessarily help those who want to play on the world stage. In other countries, squash comes first and players are willing to postpone or forgo education or study on a part-time basis in order to put in the amount of time and dedication needed to play professionally.

American players who opt for college and then the tour are usually five to six years behind international players who have stepped into the professional arena as young as 16 or 17. This is one of the reasons why there has not been an American world squash champion. Chris Gordon is the first American junior to put college education aside to play on the tour. Lily Lorentzen is another American junior who took the plunge into pro squash while postponing college. Perhaps one of them will succeed in becoming the first American World Champion and set a precedent for others to follow.

If you're pondering this issue, consider another approach. Your child could extend the college years and take only one semester of classes each year. Doing so would allow more time for training and traveling to international competitions. Getting a degree in five or six years instead of four might be a good compromise that will satisfy aspirations for both a college education and a squash career. Studying on a part-time basis has enabled players in other countries to compete on the tour and earn their degree.

College for Your Squash Player

Should your kid opt for college he can look forward to an exciting four years of team play. Top advice for squash players applying to a US college? Keep your grades up!

A strong academic record and proven squash success are what it takes to get into the college of your choice. Take a look at the 80 or so colleges in the College Squash Association and you'll see that the top squash schools are also the most academically challenging.

In the competitive frenzy of the college application process, squash can definitely give kids an edge. In fact, more schools outside of the Northeast are building courts and realizing that squash could enhance their college. Duke and the University of Notre Dame are examples. Fortunately, squash is no longer limited to Ivy League colleges, which set some of the toughest admissions requirements. Dave Talbott, coach at Yale, says he sees an enormous increase in applicants each year, with many kids hoping that squash will get them in the door. The reality, according to Talbott, is that Yale accepts about 1 in 12 applicants. As squash continues to grow in the Midwestern and Southern states, there should be more opportunities for college squash in non-Ivy League schools.

Yet there's plenty of competition for admission since worldwide recruitment is heavily underway. Setting the precedent for international recruiting efforts is Trinity College in Hartford, CT where coach Paul Assaiante scouts the globe for top male players who can also meet academic requirements. After receiving the green light from the admissions department and college president, Assaiante fielded a men's team that embarked on a six-year winning streak, setting records in college squash history. You can learn more about the dynamics of this recruiting effort in *Playing the Game, Inside Athletic Recruiting in the Ivy League*, by Chris Lincoln.

Money for College

Generally, US colleges with varsity squash teams do not offer squash scholarships but will sometimes provide financial aid based on need. Ivy League schools, which are known for their strong squash teams, also award need-based financial aid. Each college operates independently with regard to financial aid applicants.

Squash is not a full-fledged sport in the NCAA for men or women; however, women's squash is considered an NCAA emerging sport, meaning that although there are schools with active varsity teams, there are not enough to support an NCAA championship. An emerging sport also means that colleges are allowed to use student-athletes to help meet the NCAA's minimum sports-sponsorship requirements and minimum financial aid awards. While there are NCAA scholarships for emerging sports, they do not apply to squash because most of the schools with squash teams do not offer athletic scholarships. This is the case with some of the smaller colleges and Ivy League schools. Larger schools where squash is becoming more popular may offer athletic scholarships but not for squash, because squash is still a club sport and not yet at the varsity level, although teams compete within the College Squash Association. Because squash is an NCAA emerging sport, all NCAA institutions wishing to sponsor the sport at the varsity level must abide by NCAA regulations, which include limits on playing and practice seasons, recruiting regulations, student-athlete eligibility and maintaining amateur status. Colleges with men's squash teams also follow NCAA rules. (More info: ncaa.org).

The Road to College in the US

Taking the necessary steps early will offer your child the greatest number of options and help him make sound decisions. The freshman year of high school is the time when parent, child, and coach should obtain information and begin to develop a roadmap. At the beginning of the senior year, your child will make his final decision. In the interim, the parent and coach can offer a lot of help to a kid on the road to college.

Getting into the college of choice is not a foregone conclusion. Stay on top of things and do the following:

1. *Collect information:* In the first year of high school or when your child is 14 or 15, you and your child should absorb as much information as possible about the college admission and financial aid processes. Keep your options open and contact the College Squash Association (More info: SquashTalk.com/college) to find out about schools with squash teams. Contact the schools directly to get information.

2. *Compile lists:* Colleges with squash teams follow NCAA rules so you'll need to look at the NCAArequired core courses. Make a list of the nearly 15 or so core courses and be sure they are completed during high school. Consult a high school counselor and compile a list of at least 50 colleges that interest you.

3. *Preliminary tests:* Be sure your kid takes the PSAT/NMSQT (More info: collegeboard.org) tests during the freshman and sophomore years. Use the reports to analyze your child's strengths and weaknesses and to prepare for the SAT. As a bonus, the PSAT results also automatically put your child in the running for the merit scholarships and corporate scholarships awarded by the National Merit Scholarship Corporation (NMSC. More info: nationalmerit.org). International students applying to American schools should take the ACTS and also find out if their grades are transferable to meet American standards.

4. *The All-important junior year:* The child should now take the SAT (More info: collegeboard.com) and ACT (More info: act.org) tests. The USSRA tries not to schedule tournaments during SAT testing weekends. You should also look at the NCAA Clearinghouse Website, which gives important information on eligibility requirements and NCAA rules. (More info: ncaaclearinghouse.net. Register with the NCAA Clearinghouse at the end of the junior year, which is also the first time that colleges are allowed to offer

students an official recruitment visit.   Monitor core course selections.

5. *Apply:* During the child's senior year, finalize the college list and apply. The college coach may also help with the application. Find out about private and local scholarships and apply for them. Include in your child's portfolio the following:

   a. The player's record. Generally coaches value results in interscholastic competition as much as sanctioned tournaments, especially because in the US so many top juniors play at prep schools and do not travel to sanctioned tournaments.
   b. A 5 to 10 minute video of the child practicing and a match play situation.
   c. Newspaper clippings and other media coverage.
   d. Letters of recommendation from both past and present coaches.
   e. Details of sponsorship by racquet manufacturers.

6. *Meet the coach:* Arrange recruiting visits to the colleges and get to know the coaches. Show the coach your interest is genuine by contacting the school several times. Too many kids assume a coach just isn't interested in them, when, in reality, the coach may be questioning the kid's interest because there's been insufficient follow-up.

7. *Final selection:* Experts advise selecting a college based first on academic strength, then on the size and location of the school, the quality of the coach and team, graduation rate, and, finally, the financial aid available. Don't let the best financial aid package unduly influence your decision. Even if there is little or no money available for your child's freshman year, that doesn't mean there will be no money for subsequent years.

A lot of students have to work or take out student loans to pay for college, but with reasonable grades, a decent squash record, and an organized plan of action, your squash kid can play his way through college.

Visiting Colleges

Based on NCAA rules and Ivy League regulations, here are guidelines from the College Squash Association regarding visiting schools:

1) As a candidate for admission, you are not allowed to practice with a college squash team. You may attend and watch, but you may not play in a practice.

2) A college coach is not allowed to give you a "try out". That is, the coach may not ask you to play in front of him or to otherwise assess you skills by having you perform athletically in front of him (for example, the coach is not allow to test your speed, fitness, or skills.)

3) Once you become a college candidate for admission (in other words your freshman year of high school, i.e., 9th grade) you may not be coached by a college squash coach, unless he is also your *regular coach at the club* where you regularly play, and is coaching you *at that club*. A college squash coach is not allowed to coach candidate scholar/athletes at all at the college squash facilities under any circumstances.

You are allowed five official visits during senior year to Division I and II schools. There is no limit on the number of official visits in Division III and those do not count in the total of five visits taken to Division I and II schools. A particular school can provide a prospect only one official visit to their school, which applies in all three divisions. You are allowed to bring your squash racquet on your visit, and you might even play informally with friends at the school. (More info: SquashTalk.com, ncaa.org)

13

Careers in Squash

"Your dreams tell you what to do; your reason tells you how to do it."
JONAS SALK, developer of the polio vaccine

A kid may excel at squash. How can players incorporate their talents into a future career? A good squash player can choose to become a scientist, entrepreneur, cop, or musician. Who's to say a top junior won't bring his squash excellence into a top college, major in business, and become a wildly successful entrepreneur?

That said, realize that squash can play a major role in achieving success in any field. The self-discipline, focus, organizational skills, strategic thinking, physical fitness and, most importantly, friendships developed playing squash are all invaluable, no matter what career path one ultimately follows.

Defining Career Success

Career counselors will tell you that kids who develop early career plans are most likely to succeed. Most kids start to weigh career options during their high school years. Grown-up support from the parent, coach, and career counselor can come in the form of helping the squash kid develop a plan that includes at least four or five career options. Parents need to consider the financial implications of each choice and what will it take, financially, to prepare for and achieve each career option.

A chosen career path can affect just about everything: how much time you're willing to devote to a specific activity; what you read; what your hobbies and interests are; the people to whom you're attracted. Career planning experts advise their clients to think big and be prepared to adjust their plans as they move forward.

Any career plan should include a definition of success. That definition might include money and fame. Whatever your kid chooses to include, encourage him to add a healthy dose of personal happiness and community service to his own definition of career success.

Teaching Professional

A player with even a modest playing record can aspire to be a great teaching professional. Sue Wright's coach, who was also her father, was a club player who knew the game well and could teach it to others. Wright became the No. 3 player in England and a noted coach herself.

To be successful, a squash teacher must possess qualities more critical than a top playing record: keen observation and deduction skills; knowledge and love of the game; patience; the ability to motivate; and a capacity to focus on a single individual, even in a group setting. A teacher must recognize that every player has his own fingerprint of assets. The best coach is one who can build upon those assets. For teaching young children, one quality stands above all others – the ability to make lessons fun.

To get started on the path to earning a squash teaching credential, contact the squash organization in your region or the World Squash Association. (More info: worldsquash.org) You don't have to live in an area to become certified in that region. You can pick a location and squash organization that suits you, like the United States Squash Racquets Association (USSRA. More info: us-squash.org) or Squash Canada (More info: squash.ca), England Squash (More info: Englandsquash.com), the Asian Squash Federation (More info: Asiansquash.com) or Squash Australia (More info: squash.org.au).

Certification

The USSRA certifies about 30 new coaches each year. Certification is earned on the basis of completing a weekend-long workshop offered one or more or more times each year in various cities, and performance on tests through the American Sports Education Program.

Certification is available in four levels in the US. Those interested need to join the association first, complete Level 1, gain teaching experience and then progress to Level 2. A Level 1 program is a 20-hour course designed for coaches of novice or beginner players. A Level 2 certification is a 24-hour clinic for those who have completed Level 1 and are ready to coach intermediate players. A Level 3 certification, for coaching advanced players, is also a 24-hour program over three days, but requires more in-depth study. The Level 4 program is geared toward coaching elite or professional players.

The curriculum, approved by the World Squash Federation (WSF. More info: worldsquash.org), includes three components: technical, practical and theory. For the practical, coaches are observed on videotape teaching a lesson. Intermediate coaches are required to write a complete lesson plan for a team. All coaches must take a written test at home using the American Sports Education Program books. Fees range from about $250 for Level 1 to $400 for the higher levels.

Squash organizations in various countries have similar programs, with coaching standards set around the world by the World Squash Federation. However, some organizations are moving away from the traditional linear progression of certification towards a more lateral approach that enables coaches to focus on a specific area.

Squash Canada is making a transition from its five-level certification program to a competency-based education and training (CBET) approach in which coaches are trained and may achieve certification to coach in a specific coaching environment. For example, a coach may train to work with competitive players, both as a developmental and high performance coach, while another may prefer to work in a community squash environment, working with new players.

In the future, the new program will make a distinction between coach training and coach certification. Coaches who need training can acquire or refine the skills, knowledge and attitudes needed to coach effectively in a particular context. When they are ready, coaches may decide to be evaluated for certification.

The WSF regularly holds a Development and Coaching Congress where coaches from around the world share ideas and methods. The four-day conference includes keynote speakers and workshops. The sixth Development and Coaching Congress was held in Egypt. Previous conferences took place in the Netherlands, Malaysia, Hong Kong, Brazil and Australia. (More info: worldsquash.org).

School Sports Management

College and high school athletics are other areas in need of good squash teachers. In the US, the College Squash Association (More info: SquashTalk.com) represents about 80 squash teams.

Most coaching positions at top colleges must meet high standards. Coaches are usually required to have a Bachelor's degree or world class coaching experience or both. Some schools prefer a Master's degree plus prior coaching experience. A national ranking during the candidate's playing career should help. Since recruiting players is a major responsibility of the college coach, experience in this area is key. School coaches also need good communication skills and the ability to work with people of all backgrounds. Managing a team requires a lot of administrative work, so organizational skills are essential.

There are also about 80 high schools and prep schools in the US with squash programs. Coaches at these institutions have a wide range of experience and educational credentials. Some are former competitive players, others former teaching pros and some simply high school teachers who play squash.

National Team Coach

One of the more prestigious coaching opportunities is with a national team, where the coach represents his or her country and works with individuals selected to compete in international team competition. There are a number of opportunities, including coaching men's, women's, and junior teams competing in the Commonwealth Games, Asian Games, Pan American Games, Canadian American Games and world championships.

A National Team Coach can come from a variety of backgrounds but must have an excellent reputation and a proven track record as a coach. Committees appointed by national squash organizations review the backgrounds of interested candidates and make the final selection.

Sports Marketing

Sports promotion, athlete representation and event marketing are just some of the avenues for a Sports Marketer. Love of sports is just one of the qualifications needed to succeed in sports marketing. A Bachelor's degree in law, business management or advertising, combined with solid experience, is key to doing well in a sports marketing career.

While squash is not a part of larger sports marketing firms such as IMG, there are squash entrepreneurs who have established themselves as squash marketers. Companies such as John Nimick's Event Engine focus on event marketing and managing sports events. Nimick, who was also a world-class hardball player, started his company about 10 years ago after working with the Professional Squash Association, PSA. Paul Walters started his company, iSquashMarketing, more recently after spending many years at Dunlop. Walters has added another component to his organization, athlete representation.

Event Management and Marketing

Managing and marketing squash tournaments like the Tournament of Champions in New York City's Grand Central Terminal requires considerable experience and expertise. Now in its tenth year, the tournament features a top level PSA men's and WISPA women's division, making it the largest combined tournament in the world. The Tournament of Champions offers more than $120,000 in prize money and is considered the true "Grand Slam" of squash.

Live entertainment, food and beverages, a hospitality area, a special clinic for urban squash groups and a "Kids Day" are all part of the attractions at this exciting squash event. For an entire week, millions of people in and out of Grand Central Terminal can view the matches held on an all-glass court specifically designed for the area. Separate tournaments for recreational squash players called the Grand Open and for up-and-coming juniors called the All-Ivy complement the week- long New York City squash festivities.

In spite of the tremendous coordination of such an event, the organizing company, Event Engine, runs a tight ship. There is one full-time Tournament Director, one full-time Director of Operations and three different market-specific Marketing Directors. The rest of the staff is part-time, freelance or volunteer.

The Tournament Director oversees the entire event, works to secure major sponsorship from corporations, and signs up star players. The Director of Operations runs the actual event and handles logistics. The Marketing Directors sell tickets and patron packages in each market and handle local promotions, while a freelance publicist coordinates advertising and public relations in advance of the event.

Along with the event staff, many volunteers are needed to make any such tournament a success. Volunteering is a great way to build a resume and will give you an up-close-and-personal view of event management and marketing. It can also lead to a wealth of contacts.

Athlete Representation

Aside from hard-nosed contract negotiations on behalf of a professional athlete, representation for financial counsel, endorsement marketing, and public relations are becoming more prevalent. A representative may do all of these things for a client or choose to specialize in one aspect.

Between state requirements and fierce competition, breaking in as an independent player agent can be daunting. There are hundreds of medium-to-large sports marketing companies plus a good number of small companies and independent operators.

Squash players, for the most part, don't always have official managers and some handle their own affairs or use the services of a family member or lawyer. Recently, however, more and more of the top players are finding it beneficial to be represented by an agent. Paul Walters founded the company iSquashmarketing not only to develop and produce squash events, but also to manage professional players and their contracts.

Walters' services include contract and endorsement negotiation and all "off-court" business and marketing endeavors. The firm also assists with career planning, licensing, legal, tax and financial planning, marketing and promotions, charitable support, speaking engagements, personal appearances and public relations. In working to forge relationships between players and sponsors, Walters hopes to raise the profile of squash players worldwide.

Sales and Marketing Executive

After playing squash seriously or coaching the game, you have an in-depth knowledge of squash products and the market. Some squash players and coaches end up with a Prince or a Dunlop or other manufacturers in a sales position, selling racquets, balls and other equipment to teaching pros, clubs and retail outlets. Some have sports management or MBA degrees, yet others get there because of their love of the game, experience as a player and knowledge of squash products and their technology. If you're passionate about squash, knowledgeable about the products and have some salesmanship, this job could be for you.

Corporate Marketing

An agency's work consists of developing and executing a marketing program that utilizes sports and sports personalities to market a company or product. A sports marketing program can include a variety of components, from simple projects such as designing and manufacturing sports giveaways or distributing match schedules, to much grander undertakings like developing a sports-related advertising campaign, naming a stadium, or garnering a celebrity endorsement for the company's products.

Working for a college athletic department or local sports team will provide invaluable experience for almost any sports marketing career. Find out what you're good at, and what you enjoy most, by exploring various departments, from operations to creative design to management. Understand the game, not just the statistics. Know the players and the sports media; stay on the cutting edge; be informed about current industry trends and where they might lead in the future.

Squash Officiating

Being a squash referee is really more of a hobby than a career. There is no monetary compensation, yet referees are reimbursed for travel, meals and accommodations. If you want to supplement your "real" job with an exciting travel opportunity, refereeing could be your ticket. Being a referee is also a great way for squash enthusiasts to stay connected to the game.

There are several levels of referees: club, state, regional, national and international. To become certified in the US, you must pass a written test given by the USSRA (More info: us-squash.org). Prior participation in the USSRA Referee Certification Clinic is preferred but not mandatory for club certification. To advance to higher levels, referees must attend an advanced clinic or symposium, gain experience refereeing different levels of competition, receive recommendations and be evaluated by official referee assessors. The required number of evaluations and recommendations increases as referees move to higher certification levels.

The World Squash Federation (More info: worldsquash.org) and other international governing bodies, such as Squash Australia (More info: squash.org.au) and Squash Canada (More info: squash.ca) have similar programs for referees. There are plenty of booklets, literature and videos on refereeing so one can keep current. Referees can also study to become an instructor or assessor or lend their expertise to the media. There are publications and newsletters specifically for referees and columns on refereeing in *Squash* magazine and *Squash Player* magazine.

Athletic Trainer

The trainer's goal is to keep the player in top physical condition and prevent injuries. If a player does sustain an injury, it's the trainer's job to design treatment programs and oversee rehab.

There are many organizations that recognize trainers as allied health professionals. In the US, one avenue for athletic trainers working with squash players is the National Academy of Sports Medicine (NASM. More info: NASM.org). Another is the Tudor Bompa Training System, which utilizes Bompa's periodization methods. (More info: tudorbompainstitute.com).   The British Association of Sports and Exercise Science (BASES. More info:

BASES.org.UK), the Canadian Athletic Therapists Association (More info: Athletictherapy.org), and the Australian Institute of Sports National Athletic Career and Education Center, (More info: AIS.org.au), are sources your kid can tap into to start on the path to becoming an athletic trainer.

Health clubs, large corporations, sports academies, such as the Australian Institute of Sports, and schools hire athletic trainers. Once again, a great way to get started is by volunteering or working part-time while in school.

Fitness trainers working with squash players believe in the importance of sports-specific training, meaning that players should focus on their individual needs and goals to optimize their on-court performance.

Sports Psychologist

While trainers design fitness programs for players, sports psychologists work on mental skills. In this specialized field combining psychology and physical education, psychologists apply their knowledge and training to the needs of athletes.

Top players and coaches recognize that at higher levels the game as probably 80 percent mental and 20 percent physical/technical, according to Dr. Jenny Tranfield, a sports psychologist and top WISPA player. Tranfield conducted her PhD research in stress and coping in high performance squash coaching. She has worked with many squash players at the Sue Wright Sports Academy, the Hong Kong Sports Institute, and at schools and clubs (More info: JennyTranfield.com).

You can also link to such organizations as the Association for the Advancement of Applied Sports Psychology (AAASP. More info: AAASPonline.org); the American Board of Sports Psychology (ABSP. More info: americanboardofsportpsychology.org); the British Association of Sports and Exercise Science (BASES. More info: Bases.org.uk); the Canadian Mental Training Registry (More info: coach.ca) and the Australian Institute of Sports National Athlete and Career Education Center (More info: AIS.org.au).

Becoming a sports psychologist requires extensive study, such as the completion of a doctorate degree in psychology, research work in the field and practical experience.

Sports Administration

The governing bodies of squash can be sources for both paid employment and volunteer work. Whether you're on a small staff typical of squash organizations or one of many volunteers, you will have a valuable learning experience that could lead to other opportunities in the future. Sports administration skills are welcome at larger institutions, such as Olympic committees, national sports institutes and international sports federations.

Sports Entrepreneur

In the 1980s, Charlie Johnson was a college tennis player with an ear for music. Today, he carries over $50,000 in squash merchandise at his online store and is able to turn his inventory over as often as six times each year.

Johnson, a native of Alabama, came to New York to study music at Julliard. To support his passion for playing music, he worked as a salesman in sporting goods stores. Life led him back to Ohio where he discovered squash, became a certified teaching professional and opened his own club and pro shop in Dayton. In adapting to modern times, Johnson brought his store online in 1996, becoming the first to sell squash equipment on the Web. Because of his large inventory, Johnson is able to offer discount pricing and since he is an authorized dealer for all his products, he can offer manufacturers' warrantees to customers. (More info: cjsquash.com)

In addition to his online store, Johnson still maintains two retail outlets in Dayton and Cincinnati and also runs three large tournaments each year, including the Ohio Open and the $40,000 Dayton Open, a PSA World Tour event. He has been an active officer in the Cincinnati Squash Association and has served as a vice-president of the USSRA. His volunteer work doesn't stop there. Johnson also runs a program for 150 students of the local middle school. He provides transportation to and from his club in Dayton and squash play at no charge. In the summer, Johnson runs a successful junior squash camp. About 35 kids from the area have become competitive junior players. In spite of all the time he dedicates to squash, Johnson still manages to play the trumpet now and then.

Squash is legion with stories of entrepreneurs who transformed their love of the game into successful businesses. Gordon Anderson, former top touring professional, literally took his love of squash to the courts, starting his own court building firm, Anderson Courts. A pioneer in sports marketing is John Nimick. His firm, Event Engine, runs some of the top World Tour stops.

Ron Beck can be heralded as a squash media champion with his informative Website, SquashTalk.com, which brings squash news and information to millions of people worldwide.

SquashTalk also lets readers buy squash products, find partners, participate in forums and learn about camps, clubs and equipment.

Bryan Patterson not only started a community program outside Philadelphia, but also founded Universal Squash, a series of training camps throughout Europe. Pros opening new clubs or players starting new programs are all entrepreneurs. The future of squash and its growth depends on them. You too can be a squash entrepreneur, just by starting a program in your community

Tournament Promoter

Are you a good enough salesperson to convince your town that it needs a squash tournament? Do you know any corporate movers and shakers who will sponsor your event? If you answered yes to these questions, you're on your way to becoming a true squash impresario.

Hands-on experience while developing expertise in various tournament functions is critical. You can hire an experienced sports marketing company to worry about the marketing and operation of the event. In this business, organization and thorough planning will make the inevitable last-minute emergencies easier to cope with – a star player falling sick, for instance.

Running a tournament will not make you rich, but if you're willing to take risks, a tournament can be a fulfilling experience, year after year. To get started, contact the appropriate squash organization – the USSRA (More info: us-squash.org) for amateur tournaments, the PSA (More info: psa-squash.com) for men's professionals, and WISPA (More info: wispa.net) for women's professionals.

To run a WISPA tournament, the prospective promoter must apply to the WISPA and submit a fee equal to 3.5 percent of the event's total prize money. WISPA approves applications based on the ability of the promoter to run the event according to its rules and provides extensive guidelines for prospective promoters.

The PSA has helpful information, "Organizing a PSA tour Event, A Step-by-Step Guide," and "An Introduction for A New Promoter to the Organization of a PSA Tour Event." Both are available through the PSA Website. The first, a 27-page guidebook, outlines the steps required to host a tournament and covers everything from facility standards and health and safety compliances to scheduling matches, distributing prize money and accommodating players. The second document includes all PSA rules and a FAQ section.

Professional Player

Turning professional can be a momentous step in a young player's career. It often means giving up a lot of other things in life to pursue squash in a single-minded way. It means hours of fitness training, practice and more practice, travel and more travel. "It takes hard work, dedication and years of planning, monitoring and setting goals to become a professional squash player," says Sarah Fitz-Gerald, five-time world champion, in an announcement by iSquashmarketing. (More info: iSquashMarketing.com).

Only a handful of new professionals earn top rankings and prize monies quickly. Those who have been through it recommend players stick with the tour for at least five years to truly understand what it takes to become a professional squash player. Only after a significant amount of traveling and competing will you gain enough experience to be able to hit the spotlight.

Junior squash is different and it takes time to make the adjustments when transitioning from amateur to professional status. In the professional game, rallies are longer and a greater fitness level is required, along with more strength and speed. Yet in addition to the physical differences, there are also lifestyle changes. Pros are pretty much on their own, traveling to and from international tournaments and not always accompanied by their parents.

When To Turn Pro

Top juniors in Pakistan, Egypt, Malaysia and other international squash-playing countries sometimes end up turning pro as young as 16, usually forgoing further schooling. In the US where there is a stronger emphasis on college education, some juniors try a pro career after playing intercollegiately. Many in the squash world agree that this is too late. "They end up four years behind everyone else," says Damian Walker, who grew up in England and turned pro at 17.

Walker, like many of his counterparts, believes that this is the reason why an American has yet to become a world squash champion. *Squash* magazine sums it up: "It won't happen until someone decides to take a pass on college and goes after professional squash while they are still teenagers."

Now there is someone willing to take that step. American Chris Gordon decided to follow the path of his international competitors, skipping college and moving to London to concentrate on squash. His goals include winning major international titles, such as the British Junior Open, and earning a ranking in the top 75 in the

Professional Squash Association. If he succeeds, the US will surely shine in the global squash arena.

The decision to turn professional should be made based a combination of ability, effort and attitude. The kid, parent, coach, athletic trainer, and other mentors should meet to make a clinical assessment of the following:

- *Ability, Effort and Attitude*: Success at the professional level is dependent upon these three areas. You definitely need talent, but you also need to work hard at it. Along with work is the attitude that this is what I want to do and nothing will stop me. Judge your kid's ability based on consistent performance in high-level competition. Make allowance for potential improvements based on physical growth and high performance coaching. Give him the opportunity for plenty of practice time and fitness training. If the team, that is the parent, coach, trainer and other mentor, is convinced the kid is ready for professional competition at all levels—strokes, strategy, physical conditioning, and mental maturity—perhaps he should go for it.
- *Financial Plan*: Do you have the funds to support world travel? Is there a racquet or shoe company willing to sponsor your child? If not, is there a plan to cover expenses?
- *Long Range Plan*: Is your child willing to skip a college education to pursue squash? Are you okay with her decision? What happens after the tour experience is over? Or, perhaps, you want to try the pro tour for a short period, just for the fun of it, and go back to school afterwards. This is the choice top American junior Lily Lorentzen made. In putting off college temporarily, Lily gave the tour her best shot and in doing so, she's learned what you can't always learn in school. World travel can be an education in and of itself.

Prize Money vs. Lunch Money

Becoming a professional player means you have chosen to make your living playing squash. This is a lot different from playing squash for recreation. Many new pros sometimes discover that "prize" money can be lunch money.

"It's a matter of having a living, not making a living," says pro Damian Walker. A new squash professional is basically on his own unless he comes from a country that has government subsidies to support its athletes. In France, for example, top pro Thierry Lincou gets half of his expenses reimbursed by the government. Up and coming pros can expect a smaller stipend.

In the US, there are some grants through the Olympic Development Program and support from the USSRA for national teams. But for the most part in the US, aside from perhaps free apparel and racquets, the player pays for his flights, laundry and other personal needs on his own. He can, however, expect a hotel room at PSA and WISPA-sanctioned events and perhaps meals, depending upon the level of tournament. Players also pay a percentage of their winnings back to the PSA or WISPA. The amount varies depending upon the size of the event and the allotted purse. In a tournament with a 16-man draw and a purse of $100,000 or more, for example, players contribute a fee to the PSA based on 10 percent of the on-site prize money. WISPA players contribute a fixed five percent of prize earnings.

It's estimated that many pro players spend over $10,000 annually just in airfare. Add the cost of a traveling coach and stringing jobs and a professional player is looking at $20,000 just to break even.

When a winner of a major PSA tournament gets $25,000, it can really mean around $12,000, after taxes and contributions to the PSA. If a rookie can only win a first round match in a smaller event, he earns a few hundred dollars and will be seriously in the red when you add up flights and expenses. It's easy to see why young professionals may need financial support to sustain themselves during the initial years, as they get their feet wet and gain valuable professional experience.

Many squash professionals supplement their earnings in other ways. In Europe, pros participate in professional league play, where earnings can range from $80 to $500 per match. Some play matches three times per week. Others find that teaching squash is a good source of additional income. And some are able to market themselves and secure local sponsors, either companies with an interest in squash or individuals who are willing to lend their support. Those savvy enough can cut down expenses by getting to know the right people, those who can perhaps provide housing and meals.

Unless one rises to a top ranking quickly and is able to earn major sponsorships it is prudent to find additional means of support. Develop a sound financial plan for the early years. Having a good financial plan will help junior better focus on squash. With financial support in place, matches will becomes less about the paycheck and more about the game. Ultimately, this will improve rankings and earnings.

Amateur Status

Believe it or not, there's at least one major advantage to being an amateur – college squash. If a player plans to attend college in the US or is currently attending college, he must check with the NCAA on the restrictions and guidelines concerning the acceptance of prize money. (More info: ncaa.org). Failure to follow NCAA rules could jeopardize one's college squash career.

Ranking vs. Earning

The good news is that no one can stop you from winning a tournament, and the winnings are the same, whether you're currently ranked No. 100 or No. 1. Private deals – endorsements, corporate sponsorships, tournament appearance fees and such work differently.

When it comes to racquet deals, some companies rely primarily on rankings, particularly performance in the major tournaments. Others also look for players who will give them the best exposure through the media and the general public. Some give supplementary bonuses based on wins.

In *Squash Player* magazine, Andy Bunting, Sponsorship Manager for Prince, says that if a player wins a tournament and the top prize is $20,000, that player could get about $10,000 from Prince. Prince also gives players a one-year bonus based on their PSA rankings. (More info: Select References 6)

Those with lower rankings may be successful in securing funding from companies and people in their own community. Some players end up moving to an area that is more supportive of squash. The old expression, 'Go where the money is,' is true for squash.

While the players at the very top seem to have an edge, players making their way up the ladder can use their interpersonal skills and good public relations to get what they want. Overall, a higher ranking does equate to higher earnings and makes players more attractive to groups interested in clinics, exhibitions and product representation. Yet, players who are well known in their community can also do fairly well with local support.

Getting Started in Professional Squash

The Professional Squash Association (More info: psa-squash.com) and the Women's International Players Association (More info: WISPA.net) are the places to start for new professionals and amateurs who want to test their readiness for the professional tour.

The PSA World Tour has over 145 men's singles events in more than 30 countries. In conjunction with the World Tour, there is also a Super Series, which include gold, silver and platinum levels and draw the highest caliber of players, Star Tournaments, which have seven different levels, Satellite Tournaments, which are geared for aspiring pro players and, finally, Challenger Tournaments, which are entry level events designed to help new competitors get a start in professional squash. Challenger events also provide opportunities for new promoters get involved with running a tournament.

Beginning in 2005, PSA introduced a junior membership whereby players under 19 can enter sanctioned tournaments, earn world ranking points and keep current on the rules and requirements for competing in PSA events. Once junior members reach 100 in the world rankings, they can upgrade to a full member.

The prize money is a good indicator of the level of competition you can expect in professional tournaments. At the lower end, events with $3,000 in total prize money feel like a frat house, with college and junior players competing to earn valuable professional ranking points. Guess how much of that prize money goes to the winner – about $600.

Prize money in PSA events is distributed to players by a percentage breakdown as they are eliminated from the tournament. The breakdown can range from 20 percent for the winner of a 16-draw event to 1.75 percent for the player placing ninth or tenth in a 64-draw tournament.

WISPA events also take place all over the world and have a similar structure to the PSA. Prize money ranges from $500 to $75,000. The WISPA World Tour incorporates many levels of competition, including Tour Platinum, Tour Gold, Tour Silver, Tour, Super Challenger, Challenger and Rising Stars.

The last category, Rising Stars, is designed for women under 19 who want to get started in professional play. WISPA offers an introductory Rising Stars membership so young players can earn full ranking points from Junior Opens. These points can then be carried forward once players are no longer 19 and upgrade their membership.

Both WISPA and the PSA use a sophisticated system for awarding ranking points, based on the prize money offered, the level of the event, size of the draw and how far players advance.

For example, a WISPA tournament with a $35,000 purse will award a total of 14,000 ranking points. The winner gets 2,450 points, the runner-up, 1,610, and those who make it to the round of 32 get 175.

To calculate a player's ranking, divide the total number of points accumulated in any 52-week period by the number of tournaments played. It's a good idea to monitor the calendar and look at the number of tournaments played during the previous year and their results. Make sure to get entries in for the same tournaments in the current year and see how you can improve your results.

Life on the Tour

Life can be very good for the top two players in the world, who can earn from $750,000 to $1 million a season, including endorsements. Those in the top 20 also manage to do fairly well. Those ranked lower can also be successful but they need to work a little harder at making themselves known. They may be able to secure local sponsors, earn money in leagues, give lessons, find free housing when traveling and perhaps take in about $5,000 to $8,000 each year from tournaments. After that, they're playing for the love of it.

The travel opportunities, friendships, and media attention are appealing. Yet, the lifestyle can be tiring and lonely. Living out of suitcases, traveling in different time zones and missing home can affect young players. It can be more fun to partner with a group of training professionals to avoid loneliness. There is always strength in numbers.

Australian pro Nathan L'Huillier lists the most important criteria needed to survive life on the tour:

- *Networking*: Learn the power of conversation in order to encourage others to help you.
- *Dedication*: Commit 100-percent to your sport.
- *Sacrifice*: Be prepared to give up things that may be important to you.
- *Self Believe*: If you don't believe in yourself, who will?
- *People Skills*: Know when it is your time to shout for drinks or pay for the taxi.
- *Time Management*: Be flexible and willing to compromise your time for your job.
- *Strength of character*: Take the good with the bad.

Make the decision to turn pro based on realistic analysis rather than emotion. Have a sound financial plan to support the initial learning curve. Hone your public relations and marketing skills for they will be helpful. These things are key to making your young player's professional years some of the best years of his life.

Sports Media

Squash is a true global sport and regularly makes the headlines in countries around the world – the UK, Canada, Australia, Malaysia and more. International newspaper and wire services keep up with the World Tour, while the local press soaks up regional events.

Squash Player magazine, published in the UK, is as glossy as it can get. Star players like James Willstrop, sporting bare torso, appear on the cover. SquashNow.com, SquashTalk.com, iSquashMedia.com, Squashsite.co.uk and Squash247.com keep squash fans in the loop all over the world. In the US, you can also keep up to date with *Squash* magazine, which is included with a USSRA membership. Those who know the sport and like to write might find opportunities among the squash media.

Sky Sports in the UK, TSN in Canada and the inclusion of squash on The Tennis Channel in the US present opportunities for knowledgeable television commentators. Most specialized jobs require a degree in journalism. Popular players often find their way into print and broadcasting journalism because of their celebrity and knowledge of the game.

Squash legend and six-time British Open champion Jonah Barrington joined England's former women's world No 3 Sue Wright to provide commentary for the British Open during its television debut on Sky TV in 2000. With any luck, the efforts to bring squash into mainstream sports will result in more televised events in the future. Specialists in Web technology predict that the future of sports coverage lies in online TV. Wayne Reuvers, CEO of Live Technology, believes that Web- based live TV is a perfect opportunity to showcase squash to fans worldwide. This new field, a blend of high technology and media, will open up many opportunities for professional players and sponsors and those seeking an exciting new career.

14

Building a Squash Community

"Take your passion and make it happen."
FLASHDANCE, lyrics from the song "What a Feeling"

L et's start with a worst-case scenario. Your community, umm...
Pleasantville...has no courts and no players. Worst of all
nobody is interested in squash, except you. What do you do?
How do you pique community interest? And how can you go about
building a squash-loving community?

Hello, USSRA. The United States Squash Racquets
Association is the governing body of squash in the United States
(More info: us-squash.org). The USSRA consists of eight regions - Far
West, Central States, Great Lakes, Southeast, New England,
Pennsylvania, New York and Mid Atlantic. In addition, there are 34
districts offices that stem from these regional hubs. Many thousands of
volunteers run these organizations, coming together to support squash
programs all over the country.

The USSRA's "Your Squash, Your Teams, Your Community"
is the largest initiative ever launched to promote and develop the
growth of squash in the United States. The USSRA mission is
threefold with a focus on making squash more available to new
players, supporting national teams and assisting efforts to grow urban
squash and community programs. An ambitious goal of targeting
25,000 new members in five years is now underway.

Squash is a truly a sport for life. The legendary Hashim Khan
continues to play at 90. The USSRA supports a healthy community by
encouraging active living for all ages.

Linking with the USSRA

If you're a coach or a squash player, chances are you're already linked
to the United States Squash Racquets Association. For a parent new to
squash, linking with the USSRA can help you locate organizations in
your area dedicated to promoting squash and find programs to develop
a squash pathway for your junior.

If a regional USSRA association does not serve your area, you
can help start one. Twenty years ago, there was only one squash court

in Arizona. Today, the Arizona Squash Racquets Association represents 30 courts of various sizes, including two outdoors, and about 300 active members. The AZSRA hopes to see continued membership growth, since it has targeted about 1,000 people who have played squash in and around the area. Plans are currently underway to host the largest WISPA event in the US, a WISPA Gold 35 near Phoenix. Thirty-two of the world's top women players will compete for a purse of at least $45,000 on a covered, outdoor, all-glass court in the center of Fountain Park. With the tallest continually running fountain in the world as a backdrop, the arena will seat 1,000 fans. It will take a group of passionate squash enthusiasts to get together to make it all happen.

There is a minimum requirement of three clubs or facilities with squash courts and 35 members to become an official USSRA association. If there is interest in squash in your community and one or more places to play, you could encourage facilities to join forces to help grow the sport.

Developing Squash Facilities

It's not easy, but it's not impossible. Spearhead a drive to build courts in your neighborhood. It's happening out there. Once you open the doors, you'll find Jennifer, Johnnie, and friends duking it out after school with racquets and a ball. Access to a squash court is the first step in getting kids hooked on squash.

In planning a facility, it's important to choose an area where there is a high concentration of existing players and kids who would benefit from learning the game, advises Dave Carr of McWil Courtwall, an international builder of indoor racquet courts. Do your research on demographics. Will people in your community support your efforts?

Bring together all the groups and organizations with a vested interest in developing squash facilities in the area to create a committee. Here are a few possible special interest groups:

- School and community organizations
- Recreation departments
- Squash club management from other neighborhoods
- Professional squash teachers

Facility

Traditionally, squash facility formats have included private clubs, colleges or prep schools and commercial clubs that are open to the public. For squash to grow in the United States, it needs to shed its lingering baggage as an elite private club sport and be accessible to all segments of the population. Its future lies in commercial clubs and community facilities that make the game a reality for the average family.

Maybe an entrepreneur believes you have a viable place in which to build squash courts. Perhaps there is a school that would like to share its facilities with the community. Chestnut Hill Academy, a private prep school outside of Philadelphia, built six squash courts with donations from parents. When the school team is not using the courts, the facility is transformed into a squash club, Chestnut Hill Academy Springside Squash and open to community for a moderate annual family fee. In turn, the club is a revenue source for the school. Bryan Patterson, the pro who spearheaded the move to community squash, runs a full squash program you'd expect from a private club: lessons, clinics and leagues. Several top juniors have evolved from the program. St. Luke's School in New Canaan, CT will soon offer a similar program for its community.

Building a Squash Court

A squash court is not often found in the backyards of most homes, unless the homeowner is a true squash lover who can afford it. Gordon Anderson, former top touring professional and president of Anderson Courts and Sports Surfaces, a Buffalo-based squash court construction company, has built 130 courts at private homes.

Squash player and real estate developer Edward J. Minskoff has an Anderson court at his weekend home in South Hampton, Long Island. The court is housed in a separate guesthouse on his 4-1/2 acre property. Minskoff enjoys playing with his 10-year-old daughter and teenage son and many squash playing friends in the area. "It's a pure hobby that I enjoy," he says.

You need to have enough space and a substantial budget to build your own court. Yet, private court owners believe the investment is sound because the court can be used year-round and can last a lifetime. Unlike a club where there are many opportunities for play, having your own court means you need to make arrangements for games. However, once word gets out that you have a court, players will likely be calling you.

The standard squash court dimensions are 21 feet wide by 32 feet long with a minimum of 18-1/2 feet in height. With the required framework, you need to add another 8 to 9 inches to each dimension. The court itself can cost from $30,000 to $40,000; however, on top of that you need to budget for a building to house the court, unless your home has an expansive empty wing. With exterior construction, architectural fees and the necessary mechanical and electrical requirements, your total cost can add up to as much as $125,000.

If you want to add a bathroom, shower, or lounge area, costs can reach up to $200,000. A private court is certainly not a reality for everyone. Your junior will probably have more fun playing at a club, which is more affordable and offers more playing opportunities.

Building courts to be used by the public is of course an even larger investment, but if you've chosen the right location and can sustain interest in your squash program, your club will most likely become profitable. Compared with building other sports facilities, squash courts take up less space and require less maintenance. Squash courts can be built fairly quickly, so you don't have to wait so long for a return on investment.

Dave Carr of McWil recommends you look for a building on flat land with at least 20-foot high ceilings in a fairly stable climate. "Never build just one court," he advises, since more are necessary for tournaments and leagues. "Schools should have no less than four courts if they want to have matches."

Westchester Squash in Mamaroneck, NY was the first non-private facility in the Westchester area that opened to any and all interested players. One success story led to another as Damian Walker, a world-ranked player from England, built three courts in a leased office space not too far away in Stamford, CT. Soon after opening, The Squash Alley developed a large following.

You could also think creatively like Steven Polli, an avid player with his own construction company, who built an outdoor court for his community in a park next to Lake Champlain in Burlington, VT. "Squash is inherently an outdoor game," said Polli, who noted that the sport originated outdoors at the Harrow School in England. Polli got permission for the project from the City of Burlington and raised the $18,000 for materials from donations, foundation grants and Black Knight. He then spent an entire summer building the court himself with the help of a structural engineer, workers from his company and volunteers.

The floor and walls are 10-inch thick smooth concrete, and there is no ceiling, since a ceiling is not necessary in squash. The court is positioned so the sun will not shine in players' eyes and the walls are made sound enough to sustain high winds. The ball reacts well to the outdoor climate, according to Polli, who sometimes shovels off the snow to play the game in the winter. Polli is working on a prototype of a new prefabricated aluminum court that could be installed in other outdoor locations.

To find a court builder, contact the World Squash Federation (More info: worldsquash.org) or Squash Talk (More info: squashtalk.com), which provide listings of accredited court builders.

Developing Volunteers

Volunteers have always been the backbone of the squash world and organizations such as the USSRA and its regional associations. You can count on your fingers the number of staff at the USSRA headquarters. The association does its job with the help of many volunteer committees, board members and officers.

The only way for community squash to get started and thrive is for volunteers to step up to the plate. Volunteering can fit easily between career and family and can enhance rather than replace a family's interests and the time they spend together.

Parents can be key in helping raise funds for junior programs, particularly getting money for kids to travel to tournaments. Entire families can get into the act at their local squash club tournament. Parents can help with player registration, posting draws and match results, organizing social events and providing refreshments. Younger children can also get involved by helping retrieve balls that have gone outside the court, handing out towels to players and even drying off a sweaty court.

Recruiting Volunteers

Recruiting and keeping volunteers motivated is job one for any community program. Volunteers give their time because they enjoy what they're doing. Offer them jobs they really want to do and remember what motivates them to volunteer.

You'll find that volunteers, in addition to being nuts about squash, can also be motivated by all sorts of factors, including a desire to feel needed, share a skill, get to know a community, gain recognition, become an "insider," explore a career, gain status, or simply fill up free time. Volunteers will continue to serve as long as they are given recognition and feel that their efforts are making a difference.

Recruiting volunteers is an on-going effort at SquashBusters in Boston, the successful urban youth squash program. A volunteer coordinator seeks out squash players from the network of clubs and schools in the area, invites them in to see the program in action and then asks for support. Because squash players share a passion for their sport, they are often happy to volunteer, especially when they see the impact squash has made on children's lives.

Training Volunteers

Once you've successfully recruited volunteers, keep them happy and effective by providing education and growth opportunities. At SquashBusters, squash players undergo a formal training program with a staff squash professional to learn how to coach youngsters. Each day, volunteers receive a comprehensive lesson plan prior to working with the kids.

Even a non-playing parent can be trained to be a better volunteer, particularly in learning to be a referee. In fact, learning to be a referee gives a squash newcomer a real understanding of the game. And those who play squash know that rules are updated every few years, so even for seasoned players, referee refresher courses are recommended and useful. Contact the USSRA to find out about the courses and requirements for certification.

Finding Money for Community Squash

Community squash, although a fairly new concept in the United States, is beginning to take root. A new community squash center is no different from a start-up company making the venture capital rounds. Discovering and developing funding sources; making plan presentations and demonstrating value are all integral to any business operation. Those who are business-savvy and passionate about squash are planting the seeds.

Preliminary Steps

A perfect example of community squash becoming a reality is squash enthusiast Wally Glennon's Squash in the Hamptons, a $500, 000 project involving South Hampton Youth Services, Inc. Glennon introduced the concept of including squash courts in the expansion plan for the organization's recreation center. Glennon got the green light to build four singles courts and one doubles court, but was told he would have to finance the project himself. Together with a committee of dedicated volunteers, Glennon embarked on a major fundraising drive.

Fortunately for Glennon, Southampton Youth Services is a non-profit organization and operates under 501c(3) tax exemption status. Therefore, sponsors of the squash courts project are able to deduct their donations from federal income taxes. Those looking to open a new squash facility should ideally look to partner with a non-profit community organization or a school and enlist the help of a good tax attorney.

Money Sources

There are many sources of funding for community programs, but there are always more needy agencies asking for help than there are dollars available. You can make the fundraising process less intimidating with a few key strategies:

Start with the sources you know

As a squash player, you're most likely to find support from players in your area. Squash players, on the whole, tend to be fairly philanthropic in nature. Those who love the game are willing to give something back to the sport.

Glennon tapped into the many New York City business executives and families who had weekend homes in the Hamptons and were also squash players. He also reached out to the Metropolitan Squash Racquets Association, which distributed information on his mission to members. His committee of twelve people all looked to their personal and business connections for support.

Enlist support of non-squash foundations

Over 70,000 foundations nationwide grant money to non-profit organizations (More info: fdncenter.org). Investigate ways you can incorporate local non-squash issues into your programs to greatly increase the grant options available to you. Private foundations, particularly family foundations, were key for Glennon in getting his project underway.

Urban squash programs are other great examples. These organizations are successfully tackling issues related to after-school hours and low academic performance and combine them with squash opportunities. Programs in Boston, New York and Philadelphia offer excellent after-school squash and academics programs that serve disadvantaged youth from inner city neighborhoods.

Enlist the support of the Women's Sports Foundation's Community Action Program by adding programs targeting girls' participation (More info: womenssportsfoundation.org).

Take advantage of in-kind support

Donation of products and services are just as beneficial as cash. Goods and services you don't have to buy or rent can save you a bundle. Here are a few:

- Squash courts from schools and colleges. Even private clubs may be able to donate court-time for an occasional tournament or fundraising event.
- Racquets and balls. Talk to a manufacturer's regional representative.
- Help with promotional materials and publicity.
- Professional services: legal, tax, and computers.
- Meeting rooms.
- Instruction by local pros.
- Local restaurants, pizza parlors, ice-cream shops, and water-bottlers.

Hold a fundraising event

A special event can do wonders to supplement your budget. For a project such as Squash in the Hamptons, raising $500,000 takes more than a car wash or bake sale. It takes a bigger event to bring in bigger bucks. A key to a successful fundraiser is to reduce out-of-pocket expenses by generating in-kind support or services at reduced prices for the event.

SquashBusters, the Boston-based after-school urban squash program, raises some of its funds through an annual adult tournament. In its first year, the tournament drew 95 participants playing in eight flights and raised over $7,000. SquashBusters secures local sponsors for the event and holds a silent auction comprised of donated goods and services to raise more funds. Entry fees are $50, of which a portion is tax deductible.

Glennon staged a two-day exhibition at the site of his planned facility with 2002 New Zealand national champion Daniel Sharplin, Christopher Gordon, who is now playing on the pro tour, Anders Walstedt, former US National Champion, former US All-Americans Dana Betts and Lissa Hunsicker, together with Lee Witham, Princeton Club pro, Johnny Smith, the co-captain of Trinity College's 2003 national championship squad and director of Squash and Community Services at Streetsquash, and top American junior Emily Park. Glennon took the initiative of underwriting the costs of the event and was able to work with McWil on using the company's all-glass court at a competitive price.   Although the event was free to the public, it was successful in raising awareness for the project, generating publicity and thus securing additional donors.

The Briggs Cup, named after US Hall-of-Famer Peter Briggs, was the first tournament in the US organized specifically to raise money for a charity, CitySquash. The event, held at the Apawamis Club in Westchester, a private club where Briggs is based, attracted the world's top doubles players vying for a $100,000 purse, the largest in the history of American squash. Because of the generosity of many enthusiastic club members, the tournament raised over $100,000 for the urban youth Program.

Incentives

If a supporter writes a substantial check, it's nice to recognize these major donors in some way. Glennon made arrangements to dedicate part of the facility, such as the courts, lounge and pro shop, to the various sponsors. Thus, those who supported the project will always be remembered and honored for their contribution.

Grants

Following its centennial celebration in 2004, the USSRA is on a mission to re-evaluate its programs and policies. The association recognizes the magnitude and impact of the urban youth programs and wants to conduct case studies of these programs to grow this area further. Grants are in the discussion phase along with the development of a starter kit for those who want to develop programs. The next stage is for the USSRA to connect with people who have roots in squash and link them with facility designers and clubs so that they can help grow the sport and, ultimately, develop a pathway for new future programs. .

Coming up with cash isn't always easy, but it's not impossible. Put a good group of people together, develop a plan, and go after your contacts. With a little luck, you'll be on the road to your goal.

Worldwide Community-Based Squash Programs

While community programs are still growing in the US, there are many squash success stories in communities all over the world. Here are a few:

Mini Squash

Kids aged 5 through 11 are enjoying this phenomena in the UK. With portable inflatable courts, mini racquets and special balls, kids are getting a fun introduction to squash at early ages. With three levels of play, Mini Squash encompasses league competition, tournaments, school programs and special events.

Mini Squash has been featured at major pro tournaments, been part of road shows and has accounted for more fun than squash players could ever imagine. There are specific rules, coaches' guides and program manuals. (More info: minisquash.com).

Squash Canada's Instant Squash

Although not specifically designed for juniors, Instant Squash has been an effective way of encouraging new players to try the sport. The club-based program provides a package of everything one needs to get started – racquet, ball, eye guards and, in some cases, a t-shirt or a gift. The handy club finder on the Squash Canada Website enables new players to locate a club or facility in or near their neighborhood and register on-line. (More info: Squash.ca.com).

Squash Canada's Skill Awards Program

The Squash Canada Skill Awards Program (More info: squash.ca) is intended to motivate and reward players, to increase the volume of participants in the game and improve their standard of play, all while having fun. The program is designed for ages 7-14, although coaches may include players outside that age group as they see fit. To teach the program effectively, the coach should be certified at a minimum of Level 1. There are 12 levels:

- 1-6 – beginners
- 7-10 – intermediate
- 11-12 – advanced.

Squash Ontario School Squash

This program provides a great opportunity to introduce squash to elementary and middle school kids in a way that fits well into their daily schedules. The Canadians employ two formats, Courting Schools Program and School Squash Equipment Loaner Program, designed to bring squash directly to schools as PE Classes or after-school programs.

Together with Black Knight and the Ontario Ministry of Sports, Courting Schools provides clubs with equipment and program guides to entice school groups into the facility. Clubs benefit from better court usage during "down" time and the ability to introduce squash to potential new members.

The School Squash Equipment Loaner program provides schools with racquets and balls to be used in a gym or playground setting, along with a teacher's manual. For a change of pace from the typical gym class, kids can learn the fundamentals of the squash stroke right in their own school. If teachers need extra help, they can request a squash instructor to join them. Canadian clubs outside of Ontario also have similar programs. (More info: SquashOntario.com).

Come 'N Try Clinics

The Victorian Squash Federation offers a similar program to bring squash into all primary schools. After attending introductory clinics on school premises, all participants are invited to their local squash center for a free clinic and the opportunity to become part of their local squash community.

Squash-It is an extension of the program in which the Victorian Squash Federation helps to arrange inter-school competition at a local facility, at no cost, for children in grades three to five. At the end of the season, the winning school receives a special squash plaque and all kids receive certificates. (More info: victoriansquash.com.au).

Scholastic Squash

There are more than 80 schools in the US with squash teams. These are mostly private schools with a coach who oversees inter-scholastic competition. Some schools are fortunate enough to have their own squash courts. Those schools can use their facility as a source of revenue by opening doors to the community. Schools without courts have been able to partner with a nearby club, which allows students to use courts before prime time hours.

If your child's school doesn't have a program, speak with the athletic department about starting one. See if there is another school or club in the area where you can share the squash courts and coaches. Squash professionals who want to grow the game and have available courts may be willing to open their doors for you.

Urban Youth Programs

If you think squash is limited to the upper crust in the Hamptons, think again. Thanks to urban squash programs in the US, squash is entering the lives of inner city kids who have never even heard of the game. Combined with tutoring, these programs have been sprouting up successfully in many inner cities. Putting kids on a squash court while offering support and instilling confidence, these urban programs have helped shape promising futures for many youngsters. Those in the squash world believe these volunteer-driven programs are the wave of the future for the sport in the US.

SquashBusters

Ten years ago, squash in the inner cities wasn't even on the radar screen. But leave it to Greg Zaff, the pioneer of urban squash, who had a vision that the sport he loved could help and enrich the lives of inner city kids. When Zaff, former No.2 player in the US, started the first urban youth program in 1995 in Boston, no one knew that the concept would take off and make such an impact on so many lives. Zaff's SquashBusters has come a long way from the time it borrowed courts here and there and sometimes settled for a gym. With eight on staff, SquashBusters serves about 250 middle and high school students in a permanent home in the $9.5 million SquashBusters Badger and Rosen Facility at Northeastern University in Boston. (More info: SquashBusters.org).

StreetSquash

Inspired by the success of SquashBusters, George Polsky, a former co-captain of the 3-time national champion varsity squash team at Harvard and a US National Team member, jumped on the band wagon to help kids in Harlem. In 1999, he established StreetSquash, which now works with 120 kids in middle and high school. Kids learn squash through private lessons and programs at New York clubs, attend summer camps and participate in USSRA junior tournaments. The academic component provides college prep for high school students with a two to one ratio of kids to tutors. A multi-faceted program, StreetSquash also runs a literacy project to improve reading and writing skills. StreetSquash has embarked on a drive to raise $9 million to build a new 10-court facility in Harlem to better serve its students. (More info: Streetsquash.org)

SquashSmarts

Following in the footsteps of Boston and New York is SquashSmarts, which partners with Drexel University in Philadelphia. Formed in 2000 by area squash enthusiasts whose mission was to use squash to address the needs of Philadelphia's Public Schools (55 percent of children do not reach grade 10), SquashSmarts provides middle and high school students with ten hours per week of focused attention on academics and squash. To that end, SquashSmarts and Drexel developed an Academic and Technology Center where 30 kids can work comfortably in a safe environment throughout the year, actively involved in Community Service projects and experiential learning courses like Philadelphia Outward Bound. In one year, SquashSmarts kids improved their academic testing by nearly 20 percent, increased their attendance scores from 60 percent to 85 percent, and brought home their first Urban Individual National trophy!
(More info: SquashSmarts.org).

CitySquash

A dad of two happy squash players, Dr. Sanford Schwartz wanted to bring the joy of the game to those less fortunate. He was able to underwrite a program in the Bronx, staff it with former top collegiate players and get CitySquash off and running. Now there are over 1,000 people who give time or money to the program. CitySquash, which operates out of Fordham University and Concordia College, also sponsors kids to travel to USSRA tournaments. Since the program began in 2001, two-thirds of the participants have enhanced their academic performance by raising their average to at least 80 percent. Six were able to achieve a 90 percent average or above. In addition, several have advanced in national tournaments and have earned USSRA rankings (More info: citysquash.org).

Urban Squash National Championships

Urban squash programs allow kids to compete against other schools and teams in the area, as well as visit their sister programs. The Urban Squash Individual Nationals and the Urban Squash Team Nationals give the more than 200 urban youth program participants a chance to travel and compete on a national stage for age division titles. These unique events have collectively become a climatic end-of-season finale and they've even grown to include an academic event – the Urban National Poetry Competition.

Kidzsquash

The success of the urban squash programs prompted the Vassar College varsity squash coaches to reach out to the Catharine Street Community Center to establish Kidzsquash, which has introduced squash to nearly 50 children in the Poughkeepsie vicinity since 2004. The program represents a collaboration of effort between Vassar College, The Poughkeepsie Tennis Club and the Catharine Street Community Center. (More info: CatharineCenter.org and Vassar.edu).

Urban youth squash is definitely catching on. In the Washington, D.C. area, some creative volunteers have successfully launched Squash Empower, which operates out of the National Capital Y serving middle school students from The School for Arts in Learning, (SAIL), an institute for children with special needs. Patron and supporter Chris Walker, Australian pro Connie Barnes and a host of others helped organize an Australian-themed gala fundraiser at the Australian Embassy, complete with auction items that included a lunch with famous squash player Peter Nicol and an on-court session with the star at Harvard. (More info: Squashempower.org).

Another group of DC area pros and players started DC Squash Academy, an after-school enrichment program for middle school students. Top pro Natalie Grainger is on board to plan and implement the squash curriculum. This group even has some US senators and Congressmen involved. (More info: info@dcsquashacademy.org). And the first program to open outside the east coast is METROSquash where kids use the facilities at the University Club of Chicago. (More info: metrosquash.org).

Special Needs Programs

The World Deaf Squash Association has been coordinating an active program for deaf players in several countries, including Australia, England, The Netherlands, Scotland and South Africa. Most of these countries organize national teams and leagues and competitive play. There are challenge matches among nations and opportunities for international competition. The World Deaf Squash Association also helps ensure that coaches understand the special communications needs of deaf players. (More info: deafsquash@aol.com).

Great Things Can Happen

CitySquash's Tanesha Jackson, an eighth-grader at Middle School 45 in the Bronx, was awarded a full scholarship to the Hill School, a private boarding school outside of Philadelphia. When Tanesha heard the good news, she cried tears of joy and so did her mom, Maria, who has dedicated her life to her seven children. "Thank you, God," she said over and over, "thank you, thank you, thank you, thank you."

This opportunity will change Tanesha's life forever. An African-American, Tanesha lives on 161st Street in the Bronx, some forty blocks from Middle School 45, in one of the toughest parts of New York City. When it was time for her to enter sixth grade, her mom fought tooth and nail to get her into Middle School 45, which, in spite of the considerable distance from their apartment, was attractive because of its successful chess program. Maria succeeded in getting her baby girl into M.S. 45, but as fate would have it, Tanesha never joined the chess team.

Tanesha was one of hundreds of sixth graders invited to try out for CitySquash's inaugural class several years ago. She not only made the team, she quickly established herself as one of the best players and went on to win her division of the National Urban Championships two years in a row. She is bright, talented, vivacious, fun and determined to succeed in life. Just as she is fortunate that Hill has given her this opportunity, Hill is fortunate, too

It is not CitySquash's mission to place team members in private high schools, but the organization is excited for Tanesha and believes that she will not be the last CitySquasher to get to go to a school like Hill. Word is spreading among private day and boarding schools that Citysquash has talented athletes and bright, hardworking students.

Way to go, Tanesha!

Publicity for Community Squash

Mojo promo is what you need to get the word out, although you don't need to blow your entire annual budget with advertising. When Wally Glennon staged an exhibition to introduce his new squash court project in South Hampton, he contacted the local newspapers and television station to cover the event. The press came and several positive articles resulted, as well as a segment on the local television news. He also informed SquashTalk, which ran feature coverage on Glennon's event and mission on its Website for the worldwide squash community. Here are some additional ways of generating publicity:

- Word-of-mouth: The least expensive vehicle is to let your friends do the talking and spread the news.
- Distribute flyers: This tried and tested method is cheap and effective. Common sense dictates posting flyers on court bulletin boards and at community centers, health clubs, sporting goods stores, pro shops, squash clubs, youth associations, schools and colleges.
- List your events and programs with the community calendar of local newspapers and television stations.
- Develop an informational Website with prominent sections for upcoming events and memberships. Remember to register with leading Web directories like Yahoo.

Find a human-interest angle. Inner city children learning squash and developing a new outlook on life have been making the headlines of major publications, such as *The New York Times* and *Newsweek*.

Community Tournaments

Thousands of tournaments take place each year, many sanctioned by a regional governing body such as the USSRA. Others are simply operated by individual clubs, schools, and community associations for social play, fundraisers, and so on.

The Dunlop Power Tour bronze events out of Squash Ontario are an excellent example of entry-level tournaments. Aimed at new and first-year players, ages 6 to 18, the program provides a fun introduction to competitive play with one-day events complete with t-shirts and Big Mac coupons for all participants. Players are divided into categories based on levels. The format is flexible with matches of three or four out of five or by timed intervals, either with round robins or draws. Entry fees range from $5 to $20, all in the spirit of providing cheap, simple fun.

Kids can also gain valuable tournament experience locally, before they get into the higher-level sanctioned tournaments. Your community can partner with a coach, perhaps with the help of a local sponsor, to organize a tournament program. A typical series of events running throughout a season can be funded with affordable entry fees and sponsorships.

The Jericho Tennis Club, a recreational facility in Vancouver, is known for making squash competition fun for new players. Each year, its successful Junior Novice B tournament attracts many juniors from various clubs throughout the lower Mainland. Junior Jazz, on-going program of Squash BC, gives juniors a menu of choices for competition at many levels, including active league play. In Quebec, kids can participate in Jesters Junior Evenings, where they play with kids from other clubs and schools and enjoy refreshments and door prizes.

In the US, new and developing juniors have an opportunity to compete in Bronze and Silver events, formerly called Future Stars, which are sanctioned by the USSRA but limited to those who have not yet earned rankings or have a ranking below certain levels. The bottom line is that community-based squash tournaments can offer your community competitive and social opportunities for all ages and skill levels.

Creating a Squash Tournament

Kids love to compete, even the very young, provided the competition format is non-threatening and doesn't over-emphasize wins and loses.

If your area lacks opportunities for juniors to compete, or the competition format doesn't suit you, consider organizing your own tournament. You'll need to recruit players, interest sponsors, find courts, and get some mojo publicity. This can all be fairly easy if it's a small tournament.

Players

You can find eager participants at schools with squash programs, clinics conducted by local pros, and nearby squash clubs. Tournaments can be run with any multiple of two players. It's more interesting, though, when you have two groups at different skill levels. The maximum number of players depends on the number of available courts. For a facility with four courts, you wouldn't want any more than 6 draws of 16 kids. A new director may find numbers beyond that unwieldy. If you have an odd number of players, fill the draw with byes and award those byes to seeded players, such as top-ranked juniors from the area or give the byes out randomly.

Format

Choose a format appropriate for the skill level of registrants. When working with peewees with less than a year of squash under their belts, use the Dunlop Max blue ball, which is bigger and bouncier than the standard tournament ball.

Organizing kids into teams of equal abilities and size to play in a round robin format can be fun. Or if time is a factor, matches can be of a certain length. When time is up, players stop and play the next opponent. Points are tallied at the end. These formats are less threatening than the elimination format in which a player drops from the tournament as soon as he loses a match.

Emphasize the fun factor. Award not only the winner, but also the player who exhibited the best sportsmanship throughout the tournament, the most improved player, and the kid who chased down every ball. Hold an end-of-day carnival event where everyone is welcome. Distribute gifts to all competitors, event participants, and volunteers!

Giving Back

John Nimick of Event Engine runs the prestigious Boston Open, which until recently had been held in Symphony Hall in Boston. While the event offers $50,000 in prize money to the world's top pros, it also serves as a fundraiser for SquashBusters, the official charity. The kids from Boston's inner city who participate in the urban youth program have the time of their lives in a special on court clinic with the pros. They also help with the tournament, serving as the court crew – wiping down the court and retrieving balls. It's a win-win for all involved.

Bringing in school kids, or honoring a local pro or a volunteer are examples of giving-back that could be incorporated into a tournament. It's great education for the kids and helps them see beyond wins and losses.

As you gain experience at local tournaments, you might want to try holding an USSRA-sanctioned event for juniors, such as a Bronze tournament. Follow up success there with a Silver or Gold event. Who knows? You might one day reach the pinnacle of tournament directing by hosting a WISPA or PSA event in your town.

Squash Software to the Rescue

Today is tournament day. The draw sheet has 48 kids at three different skill levels. Two kids reported sick and three say they ought to be playing at a different level. Little Karrina is wondering how she got put in the Boys 10s. As tournament director, you've got to straighten out the draw sheet quickly. You can scratch your head and choose to do it yourself, or let a computer equipped with squash software do the scratching for you.

Welcome to tournament management software. These systems can create and revise draws on the fly. Just type in or revise the names, skill-levels, number of courts and rounds and the system does the rest, including printing out a complete new line-up and court assignments. There are several software companies that offer these programs, which can sometimes be downloaded for free with an opportunity to purchase optional add-ons.

In 2004, the USSRA introduced RailStation, a Web-based service for leagues, ladders, tournaments and rankings. It can be used at no cost, but you need to contact the USSRA to arrange for online instruction.

As your program grows, tournaments can get fancier. You may want the system to handle first-round consolation, in addition to elimination and round robin events. The tournament may be held at multiple sites simultaneously. RailStation has the ability to coordinate multi-sites, seed players and even take entry fees via credit card.

Building A Junior Squash Business

If you're the entrepreneurial sort or want to make profitable use of free time, consider starting a business delivering squash programs to kids. Frankly, one could find other, more profitable avenues of pursuit. But if you love squash, a junior squash business will yield profits beyond those reflected on the balance sheet.

Silicon Valley, the capital of high-tech entrepreneurialism, is high strung and exciting. Notwithstanding the dot-com crash, recent college grads and seasoned entrepreneurs still engage in nerf gun battles and work through the night. These overachievers are known for building stuff in their garages and turning it into something millions use worldwide. Think what could happen if just a portion of that fervor was directed to squash.

We're not talking about creating and maintaining sports champions, but the under-served markets at the grass roots level: the business of developing recreational players; the business of transforming french-fry logged, obese kids into fit squash enthusiasts. Developing recreational players can be both a passionate experience and a business opportunity.

The Valley teaches us two rules of entrepreneurial wisdom:

- Think big. Start small.
- Lone rangers go nowhere.

A parent, a coach, and an MBA can pool their talents to build a viable squash business for your community. It takes perseverance, pure love for squash and a little bit of luck along the way to hit a winner.

15

Inside Squash Organizations

"People understand contests. You take a bunch of kids throwing rocks at random and people look askance, but if you go and hold a rock-throwing contest – people understand that."
DON MURRAY, football coach

P eople, organizations, and money, in that order, make the squash world go round. When we, as parents and coaches, understand their roles and motivations, we're in a better position to help our kids develop a roadmap for their future. Knowing how the system works makes our own contributions to the squash world more effective.

Here then is the inside skinny on squash organizations, ordered in the way a parent and kid may encounter them.

USSRA

If there's one organization an American parent or coach raising a squash kid should support, this is it. Founded in 1904, the United States Squash Racquets Association (More info: us-squash.org) is a volunteer-based organization with around 9,000 individual members and hundreds of clubs and facilities members across the country. As the national governing body for squash, the USSRA strives to promote and develop the growth of squash, from the grass roots level to the professional game.

The USSRA And You

The USSRA is a much smaller operation compared to the National Football League (NFL) or the US Tennis Association (USTA), although the enthusiasm and passion shown by the staff, volunteers, coaches and players will easily put it on par with any other sports organization. The USSRA is a non-profit organization that operates under a 501c(3) tax shelter. Contributing to the USSRA are you and your fellow members, organizational members and clubs, sanctioning fees from tournaments, support from the US Olympic Committee and endowment funds made possible by donations from dedicated squash friends.

The USSRA offers important membership benefits, especially for a parent. By joining the USSRA, you and your child automatically become members of one of eight regional associations and 36 district associations throughout the country. This puts you in contact with the squash playing community in or close to your area and provides access to USSRA-sanctioned tournaments.

Annual membership in the USSRA costs $35 for a junior or an adult. Membership includes a subscription to *Squash* magazine, discounts on entry fees for sanctioned tournaments and the ability to earn a national ranking. The association also provides access to coaching and referee certification programs, as well as the ability to purchase USSRA equipment, clothing and accessories. And, more importantly, your membership helps support local and national programs.

As the editor of *Squash* magazine asked recently, why aren't more of the 500,000 or so players in the US, members of the USSRA? If you're keen on squash, support the national organization for the sake of the sport's future.

There are also opportunities to connect with the USSRA other than membership. Volunteer at your local district organization. Serve on local and national USSRA committees. Speak up and set the course for the future of squash. Bottom-line: get involved. You owe it to all the squash kids out there.

Organization

Promoting squash nationwide and serving the needs of its members requires the effort of many individuals and organizations. The USSRA operates through eight geographical sections. Each section maintains its own volunteers to administer USSRA programs and coordinate the efforts of 36 district associations.

A 35-member board, which includes an 11-member Executive Committee, eight regional representatives, eight special interest groups, four members at large and more than five athletes guide the USSRA. All but two members of the Executive Committee are selected by a Nominating Committee, which also selects the President, Treasurer, Secretary, Chairman and other positions. There are two active athletes selected by an Active Athlete's Committee. Members of the Executive Committee have one-year terms, but they sometimes serve longer.

The Board and the Executive Committee meet twice a year but keep in touch electronically. A small paid staff of six people at the organization's headquarters in Bala Cynwyd, Pennsylvania effects national coordination and administration.

Recent changes in USSRA leadership promise to deliver more to members. The first step is tightening up finances and seeking additional funding to make more programs available to players. Stand by and keep your antenna up, a new and improved USSRA is about to unfold.

Professional Tournaments

US Open – Men's

The largest and most prestigious event of the 15 US Championships run by the USSRA is the $50,000 US Open, which the association owns and licenses. This men's competition, which is also a stop on the PSA Super Series Circuit, used to take place at Symphony Hall in Boston, home of the Boston Symphony Orchestra, but since 2005 it has been held at Harvard University.

The tournament started in 1954 as a hardball event bringing together professionals and amateurs. The Khan family dominated the event until the early 1980s. In 1966, the US Open merged with the Canadian Open and was called the North American Hardball Open.

Adapting to the times, it became a softball event in 1985. The North American Open continued only briefly, but USSRA officials would like to bring the tournament back once again. In keeping with its historic tradition, the US Open holds both pre-qualifying and qualifying tournaments that provide opportunities for local players.

US Open – Women's

The Women's division of the US Open is the Carol Weymuller US Open, named after the popular player and coach. The tournament also started as a hardball event in 1975 and was called The Heights Casino Open, named after the club where Weymuller played and coached. In 1980, it became a softball event and renamed to honor Weymuller. The USSRA and the Heights Casino collaborated to elevate the status of the tournament to a National Open Event.

The Howe Cup

The Howe Cup is one of the oldest and most treasured prizes in all of US women's squash. Originally an inter-city competition among teams from the New York, Boston, and Philadelphia metropolitan areas, the Howe Cup has grown into a national competition with both inter-city and intercollegiate divisions.

The Teaching Pro Championships

This is a national event revived in 2004 at the Tournament of Champions in New York City. The tournament offers $5,000 in prize money and is open to teaching professionals and full-time coaches who reside in the US and are USSRA members.

In addition, the USSRA sanctions the National Men's and Women's Championships, National Men's and Women's Doubles Championships, and National Mixed Doubles.

Amateur Competition

While professional tournaments showcase the stars and rev up the fans, amateur competition ensures the growth of squash at the community level.

The US Junior Open attracts about 450 players from 15 countries in all four age divisions: Under 19, Under 17, Under 15, and Under 13 for boys and girls.

For the rest of us, well, there are hundreds of USSRA-sanctioned competition opportunities. There are adult tournaments designed for every skill level and age group, from 19 to 90 in five-year intervals.

Juniors can compete according to their age and skill level in events from Bronze tournaments for players ranked 65 and below, to Silver tournaments for players ranked 33 and below to Gold tournaments, open to all players in Under 19, Under 17, Under 15, Under 13 and Under 11 age divisions. This three-tiered approach, introduced by the USSRA in the 2005/6 season, was designed to appeal to all levels and meet the growing contingency of new players.

The introduction of a National Father and Son Doubles Tournament, with a senior division for those with sons 18 and older and a junior draw for dads with sons 17 and under, has meant even more fun. Held in New York in 2005, the inaugural event included a host of social activities.

The USSRA also supports teams in sub Olympic Games, such as the Pan American Games and the World Championships for men, women and juniors. The USSRA continues to lobby to make squash an Olympic sport.

Inter-Scholastic Competition

The USSRA has about 80 high school and prep school teams in its membership. Each year, the USSRA holds one High School Championship per region, district or state. The 2005 National High

School Squash Championships grew three-fold over the previous year and attracted 43 seven-player teams.

The 84 college teams of the College Squash Association are also members of the USSRA. (More info: SquashTalk.com).

Hardball Doubles

Even though the squash world has adapted to the soft ball game, there are many who relish the hard ball game of yesteryear. Each season the USSRA sanctions a junior hardball doubles tournament and encourages juniors to try this fun and challenging game.

League Play

Each local squash association runs its own programs for players. Often these include leagues organized by skill level. Because these events are not sanctioned by the USSRA, membership is not required, but players need to join their local association in order to participate. Fees are determined by the association and vary per region.

Squash Academies

A national academy is on the wish list of many squash organizations, particularly the USSRA. As dreamers dream, take a look at the many programs that are beginning to evolve into squash academies. And that transformation is happening worldwide.

In the US, you'll find the Talbott Squash Academy, run by the famous Mark Talbott, in Newport, RI and the Princeton Squash Training Center, led by Princeton coaches Gail Ramsey and Bob Callahan. Openings in these summer programs are some of the most sought after among top junior players.

In Australia, there is the government supported Australian Institute of Sport, where squash is under the direction of renowned coaches Rodney Martin and Geoff Hunt, who have worked with several of the world's top players and up-and-coming stars. The National Squash Academy at Grantham College in the UK is supported by England Squash. The program is run by former world No. 2 Peter Marshall. Paul Walters, the entrepreneur behind iSquashMarketing, has developed a division of his company called iSquashAcademy, a global program for top players led by five-time world champion Sara Fitz-Gerald and British Open champion Lee Beachill, who reached No. 1 in the world rankings in 2004.

A national academy is the dream of many squash playing nations. Slowly, camps and training programs are developing and growing to make this dream a reality.

Dear Santa,

What I want for Christmas this year won't be so easy for you and the elves. When I visited my cousin in Philadelphia last week, I played squash for the first time. It was loads of fun. But there are no squash courts where I live so I can't play. My cousin plays three times a week and is even in tournaments. I really wish I could get good enough to do what he's doing. Is there any way you can get some squash courts built around here?

We also watched some professional players in an exhibition. It was really cool. I'd love to see those players again. My cousin gave me a video, but it doesn't seem to really capture what I saw live. Could you find me a video that really shows how the players move, how they reach for the ball and how hard they hit?

While you're working on this, I'd also like a Dunlop Junior TI and maybe you could throw a ball or two and a bandana in my stocking.

Thank you, Merry Xmas.

Bailey

College Squash Association

The former Inter-Collegiate Squash Association was officially renamed the College Squash Association in 2002 (CSA. More info: SquashTalk.com/college). An impressive group of coaches from top squash colleges run the association and serve on the board. Prince Sports, a loyal sponsor, has signed an expanded three-year agreement to continue its support. The Marsh Companies and Dunlop balls are co-sponsors.

The CSA administers rankings for all collegiate squash and runs a national team championship and individual championship for men and women (the intercollegiate Howe Cup) in February to mark the end of the season.

The CSA is comprised of volunteer college coaches and one salaried Executive Director. In addition to support from sponsors, the CSA runs on membership dues and event entry fees.

The mission of the CSA is to promote collegiate squash and help more schools develop teams. The association represents approximately 84 college teams – 32 women's and 52 men's, including emerging teams and club teams preparing to participate more fully in the future. Although these figures are small, the CSA is still in its infancy and has high hopes for the future.

While New England Ivy League schools were the original core of the CSA, more colleges from other areas are coming on board, such as the University of Utah, the University of Rochester, Hamilton College in Clinton, NY, Colgate University in Hamilton, CT, the University of Virginia and Bryant University in North Smithfield, RI.

A west coast presence is even stronger now since Mark Talbott, considered squash's greatest American player, moved to Stanford University as Director of Squash after six years as coach of the successful Yale women's team. In addition to the west coast, the Southeast and the Chicago area are also emerging squash arenas, thanks to the persistence of the CSA.

Coaches in transit, recruitment efforts and ground breaking for new college squash facilities are just some of the exciting happenings at the CSA.

Tournaments

There are end-of-season men's and women's team and individual championships offering many divisions of play, plus a number of invitational and other tournaments throughout the season. Traditionally, Ivy League schools have claimed the top ranks in both women's and men's college squash, but for six consecutive years, Trinity College in Hartford, CT has been the reigning champion of the men's teams, winning 105 straight matches. This incredible streak was due to the worldwide recruiting efforts of head coach Paul Assaiante. The women's team has also proved strong, led by coach Wendy Bartlett. Throughout the men's team's six victorious years, Trinity has sported 41 international male and female players. This international contingency is characteristic of college squash. And if your son or daughter ends up on a college squash team in the US, chances are the coach will not be American but will have sterling squash credentials and a passion to spread the squash credo.

NESCAC

The New England Small College Athletic Conference, founded in 1971, includes eleven selective liberal arts colleges that share the philosophy that a strong sports program can support an educational environment committed to academic excellence. These colleges have competitive squash teams with excellent coaches and compete against each other. They include Amherst, Bates, Bowdoin, Colby, Connecticut, Hamilton, Middlebury, Trinity, Tufts, Wesleyan and Williams. (More info: NESCAC.com)

IHRSA

Over 33 million Americans pump up, rally, tee off, and lap their way to good health at 18,200 health clubs. Those numbers are good enough to sprout an association. The International Health, Racquet & Sportsclub Association (IHRSA. More info: ihrsa.org) is a not-for-profit trade association representing privately owned health and fitness facilities, gyms, spas, squash clubs and their suppliers worldwide.

Headquartered in Boston, IHRSA has over 6,500 member clubs and publishes research findings related to the club market.

NCAA

The National Collegiate Athletic Association (NCAA) is a voluntary, membership-led organization made up of more than 1,200 colleges and universities, conferences and other groups that make their own rules and regulations. There are three divisions within the NCAA – Division I, Division II and Division III. The primary difference between Divisions I and II and Division III is the awarding of scholarships based on athletic ability. Divisions I and II award scholarships for their athletic programs, while Division III does not give athletically-related financial aid. The purpose of the NCAA is to ensure that college sports are fair, safe, equitable and sportsmanlike and to further integrate intercollegiate athletics into American higher education, making academics central to the experience of student-athletes.

Squash is not a full-fledged NCAA sport, yet women's squash is considered an NCAA emerging sport. This means that although there are active women's varsity squash programs at NCAA schools, there are not enough schools sponsoring women's squash to hold an NCAA Championship. Yet as women's varsity squash continues to grow, perhaps that will change in the future. An NCAA emerging sport is one intended to provide additional athletic opportunities for female student-athletes. Once identified as an emerging sport, all NCAA institutions wishing to sponsor the sport at the varsity level must abide by NCAA regulations, which include limits on playing and practice seasons, recruiting regulations, student-athlete eligibility and maintaining amateur status. And although men's squash is not an NCAA sport, colleges with men's teams also abide by NCAA guidelines. (More info: NCAA.org).

The Professional Squash Association

The PSA (More info: PSA-squash.com) is the governing body for men's professional squash and is responsible for organizing and coordinating the Men's Pro Tour. The PSA serves as the official sanctioning body for men's world rankings. The World Tour, with $1.7 million in prize money, is a year-long series of over 145 single elimination tournaments held in more than 30 countries throughout the world. The PSA assists clubs, promoters and national governing bodies in running these events.

The PSA is run by a Board of Directors together with a small staff at its headquarters in the UK. The organization is funded by membership fees, entry registration, sponsorship dollars and by players who contribute a portion of their prize money earnings.

More than 350 players are members of the PSA. Beginning in 2005, the PSA introduced a junior membership whereby players under 19 can enter sanctioned tournaments and earn world rankings. Once they reach 100 in the world rankings, they can upgrade to a full membership.

The PSA could use some big sponsorship dollars to bring professional squash to the forefront. Although membership has been increasing, prize money has not. Adding different types of events and different ways for players to earn ranking points should make the PSA more lucrative and effective in its mission.

Tournaments

- *The Super Series:* The Super Series tournaments are the Tour's main attractions, offering the largest prize purses and the best players in the world. These events include: The Tournament of Champions, which is known as the "Grand Slam" of squash, PSA Masters, British Open, Cathay Pacific Hong Kong Open, Pakistan Open, Qatar Classic and the World Open. Super Platinum Series events have a total prize fund of $120,000, the Gold Series, $100,000 and Silver Series, $70,000. These events, which are part of the PSA TV Series, allow players to qualify for the Super Series Finals. The top eight players in the Super Series standings at the end of a calendar year qualify for the Super Series Finals.

- *Star Tournaments:* Beneath the Super Series level, Star events have seven levels and offer total compensation of over $100,000.
- *Satellite Tournaments*: These tournaments, with less than $100,000 in total compensation, attract aspiring players eager to test the waters of the pro tour.

Women's International Squash Players Association

For girls who dream of a future in professional squash, the Women's International Squash Players Association is dedicated to supporting them. Competing in the Association's sanctioned tournaments, women pros can earn prize money while gaining an incredible learning experience traveling around the globe.

For the past 20 years, the WISPA (More info: WISPA.net), based in London, has been organizing tournaments, administering rankings, and seeking out new sponsors and host countries. The WISPA also runs promotional tours where top players participate in clinics, exhibitions and press conferences in various countries, all to promote women's squash. China, where the game is developing, was a more recent squash host. Little by little, the pocketbook is getting larger and more companies are taking notice.

WISPA got started in 1976 as the Women's International Squash Racquet Federation, WISRF, after the first women's non-national open in Brisbane. The group's role was to organize and control women's world championships and serve as a link to players from member countries. In 1983, members felt they should follow the men's lead and create an association for the players. The result was the Women's Squash Players Association, WSPA. In the 90s, the official name became the Women's International Squash Players Association, WISPA. While Australian and English players were instrumental in getting WISPA off the ground, today players from many different countries participate. WISPA currently has a total membership of 180 women players.

WISPA is supported by membership fees, event registrations, sponsorship dollars and by players who contribute five percent of the prize money earned in WISPA tournaments. With only a two-person staff, WISPA has been enormously successful in growing the women's game.

The WISPA World Tour reached the $1.1 million mark in 2004, representing a 44 percent increase from 2003. This leap is a result of more new Gold events, plus an increase in tournaments at all levels. The Tour has come a long way since 1983 when prize money totaled $100,000.

Tournaments

The WISPA's World Tour, the official circuit for women's squash, enables players to earn prize money as well as ranking points. The Tour offers several categories of tournaments. Players under 19 can compete in "Rising Star" events, which include National Opens where only ranking points are awarded. A WISPA Rising Star membership allows players to start accumulating ranking points from Junior Opens. These points can then be carried forward once players turn 20 and upgrade their membership. The Rising Star level is therefore a valuable stepping-stone for new players.

Prize money earnings start at the next level, "Challenger," which includes events with $500 to $3,999 purses, limited world ranking points and flexible formats. The third level, "Super Challenger" involves National Closed Championships with prize money of over $4,000 and ranking points. Finally, "Tour" events have prize funds ranging from $4,000 to $14,999 and "Tour Gold" Events offer prizes up to $50,000. Bahrain, Qatar and Shanghai are a few of the newly added tour stops.

European Squash Federation

The European Squash Federation (ESF. More info: europeansquash.com), serves as the World Squash Federation's designated regional federation for Europe. It promotes and organizes championship events, maintains rankings, upholds and enforces the rules of squash and promotes the growth of the sport throughout Europe.

Based in England, the ESF is a non-profit association led by a Management Board and many committees of volunteers. There is only one paid employee, a secretary. The ESF is funded through annual membership fees, championship entry fees, fees for hosting ESF events and a limited amount of sponsorships.

Tournaments

For juniors worldwide, the ESF's Junior Circuit is often the first step in international competition. The circuit currently consists of events in Switzerland, Sweden, England, Belgium, Hungary, Ireland, Scotland, Denmark, Czech Republic, Slovakia, Italy, France, Wales, Austria,

Germany, the Netherlands and Spain. It's open to boys and girls eligible to play in Under 13, Under 15, Under 17 or Under 19 age divisions.

Players must be endorsed by their national squash association. Juniors from all over the world have entered these competitions and have earned rankings and prize money. The ESF also organizes junior and senior team and individual championships.

Squash Canada

Squash Canada (More info: squash.ca) based in Ontario, has a lean staff of three, but covers a lot of ground providing programs and policies to promote squash to all ages and levels of play. The organization serves over one quarter of a million players throughout the nation and has ambitious goals of increasing this number significantly while raising the level of its top competitors.

Squash Canada encompasses many areas. It selects and develops teams, officials and coaches for domestic and international competition, maintains standards for training and certification of coaches and officials, provides a high performance system and coordinates with its provinces and territories in promoting the sport.

Squash Canada also runs a university program, as well as Instant Squash and a Skill Awards Program, to introduce new players to the sport. A non-profit organization, Squash Canada is funded partially by the Canadian government and provincial membership. For a country with a population that is sparse relative to its size, Canada has an impressively well-organized squash program, one that is highly respected worldwide.

Tournaments

In addition to hosting WISPA and PSA events, Squash Canada runs a nine-event pro Circuit, which culminates in a grand finale. Squash Canada supports seven national championships, eight national teams and six squads.

Squash Australia

Representing eight state territories, Squash Australia (More info: squash.org.au) is the central authority for the sport in the nation. The organization, which began in 1934, became a founding member of the International Squash Racquets Federation, now the World Squash Federation, in 1976. Since 2003, Squash Australia has been following an ambitious strategic plan to see that squash flourishes among all levels of players in the nation and that Australian players excel in international competition.

Squash South Africa

In 1910, South Africa became the first nation to form a national controlling squash body whose function was to administer the South African Championships. Through the years, there were several different men and women's squash associations, culminating in 1992 with one unified body representing all of South Africa. Today there are 28 provincial associations within Squash South Africa (More info: squashsa.co.za).

Squash South Africa has come a long way since the days of apartheid and, despite its isolation, has become a real force in the sport. It was the first to organize a veterans' squash association, which opened the game up to older players.

Asian Squash Federation

As many as 27 countries comprise the Asian Squash Federation (More info: asiansquash.com), including the squash hotbeds of Malaysia, Hong Kong and Pakistan. The organization was formed in 1980 at the suggestion of Pakistan. The founding members were Bahrain, Bangladesh, Malaysia, Pakistan, the Philippines, Singapore and Thailand. More recently, the Asian Squash Federation has experienced strong growth in the sport in Hong Kong and Korea.

World Squash Federation

Here's where the big numbers are. Looking at squash globally, you can understand the bigger picture. Throughout the world, there are some 15 million players in 153 nations. The central authority for the game is the World Squash Federation (More info: worldsquash.org), which is responsible for the rules, promotion and growth of the sport and the annual World Championships.

WSF has 118 members comprised of national squash associations from all over the world. The federation includes five regional divisions - Africa, Europe, Asia, Oceania, and Pan America, and four sub federations – Arab, CASA (Caribbean Area Squash Association), CentroAmericana and SubAmerican Squash Federation. Both a management committee and an executive committee run the WSF, which is based in England. The WSF has a full-time Chief Executive and a small professional staff.

WSF states that its mission is to keep the sport growing and to maintain its quality and reputation as one of the most exciting and enjoyable participant and spectator sports in the world. In keeping with these goals, the WSF sets the standards for rules, coaching, refereeing, court specifications, player development and medical guidelines.

The WSF is also responsible for ensuring that squash is represented in all major regional multi-sport games and in the Olympic Games. Its high-profile campaign to include squash as a full medal sport in the Athens Olympics of 2004 was unsuccessful, but in June 2005 IOC members meeting in Singapore voted squash as their first choice sport for the London 2012 Olympics. Unfortunately, the committee then voted not to include any new sports, so squash will not be included in the 2008 or the 2012 games. Squash should be first in line for a place in future Olympiads, and the WSF will continue to campaign for its inclusion.

Squash is included in all sub-Olympic Games, such as the Pan-American Games, Asian Games, Commonwealth Games, World Games and All Africa Games.

The WSF is a small, hard-working, under-budgeted association. What it needs is to become like Major League Baseball and develop point-of-sales materials on a regular basis.

Tournaments

The WSF promotes and organizes the World Championships for men, women, boys, girls and masters at individual and team levels in both singles and doubles. These events are held every two years and run by member nations.

World Squash Day

Celebrate Squash! There is a special day, once a year, where all clubs and facilities in the world are encouraged to open their doors to welcome new players. World Squash Day was established to spread the word that squash is a great game, to raise money for important causes and, more recently, to assist squash leaders in their bid for the game's inclusion in the Olympics.

Celebrities and pros participate in special programs all over the world, including fun street games, all-night squash, tournaments for the physically challenged and a special attempt at setting the record for the world's longest rally. This challenging event involves teams of five players who must keep a rally going for as long as possible during a 60-minute time period. World Squash Day began in 2002 and was organized by Alan Thatcher, British squash journalist and promoter. The program is supported by the World Squash Federation. (More info: worldsquashday.org).

International Squash Doubles Association

The ISDA was inaugurated in 2000 as a governing body for a world professional doubles tour. Since it began, the tour has held more than 16 tournaments and boasts prize money totaling over $600,000 in pro and pro-am events. Doubles Squash is an exciting game enjoyed all over the world. (More info: isdasquash.com).

Unfortunately, the ISDA is not large enough to grow the sport worldwide and it mainly focuses on existing groups. The average age of the players is 35. Doubles popularity can experience a growth spurt if a junior doubles circuit or season is introduced.

USSRA Hall of Fame

To appropriately honor the inductees in the USSRA's six-year-old Hall of Fame, a permanent home will soon be installed adjacent to the Brady Squash Center at Yale University. A group of enthusiastic squash players have embarked on an active fundraising campaign to make this dream a reality.

The site will include plaques and memorabilia from special moments in US squash history. There will be glass cases sporting the first racquets of some of the most famous players and a hands-on computer generated game of squash facts and trivia.

Here you can learn more about Mark Talbott, five-time North American singles champion who dominated world rankings for an 11-year stretch, and Alicia McConnell, a national champion for seven consecutive years. You'll also find out about some of the pioneers in US squash, such as Stanley Pearson, a six-time national champion beginning in 1915. During the peak of his squash career from 1915 to 1923, Pearson lost only one match. And there's Hunter Lott Jr., who captured eight national doubles titles starting in 1938. A prestigious junior tournament is now named after him.

The squash world likes to show appreciation for talented players and those who made a difference in the sport. There's also a College Squash Hall of Fame, which honors significant coaches and players throughout the history of intercollegiate squash. Other organizations, such as the Women's International Players Association, WISPA, and Squash Australia, also maintain their own Halls of Fame.

World Squash Hall of Fame

Each year, the WSF recognizes players who have attained incredible achievements in squash. The "Hall" is not a building, but simply a celebration of wonderful squash talent. One of the most recent inductees was Sarah Fitz-Gerald of Australia, who won the World Open five times and the British Open twice.

Other notables are Hashim Khan of Pakistan, who captured seven British Open titles, and Jonah Barrington of Ireland, who won the British Open six times. No Hall of Fame would be complete without more of the Khan dynasty – Jahangir, who won eight world titles and 10 British Open championships, and Jansher, who captured eight World and six British titles.

16

Movers and Shakers

*"I am tired of hearing about money, money, money, money, money.
I just want to play the game, drink Pepsi, wear Reebok."*
SHAQUILLE O'NEAL, professional basketball player

Today there are hundreds of medium to large-sized corporations and thousands of one-person armies in the business of marketing and managing sports, all making up a multi-billion dollar industry. Where does squash fit into the picture? While big-name sponsors have poured money into sports like professional football and tennis, squash has, unfortunately, has taken a back seat. Yet, there are squash marketers primed to take the sport out of the shadows and into the spotlight. Their accomplishments are notable, as they've convinced sponsors that squash is indeed a viable marketing tool.

Sports Marketing

Large sports marketing companies like IMG and Octagon may still be pondering whether to take the plunge into marketing squash and its players. However, there are a number of enthusiastic entrepreneurs and small companies promoting squash all over the world. You don't need a big company to get the job done and to do it well.

John Nimick spent seven years managing the PSA and its World Tour before branching out on his own in 1999 with his company, Event Engine. Using creative new ideas and formats, these pros-turned-entrepreneurs are determined to prove that squash is a worthwhile recipient of sponsorship dollars. It's been a tough sell for squash marketers, but with their passion for the sport and expertise in event planning, their work is paying off.

Event Engine

John Nimick is a former pro player who won two North American Open Squash Championships and reached a world hard ball ranking of No. 2 in the 1980s. He also represented the US twice in international competition in the world championships.

With his expertise in pro events, Nimick has grown his company, Event Engine, to include the promotion of four of the top 10 tournaments in the world, including the Tournament of Champions in New York City, the US Open in Boston and the Canadian Open in Toronto.   He also partnered with John Beddington of Beddington Sports Management Ltd to work with England Squash to license the rights to the prestigious British Open.

One of Nimick's major accomplishments was the signing of an agreement with The Tennis Channel, a 24-hour-a-day, traditional, ad-supported cable network. Beginning in 2003, a regular schedule of squash programming was broadcast for the first time in the US. Nimick hopes to make squash "the poker of the Tennis Channel," creating a compelling interest in the sport among both viewers and sponsors.

Nimick says he wants people to come away from an Event Engine-run tournament feeling that they have been to something comparable to a major league golf, tennis or team event. In addition to featuring the top players, he invests in special events and programs such as clinics, games and contests for kids, exhibitions and a charity golf tournament so spectators will come for the whole experience, not just the squash. In the future, Nimick hopes to expand the US Pro Series and present a local regional tour that will attract many different players.

iSquash Marketing

After six years with Dunlop, Paul Walters, armed with contacts, knowledge and drive, set out on his own to create iSquashMarketing, the first global company dedicated to the marketing and management of squash.

Based in the UK and established in 2003, iSquashMarketing is a squash specialist marketing and management company with a network of business divisions, including iSquashMarketing, managing world-class events, iSquashAcademy, a top training institute for up-and-coming players, iSquashMedia, a print and Web-based media component, and iSquashManagement, representing world-class players.

With iSquashManagement, Walters established a formal program of athlete representation, helping manage pros professionally and providing assistance with financial planning, contracts and endorsement deals.

Another of Walter's innovations was the creation of a Super 8 Grand Prix, an invitational event with a strong draw held in 2004 in

Manchester, England. Walters, who sold his concept to sponsors, believes that a round robin with two pools of eight of the world's top players is a better way to showcase the men's game. The event was also supported by a British U23 Women's Super 8 event, featuring the UK's highest-ranked players. Following these events was a Junior Super 8.

Eventis Sports Marketing

Leave it to the top pros to get into the act of marketing squash. World champion Peter Nicol, along with pro partners Tim Garner and Angus Kirkland, established the company, Eventis Sports Marketing in the UK in 2003. Garner was instrumental in the British tournament circuit, and Kirkland isa former director of the US open. Along with Nicol, they make a unique team. The talented trio launched their new company with the inaugural Prince English Open, a four-star PSA tournament, held in a theatre in Sheffield.

TrojanOne

Canadians are promoting squash with equal zeal. Squash Canada is able to provide a large number of programs for its players with the help of TrojanOne, a full-service sports marketing firm. TrojanOne is responsible for all aspects of event management, including conception, planning, sales and design.

Assisting Squash Canada with the promotion of both professional events and grass roots programs, TrojanOne has been instrumental in promoting Squash Canada's university program, Ups, its outreach to new players, Instant Squash, and its incentive for juniors, the Skill Awards Program. With 32 people on board, TrojanOne is able to lend manpower to Squash Canada in its mission to grow the sport.

Growth of Squash Marketing

Fueled by their passion for squash, more pros and players all over the world are getting into the act of promoting the game. Top pro and national team coach Chris Walker has also founded a company, Squash Solutions, which promises to organize clinics or demonstrations, host exhibitions, run professional tournaments and serve as a clearinghouse for those seeking squash coaches or for coaches seeking players. Services run the gamut, as Walker, based in Connecticut, aims to raise the profile of squash in the US and seek out more sponsors for the game.

Similarly, Squash247, both a Website and marketing firm, is the brainchild of Alan Thatcher, a renowned squash figure in the UK. While Squash 247's online service provides news of the squash world, Thatcher also offers potential clients a complete sponsorship service and can organize squash events and programs of all sizes.

Grassroots Marketing

In order to attract big-name sponsors, squash has to appeal to the masses. The USSRA and squash marketers are realizing that they need to work from the bottom up and focus their attention on getting more people to play the game. TrojanOne's work with Squash Canada concentrates on the grass roots level - schools, universities and clubs.

Point Max, the Canadian sales and marketing firm that purchased Manta, the squash racquet manufacturer, in 2004, is directing its efforts toward racquet sports specialists and club pros. By supporting the business of teaching professionals and club owners rather than giving money and equipment to established touring professionals, Point Max is getting racquets into the hands of more players. The company is working to secure new sponsors and create a large tournament circuit with significant prizes for all levels of players.

Television is also key. Canadian squash television producer Jean DeLierre writes extensively on the subject in an article in *Squash Player* magazine. "The day we can prove to the largest corporations through our programs' TV ratings that squash is watched by millions, then that will be the day they will readily join us." (More info: Select References 7).

Promoters

Promoters bring tournaments and events to a community. Ranging from corporations like Event Engine, which promotes some of the largest squash events in the US, to pros-turned-entrepreneurs like Andre Maur, the winner of several World Tour titles and US Master Champion, who runs the Opens in Jamaica and Atlanta.

It's the entrepreneurial individuals with a strong squash background and a head for numbers who run this segment of the squash industry.

Idea

Come up with an idea for an event or tournament fans will pay to watch.

Facility

Identify a facility to stage the event. Depending upon the profile of the tournament, clubs, schools and colleges are all possibilities. Some tournaments are held at multiple sites in close proximity to each other. A portable all glass court will accommodate a larger crowd and can be used outside, in an arena or even in a theater. An example is the Tournament of Champions in Grand Central Terminal, which draws thousands of fans.

Players

Set a date and find players. If your event is a sanctioned tournament, PSA (More info: psa-squash.com) or WISPA (More info: wispa.net), check the calendar to avoid conflicts with existing tournaments. You'll be working with these organizations to make sure the event adheres to their guidelines. And don't forget to check with your local, state and possibly national association to ensure that the proposed dates are clear. You can request the PSA's two helpful guides: "Organizing a PSA tour Event, A Step-by-Step Guide," and "An Introduction for A New Promoter to the Organization of a PSA Tour Event." WISPA also has a packet designed for tournament promoters.

Number Crunches

Crunch your expense numbers. Prize money, facilities rental, and accommodations are some obvious expenses.

You can start sanctioned tournaments with prize money as low as $3,000 and as high as $100,000 for Super Series events. You must also pay a fee to the sanctioning organization. WISPA takes a 3.5 percent fee of the total prize money. PSA has a five percent minimum. For events with less than $7,000 in prize money, WISPA registration is $250. (More info: wispa.net). You can check on PSA's sliding scale at psa-squash.com

There are different requirements depending upon the type and level of the tournament. There are also security deposits that are returned following the event. If the event doesn't take place, the deposit is non-refundable. As with any large sporting event, there are many rules to follow and promoters take a financial risk. However, if you study the market and are able to attract an audience, your investment of time and money may well be rewarded.

Bring on the Stars

You want big name players for your tournament? Pay them upfront with cash? No way. Appearance fees and guarantees are strictly forbidden in professional squash. According to PSA rules, tournaments shall not offer players any compensation, gratuity or other thing of value for the purpose of guaranteeing their appearance.

Invitationals and exhibitions are another story. With these formats, promoters can pay appearance fees to bring in stars and boost attendance. When stars commit, sponsors might be enticed to open their wallets and fans follow.

The "S" Word

Sponsors – selling your event to them is the true test of a promoter's mettle. Always keep in mind the reasons why companies sponsor events:

- Advertising: Corporate identification, target marketing, awareness.
- Promotion: Gains attention from trade or consumers.
- Sales: Client entertainment, sampling opportunities.
- Public Relations: The catchall phrase.

It's not uncommon for a professional squash event to have 10 to 12 sponsors. However, it's not the quantity of sponsors that's important, but the level of money raised from major sponsors, according to John Nimick of Event Engine. The level varies, says Nimick, who was able to raise $200,000 for the Tournament of Champions in New York City.

Now that you've lined up your sponsors, as the promoter all you have to do is publicize the event, sell tickets, and hold the tournament. Sounds simple, right? It can be, with good organization and planning and an experienced team. Hopefully, your tournament will make money, even when a star player calls in sick and another withdraws with an injury. Welcome to the world of the squash promoter!

Post Tournament Direction

And with weary feet
He homeward trod,
His footfalls echoes
Of a thoughtful plod.
Questions nagging
At a tired mind
Was aught awry?
Or undermined?
Was the sponsor happy?
Was the program fine?
Was the squash attractive?
The games on time?
Did I upset his wife?
Did he upset mine?
Were the trophies adequate?
The meals enough?
The seeds correct,
Decisions too tough?
Will the double D's come back again?
Did they have fun?
Will my back ever straighten up,
Or will I ever run?
Did I send the press release?
Did I thank the staff?
Half of them enjoyed it –
I'll have to ask the other half!
Could I have done more than this,
Or other things instead?
I'll check tomorrow morning –
I've <u>got</u> to get to bed.

⚜

—*Richard Millman*

Sponsorships and Endorsements

While businesses pay famous players to endorse their products, they also sponsor those not yet famous in the hope that one day they'll reach celebrity status. Look at it this way: endorsement budgets are like stock investments, whereas sponsorships are investing in futures.

Sponsorship implies that a company pays a portion of training expenses, while endorsement suggests that the player is a company spokesperson or business representative. A company might sponsor many promising athletes, but hire only one or two more famous players as spokespersons. Ultimately, players earn sponsorships to help businesses get their brands in front of as many consumer eyeballs as possible, in stadiums and, if possible, on television.

A company pays a famous player a fee for making a public endorsement of its products. Beyond wearing the company's shoes, apparel, and logos, the player may be contracted to attend company functions, appear in photo shoots and commercials and lend his name to a new product.

In squash, it's usually rankings that determine the top deals. However, there is a fair amount of scrambling among racquet companies to support emerging talent on the international circuit. Top juniors can realistically expect to receive equipment from a company but little else, unless they have reached the level of Nicol David of Malaysia, world junior champion, who at age 17 managed to secure a sponsorship deal with Mulpha Sports, the Malaysian distributor of Head Racquets. David fit the right profile of a marketable player on the verge of becoming a major star.

Before he made it up the ranks, Peter Nicol approached Andy Bunting, the sponsorship manager for Prince, for support. "He sat down and worked out what he wanted to do, and decided that he needed help. He outlined very clear objectives for himself and then found ways to meet them. He went to Neil Harvey for training and worked hard for his sponsor," says Bunting in an article in *Squash Player* magazine. (More info: Select Reference 6)

Company scouts like Bunting are always on the look out for up-and-coming players at tournaments and on the ranking lists. If Bunting targets a player with potential, he'll put his local Prince agent on the case, who might be able to provide equipment and some training expenses. If the player progresses through the rankings, he may be able to earn an international contract offering equipment and money.

Endorsement contracts vary. If players on the lower rung of the rankings ladder want endorsements, they may be more successful with companies in their own communities. Pros have had support from their home clubs, along with an assortment of local companies, such as a hotel or restaurant or retail outlet. It takes good public relations and marketing skills to prove that you are worth the investment. For the most part, those willing to endorse a player are interested in phenoms who can move products by virtue of a fickle mix of on-court performance, off-court antics and, for the younger crowd, aura.

Interestingly, a variety of organizations and individuals make up the inside world of endorsements. You have the player and her immediate entourage, including coach and family members. Then sometimes there's the player agent. And, finally, there are the lawyers and accountants, Price Waterhouse Coopers, for example, to pour over the fine print.

Endorsements are a big-time business because squash enthusiasts will gladly part with a few extra dollars to pick up a James Willstrop E-Squash Carbon 3 racquet. Who knows, one day *your* squash kid may be on the endorsement list, motivating millions of buyers.

Thanks for reading *Raising Big Smiling Squash Kids*. We hope you enjoyed the read and found it helpful. Working on the book has been a very positive experience for both of us. It allowed us to revisit and re-examine the reasons why we became interested in and hooked on the game, and why Richard has spent his life in this sport.

What is Squash? Beyond the obvious, we hope we've given you more than a glimpse of all this great game has to offer. Athletics – yes! A life sport in which participants frequently play into their 70s and 80s – yes! An extraordinary amalgam of mind and body in which strategic problem solving worthy of any chessboard combines with extreme physical pressure to challenge participants in ways possibly only rivaled during war or prehistory – yes! These are all great values of our sport.

But perhaps more than any of these, Squash has the facility to help people find out who they are and who they would like to be. Through many hours of competition against a wonderful variety of personalities, Squash players test themselves, then find ways of improving, largely as a result of friendly rivalries – some of which last for years or even a life time. In short, Squash is a vehicle for the development of strong, lasting personal qualities the likes of which we have not found elsewhere.

So let's all rally for Squash by joining a regional or national association, supporting an urban youth program or helping to get things up and running in our communities. Let's help Squash not only thrive but grow, bringing more kids and parents to this great game. We hope this book inspires you and your family to play, have fun and reap the many rewards Squash has to offer.

Select References

1. Frank Satterthwaite, *The three-wall nick and other angles: A Squash Autobiography*, Holt Reinhart and Winston, 1979.

2. Hashim Khan, *Squash Racquets: The Khan Game*, Wayne State University Press, Detroit, 1967.

3. W. Timothy Gallwey, *The Inner Game of Tennis,* Random House, 1974.

4. Will Morris, *Squash Fitness: How Do I Get in Shape for Squash?* Tar Heel Squash Online Newsletter, University of North Carolina, April 2004.

5. *Interview with Tim Garner*, Squash247.com.

6. Martin Bronstein, *Players' Prince,* Squashplayer.co.uk.

7. Barnett series, *An Interview with Jean DeLierre,* Squashplayer.co.uk, Oct. 2003.

Credits

- Dr. Suess quote by permission of Dr. Suess Enterprises, L.P.
- Poems by Richard Millman, Copyright Richard Millman. Used by permission of Richard Millman.
- References to the article Inside the Head of a Squash Player at Jenny Tranfield, JennyTranfield.com by permission of Jenny Tranfield.
- Attribution to Dr. Tudor O Bompa from Periodization: Theory and Methodology of Training, 1999, Human Kinetics. Attribution reprinted by permission of Dr. Tudor O Bompa.
- Attributions to Nathan L'Huiller in the article What It Means To Turn Pro, Inform Connection, Squash247.com by permission of Nathan L'Huiller.
- Attributions to Jack Barnaby from Winning Squash Racquets by Jack Barnaby, ISBN 0205061753, 1979, Allyn & Bacon by permission of Allyn & Bacon.
- Excerpts from chriswalker.net by permission of Chris Walker.
- Excerpts from Claire Rein-Weston by Amy Boytz Duchene, Squash Magazine, Oct. 2003, page 31; Cracking Like An Egg, Squash Magazine, Oct 2003, page 12; Back To Basics by Karen Calara, Squash Magazine, Oct. 2003, page 16; Squash Risks by A. Martin Clark, Jr, SquashMagazine.com; A Road Not Traveled by Jay Prince, Squash Magazine, May 2004. By permission of Jay Prince, Publisher, Squash Magazine.
- Attributions to Ashley Kayler from Squash Tip Archive, Calsquash.com by permission of Ashley Kayler.
- Excerpts from A Sprint Or A Marathon, Dr. David Behm, Squash Newsletter; Warm Up And Flexibility, Dr. David Behm, Squash Newsletter. By permission of Dr. David Behm.
- References to Canada's Skills Awards Program by permission of Wendy Gayfer, Squash Canada.
- Excerpts from Juniors Taking Fun Seriously, Squash Player Magazine; Peter Nicol Squash Tips, Squashplayer.co.uk; Mike Todd on Malcolm Will\strop by Framboise Gommendy, Squash Player Magazine. By permission of Ian McKenzie, Managing Director, Squash Player Magazine.
- Excerpts from Eye Injuries and Sports by Dr. Michael Kellam, Visionarts.ca. By permission of Dr. Michael Kellam.
- Text reprinted, with permission, from Vinger PF: A practical guide for sports eye protection, The Physician and Sportsmedicine 2000,28(6):49-69 Copyright 2005 The McGraw-Hill Companies.
- References to Inner Tennis by W. Timothy Gallwey, copyright 1976 by W. Timothy Gallwey. Used by permission of Random House, Inc.
- Attributions to Dr. Jim Taylor from Positive Pushing: How to Raise a Successful and Happy Child by Dr. Jim Taylor. Copyright 2002 Dr. Jim Taylor. Reprinted by permission of Hyperion.
- References to Forbes.com by permission of Forbes.com.
- References to The Three Wall Nick by Frank Satterthwaite by permission of Frank Satterthwaite.
- Cover Photos of Peter Murray and Coco Siebert by permission of Stockton Photo, Inc www.StocktonPhoto.com

Index

Acknowledgments

We would like to express our gratitude to those without whose support this work would simply be incomplete. Their generosity in sharing their time and expertise benefited us enormously and, through this work, will benefit you and your squash kid(s).

Our sincere thanks to:

- Andrea Savage, New England Small Athletic Conference
- Andre Maur, Global Squash
- Andrew Shelley, Women's International Players Association
- Adrian Christy, England Squash
- Anne Farrell, USSRA
- Arnie Berman, Hi Tec
- Barry Faguy, Squash Official, Squash Canada/International Referee
- Bill McNally, Connecticut College Coach, USSRA Coach Educator and Examiner
- Brian Mathias, CitySquash
- Bryan Patterson, Universal Squash Camps
- Charlie Johnson, Charlie Johnson's Squash Shop
- Charles Kingsley, USSRA Hall of Fame
- Chris Gordon, Pro Player
- Chris Smith, SquashBusters
- Chris Walker, Player, Coach, Former World No.4, National Team Captain and Entrepreneur
- Chrissy Schluep, NCAA
- Christian Leighton, World Squash Federation
- Craig Brand, Former Executive Director, USSRA
- Crawford Lindsay, United States Racquet Stringers Association
- Damian Walker, The Squash Alley and former US Men's Champion
- Dave Carr, McWil Courtwall
- Dave Talbott, Yale University Coach
- David Behm, School of Human Kinetics and Recreation, Memorial University of Newfoundland
- David Kay, MetroSquash
- David Rawlings, Athletic Trainer
- Dominick Everett, World Deaf Squash Association
- Edward Minskoff, Squash Enthusiast
- Edward Wallbutton, Former Chief Executive and Secretary General, World Squash Federation

- ❖ Elizabeth Van Orman Dupree, DC Squash Academy
- ❖ Eric and Patty Fast, Squash parents, enthusiasts and supporters
- ❖ Frank Satterthwaite, Player, commentator and author
- ❖ Gail Ramsay, Princeton University Coach
- ❖ Gary McCoy, Evolve Sports Medicine Group
- ❖ Gordon Anderson, Anderson Courts and Sports Surfaces
- ❖ Greg Reiss, Manufacturer's Rep
- ❖ Gus Cook, International Squash Camps and Tours
- ❖ Haseeb Anwar, Squash Design
- ❖ Jack Halford, Tibbetts Ranch
- ❖ James Zug, Author, *Squash, The History of The Game*
- ❖ Jan Hebden, Mother of Junior competitor, Britt
- ❖ Jane Parker, Vassar College Coach
- ❖ Jeanie Shanahan, USSRA
- ❖ Jenny Tranfield, Sports Psychologist
- ❖ John Flanigan, University Club of Chicago
- ❖ John Nimick, Event Engine
- ❖ Dr. Jonathan Katz, Sports Psychologist, Altheus
- ❖ Ken Watson, Inventor, Big Hand Sports
- ❖ Kevin Doucet, Squash Canada
- ❖ Kevin Dunn, Point Max
- ❖ Kevin Klipstein, Chief Executive Officer, USSRA
- ❖ Lana Quibell, Mother of junior competitor, Michelle, and former resident pro and national age group champion
- ❖ Leonard Lye, inventor, Footworker
- ❖ Lianne Price, England Squash Association
- ❖ Lily Lorentzen, Harvard University Varsity Player
- ❖ Lorraine Harding, World Squash Federation
- ❖ Mark Devoy, Cornell University Coach
- ❖ Mark Talbott, Talbott Squash Academy, Director of Squash at Stanford University and former No. 1 hardball player
- ❖ Dr. Michael Schumacher, Chairman of the USSRA Medical Advisory Committee and Podiatrist
- ❖ Michelle Quibell, Yale University Varsity Player
- ❖ Mike and Debbie Barnett, USSRA
- ❖ Mike Hymer, Prince
- ❖ Norman Bloom, Prince
- ❖ Paul Walter, iSquashMarketing
- ❖ Peter Hirst, England Squash
- ❖ Peter Logue, Squash Australia
- ❖ Phil Green, Cedar Hill Squash Club in Victoria
- ❖ Robert Graham, Santa Barbara Athletic Club
- ❖ Robert Millar, Point Max

- ❖ Ross Triffitt, Bermuda Squash Racquets Association
- ❖ Sandy Schwartz, Founder, CitySquash
- ❖ Seamus O'Keefe, Game Plan Marketing
- ❖ Sheila Cooksley, Professional Squash Association
- ❖ Sherry Funston, Squash Ontario
- ❖ Stephen Cox, Pro
- ❖ Stephen Hall, Dunlop
- ❖ Steve Gregg, SquashSmarts
- ❖ Steve Polli, Squash enthusiast, court builder
- ❖ Sue Scott, European Squash Federation
- ❖ Susan Keeping, The Travel Edge
- ❖ Tim Bacon, Smith College Coach
- ❖ Tim Wyant, CitySquash
- ❖ Tina Fuselli, Arizona Squash
- ❖ Tom Generous, Tar Heel Squash
- ❖ Vijay Chitnis, USSRA
- ❖ Wally Glennon, Squash in the Hamptons
- ❖ Wayne Reuvers, Live Technology
- ❖ Wendy Gayfer, Squash Canada
- ❖ Will Carlin, Senior Writer, *Squash* magazine, former US No. 1

Richard Millman & Georgetta Morque

Make Your Next Squash Event
A Huge Success

Key-chains and bobble-heads are simply not enough to draw fans (particularly families) to squash events. New and creative ways for attracting families and players are desperately needed. Drive up ticket sales; gain new members, signups for programs and tournaments. Find out how our book Raising Big Smiling Squash Kids, loved by families, coaches and the media, can be customized and used as a promotional item to attract enthusiastic supporters to your next event.

We will show how you can order this premier edition at amazingly low prices, customized with your logo on the cover, program description and your sponsors' messages. The special edition costs less than a t-shirt and can even be free to you in some instances. Now that's a deal. Raise funds, fill up your event and be a hero in your community by supporting squash and reading!

The premier edition of Raising Big Smiling Squash Kids is a promotional item that is both positive and practical, and will benefit all the parents and kids that attend any tournament. Ultimately, this book customized with your brand, program description and your sponsors' messages will remain with these squash families for years to be used over and over again. Bobble-heads may break, t-shirts fade away and are discarded. No one throws away books!

Please call Mansion Grove House at 408.404.7277 or email premiers@mansiongrovehouse.com to set up your next special event!

Want More?

3 Easy Ways to Order Raising Big Smiling Squash Kids:
- ❖ Leading chain and independent bookstores, squash pro shops, sporting goods stores, and catalogs
- ❖ Leading online retailers
- ❖ Direct from the publisher:
  - ➢ MansionSquash.com
  - ➢ Fax: 408.404.7277
  - ➢ Mail: Mansion Squash,
    PO Box 201734, Austin TX 78720 United States

Distributor, Retailer & Squash Group Inquiries:
- ❖ Email: sales@mansiongrovehouse.com
- ❖ Fax: 408.404.7277